AQA History

AS
Unit 1

Britain, 1483–1529

Exclusively endorsed by AQA

Cathy Lee

Series editor
Sally Waller

Nelson Thornes

Published in 2008 by:
Nelson Thornes Ltd
Delta Place
27 Bath Road
CHELTENHAM
GL53 7TH
United Kingdom

08 09 10 11 12 / 10 9 8 7 6 5 4 3 2 1

A catalogue record for this book is available from the British Library

978-0-7487-8261-1

Illustrations by: Gary Rees (c/o Linda Rogers Associates), David Russell Illustration
Page make-up by Thomson Digital

Printed in Croatia by Zrinski

Contents

AQA introduction

Nelson Thornes and AQA

Nelson Thornes has worked in collaboration with AQA to ensure that this book offers you the best support for your AS or A level course and helps you to prepare for your exams. The partnership means that you can be confident that the range of learning, teaching and assessment practice materials has been checked by the senior examining team at AQA before formal approval, and is closely matched to the requirements of your specification.

Blended learning

This book forms a blend with electronic resources: this means that links between topics and activities between the book and the electronic resources help you to work in the way that best suits you, and enable extra support to be provided online. For example, you can test yourself online and feedback from the test will direct you back to the relevant parts of the book.

Electronic resources are available in a simple-to-use online platform called Nelson Thornes learning space. If your school or college has a licence to use the service, you will be given a password through which you can access the materials through any internet connection.

Learning activity

These resources include a variety of interactive and non-interactive activities to support your learning.

Progress tracking

These resources include a variety of tests that you can use to check your knowledge on particular topics (Test yourself) and a range of resources that enable you to analyse and understand examination questions (On your marks…).

Research support

These resources include WebQuests, in which you are assigned a task and provided with a range of web links to use as source material for research.

Study skills

These resources support you to develop a skill that is key for your course, for example planning essays.

When you see an icon, go to Nelson Thornes learning space at www.nelsonthornes.com/aqagce, enter your access details and select your course. The materials are arranged in the same order as the topics in the book, so you can easily find the resources you need.

How to use this book

This book covers the specification for your course and is arranged in a sequence approved by AQA.

The features in this book include:

Timeline

Key events are outlined at the beginning of the book.

Learning objectives

At the beginning of each section you will find a list of learning objectives that contain targets linked to the requirements of the specification.

Key chronology

A short list of dates usually with a focus on a specific event or legislation.

Key profile

The profile of a key person you should be aware of to fully understand the period in question.

Key term

A term that you will need to be able to define and understand.

■ Did you know?

Interesting information to bring the subject under discussion to life.

■ Exploring the detail

Information to put further context around the subject under discussion.

■ A closer look

An in-depth look at a theme, person or event to deepen your understanding. Activities around the extra information may be included.

Sources

Sources to reinforce topics or themes and may provide fact or opinion. They may be quotations from historical works, contemporaries of the period or photographs.

■ Cross-reference

Links to related content which may offer more detail on the subject in question.

■ Activity

Various activity types to provide you with different challenges and opportunities to demonstrate both the content and skills you are learning. Some can be worked on individually, some as part of group work and some are designed to specifically "stretch and challenge".

■ Question

Questions to prompt further discussion on the topic under consideration and are an aid to revision.

■ Summary questions

Summary questions at the end of each chapter to test your knowledge and allow you to demonstrate your understanding.

AQA Examiner's tip

Hints from AQA examiners to help you with your study and to prepare for your exam.

AQA Examination-style questions

Questions at the end of each section in the style that you can expect in your exam.

AQA examination questions are reproduced by permission of the Assessment and Qualifications Alliance.

Learning outcomes

Learning outcomes at the end of each section remind you what you should know having completed the chapters in that section.

■ Web links in the book

Because Nelson Thornes is not responsible for third party content online, there may be some changes to this material that are beyond our control. In order for us to ensure that the links referred to in the book are as up-to-date and stable as possible, the web sites provided are usually homepages with supporting instructions on how to reach the relevant pages if necessary.

Please let us know at **webadmin@nelsonthornes.com** if you find a link that doesn't work and we will do our best to correct this at reprint, or to list an alternative site.

Introduction to the History series

When Bruce Bogtrotter in Roald Dahl's *Matilda* was challenged to eat a huge chocolate cake, he just opened his mouth and ploughed in, taking bite after bite and lump after lump until the cake was gone and he was feeling decidedly sick. The picture is not dissimilar to that of some A level history students. They are attracted to history because of its inherent appeal but, when faced with a bulging file and a forthcoming examination, their enjoyment evaporates. They try desperately to cram their brains with an assortment of random facts and subsequently prove unable to control the outpouring of their ill-digested material in the examination.

The books in this series are designed to help students and teachers avoid this feeling of overload and examination panic by breaking down the AQA history specification in such a way that it is easily absorbed. Above all, they are designed to retain and promote student's enthusiasm for history by avoiding a dreary rehash of dates and events. Each book is divided into sections, closely matched to those given in the specification, and the content is further broken down into chapters that present the historical material in a lively and attractive form, offering guidance on the key terms, events and issues, and blending thought-provoking activities and questions in a way designed to advance students' understanding. By encouraging students to think for themselves and to share their ideas with others, as well as helping them to develop the knowledge and skills they will need to pass the examination, this book should ensure that students' learning remains a pleasure rather than an endurance test.

To make the most of what this book provides, students will need to develop efficient study skills from the start and it is worth spending some time considering what these involve:

- Good organisation of material in a subject-specific file. Organised notes help develop an organised brain and sensible filing ensures time is not wasted hunting for misplaced material. This book uses cross-references to indicate where material in one chapter has relevance to material in another. Students are advised to use the same technique.

- A sensible approach to note-making. Students are often too ready to copy large chunks of material from printed books or to download sheaves of printouts from the internet. This series is designed to encourage students to think about the notes they collect and to undertake research with a particular purpose in mind. The activities encourage students to pick out that information that is relevant to the issue being addressed and to avoid making notes on material that is not properly understood.

- By far the most important component of study is taking time to think. By encouraging students to think before they write or speak, be it for a written answer, presentation or class debate, students should learn to form opinions and make judgements based on the accumulation of evidence. These are the skills the examiner will be looking for in the final examination. The beauty of history is that there is rarely a right or wrong answer so, with sufficient evidence, one student's view will count for as much as the next.

Unit 1

The topics offered for study in Unit 1 are all based on 'change and consolidation'. They invite consideration of what changed and why, as well as posing the question of what remained the same. Through a study of a period of about 50 to 60 years, students are encouraged to analyse the interplay of long-term and short-term reasons for change and not only to consider how governments have responded to the need for change but also to evaluate the ensuing consequences. Such historical analyses are, of course, relevant to an understanding of the present and, through such historical study, students will be guided towards a greater appreciation of the world around them today as well as developing their understanding of the past.

Unit 1 is tested by a 1 hour 15 minute paper containing three questions, from which students need to choose two. Details relating to the style of questions, with additional hints, are given in Table 1 and links to the examination requirements are provided throughout this book. Students should familiarise themselves with these and the marking criteria before attempting any of the practice examination questions at the end of each section.

Answers will be marked according to a scheme based on 'levels of response'. This means that the answer will be assessed according to which level best matches the historical skills displayed, taking both knowledge and understanding into account. Take some time to study these criteria and use them wisely.

Question 1 (a), 2 (a) and 3 (a)

Level 1 Answers contain either some descriptive material that is only loosely linked to the focus of the question or some explicit comment with little, if any, appropriate support. Answers are likely to be

Table 1 *Unit 1: style of questions and marks available*

Unit 1	Question	Marks	Question type	Question stem	Hints for students
Question 1, 2 and 3	(a)	12	This question is focused on a narrow issue within the period studied and requires an explanation	Why did… Explain why… In what ways… (was X important)	Make sure you explain 'why', not 'how', and try to order your answer in a way that shows you understand the inter-link of factors and which were the more important. You should try to reach an overall judgement/conclusion
Question 1, 2 and 3	(b)	24	This question links the narrow issue to a wider context and requires an awareness that issues and events can have different interpretations	How far… How important was… How successful…	This answer needs to be planned as you will need to develop an argument in your answer and show balanced judgement. Try to set out your argument in the introduction and, as you develop your ideas through your paragraphs, support your opinions with detailed evidence. Your conclusion should flow naturally and provide supported judgement

generalised and assertive. The response is limited in development and skills of written communication are weak. *(0–2 marks)*

Level 2 Answers demonstrate some knowledge and understanding of the demands of the question. Either they are almost entirely descriptive with few explicit links to the question or they provide some explanations backed by evidence that is limited in range and/or depth. Answers are coherent but weakly expressed and/or poorly structured. *(3–6 marks)*

Level 3 Answers demonstrate good understanding of the demands of the question providing relevant explanations backed by appropriately selected information, although this may not be full or comprehensive. For the most part, answers are clearly expressed and show some organisation in the presentation of material. *(7–9 marks)*

Level 4 Answers are well focused, identifying a range of specific explanations backed by precise evidence and demonstrating good understanding of the connections and links between events/issues. For the most part, answers are well written and organised. *(10–12 marks)*

Question 1 (b), 2 (b) and 3 (b)

Level 1 Answers either contain some descriptive material that is only loosely linked to the focus of the question or address only a limited part of the period of the question. Alternatively, there may be some explicit comment with little, if any, appropriate support. Answers are likely to be generalised and assertive. There is little, if any, awareness of differerent historical interpretations. The response is limited in development and skills of written communication are weak. *(0–6 marks)*

Level 2 Answers show some understanding of the demands of the question. Either they will be almost entirely descriptive with few explicit links to the question or they contain some explicit comment with relevant but limited support. They display limited understanding of different historical interpretations. Answers are coherent but weakly expressed and/or poorly structured. *(7–11 marks)*

Level 3 Answers show a developed understanding of the demands of the question. They provide some assessment, backed by relevant and appropriately selected evidence, but they lack depth and/or balance. There is some understanding of varying historical interpretations. For the most part, answers are clearly expressed and show some organisation in the presentation of material. *(12–16 marks)*

Level 4 Answers show explicit understanding of the demands of the question. They develop a balanced argument backed by a good range of appropriately selected evidence and a good understanding of historical interpretations. For the most part, answers show organisation and good skills of written communication. *(17–21 marks)*

Level 5 Answers are well focused and closely argued. The arguments are supported by precisely selected evidence leading to a relevant conclusion/judgement, incorporating well-developed understanding of historical interpretations and debate. For the most part, answers are carefully organised and fluently written, using appropriate vocabulary. *(22–24 marks)*

Introduction to this book

Britain in 1483

■ The nature of monarchy: the authority of the King

Historians studying late 15th century Britain need first to understand the role and importance of the monarch, and his relationship with both his close counsellors and his subjects across the kingdom. At this time, it was accepted that the King was appointed by God as a defender of his subjects. In his coronation, he was anointed with holy oil as a sign of God's grace. It therefore followed that to overthrow a king was a sin against God.

This God-given authority did not, however, give the King unlimited powers.

- He was expected, according to custom, to make decisions about the country and the Church having consulted other men, called taking counsel.
- He could only pass laws and raise taxation with the approval of parliament.
- The King was expected to be fair and to ensure that English justice was enforced through the established courts across his realm.
- He was expected to pay for the ordinary expenses of government through his own income.
- He relied on his subjects' support when he declared war.

The English

Figure 2 shows the hierarchical nature of English society. God and the angels in heaven, at the top of the chain, appointed the King. The King depended on the 'second estate' to help him direct society. The second estate composed the lords spiritual (archbishops and bishops) and lords temporal (magnates), and the gentry, for example knights with the title of 'Sir' and esquires, who were gentlemen who bore arms and had not been knighted. The ordinary people, known as the 'commonality', obeyed their laws and showed them deference. Below the commonality were the animals and plants. The purpose of the structure of Christian society was preparation for death and judgement; hence heaven and salvation at the top, and the fires of hell at the bottom.

The structure of English society was based on a belief held by contempories that there was a Great Chain of Being (see Figure 2) in which each person had a fixed, pre-determined role in society from peasant to nobleman. This structure, although hierarchical and rigid, was in practice becoming increasingly flexible. There was greater social mobility with the gradual breakdown of the feudal structure, the growth of commerce and trade, and the expansion of roles in royal service for educated men.

The King relied on his nobility to run the country and provide law and order, because local government and local policing were not employed or run by the King, but consisted of unpaid local people chosen by their

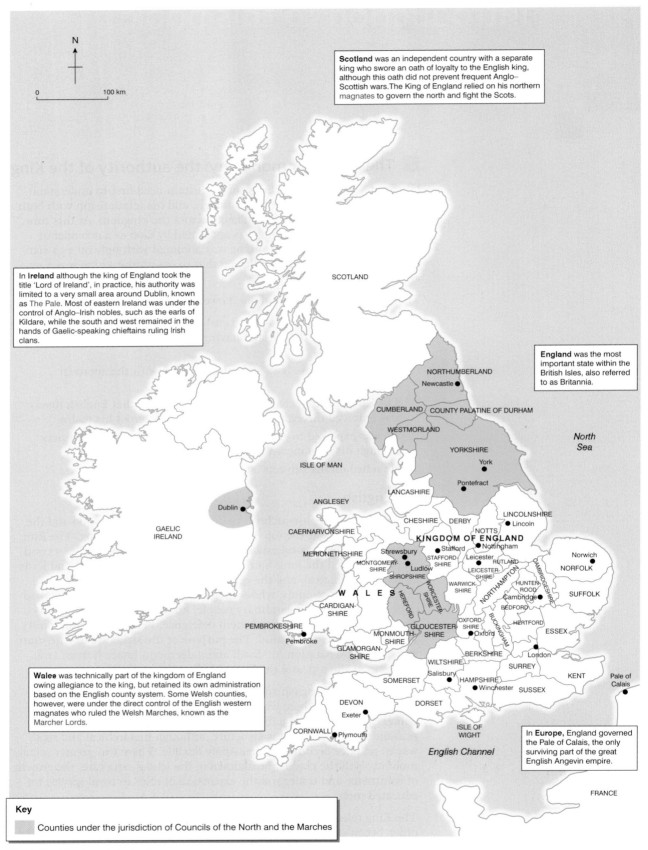

Scotland was an independent country with a separate king who swore an oath of loyalty to the English king, although this oath did not prevent frequent Anglo–Scottish wars. The King of England relied on his northern magnates to govern the north and fight the Scots.

In **Ireland** although the king of England took the title 'Lord of Ireland', in practice, his authority was limited to a very small area around Dublin, known as The Pale. Most of eastern Ireland was under the control of Anglo-Irish nobles, such as the earls of Kildare, while the south and west remained in the hands of Gaelic-speaking chieftains ruling Irish clans.

England was the most important state within the British Isles, also referred to as Britannia.

Wales was technically part of the kingdom of England owing allegiance to the king, but retained its own administration based on the English county system. Some Welsh counties, however, were under the direct control of the English western magnates who ruled the Welsh Marches, known as the Marcher Lords.

In **Europe**, England governed the Pale of Calais, the only surviving part of the great English Angevin empire.

N

0   100 km

SCOTLAND

NORTHUMBERLAND
Newcastle

CUMBERLAND   COUNTY PALATINE OF DURHAM
WESTMORLAND

YORKSHIRE
York
Pontefract

North
Sea

ISLE OF MAN

LANCASHIRE

ANGLESEY

CHESHIRE   DERBY
LINCOLNSHIRE
Lincoln
NOTTS
Nottingham
KINGDOM OF ENGLAND

CAERNARVONSHIRE

GAELIC
IRELAND

Dublin

MERIONETHSHIRE

Shrewsbury   Stafford
STAFFORD-   Leicester
MONTGOMERY-   SHIRE   RUTLAND
SHIRE   Ludlow   LEICESTER-
SHROPSHIRE   SHIRE
Norwich
NORFOLK

CAMBRIDGESHIRE

WARWICK-   NORTHAMPTON   HUNTEN-
SHIRE   ROOD
Cambridge
SUFFOLK

W A L E S   HEREFORD   WORCESTER-   BEDFORD
SHIRE

CARDIGAN-
SHIRE
BUCKINGHAM

PEMBROKESHIRE
MONMOUTH-   GLOUCESTER-   OXFORD-   HERTFORD
SHIRE   SHIRE   SHIRE
Pembroke   Oxford   ESSEX
GLAMORGAN-   London
SHIRE   BERKSHIRE

WILTSHIRE   SURREY
Salisbury   KENT   Pale of
SOMERSET   HAMPSHIRE   Calais
Winchester   SUSSEX

DEVON   DORSET

Exeter   ISLE OF
WIGHT
CORNWALL   Plymouth

English Channel

FRANCE

Key

Counties under the jurisdiction of Councils of the North and the Marches

Fig. 1 *The kingdom of England*

Fig. 2 *The hierarchical nature of English society is illustrated in this contemporary print, however, in reality, society was becoming much more flexible by the late 15th century*

communities. In these upper ranks of society there were greater and lesser noble families, but all had originally been granted land and titles in return for service in the established **feudal** tradition.

The middle ranks of English society were much more varied. They included members of the gentry such as knights and esquires who were often **retained men**. Generally speaking, most of the gentry held land, and some were also engaged in other occupations such as practice of the law. Other groups in these middle ranks included citizens with the authority to administer the growing towns and cities; yeomen aspiring to raise their family's status; and a range of tradesmen, skilled craftsmen and merchants.

Historians know least about the most numerous and lowest ranks in society, which included a wide range of labourers from peasant farmers to carpenters, as well as the shifting population of victims of rural depopulation. It is very difficult to be accurate in reconstructing their lives because they lived outside the **political nation**, and much of the surviving historical evidence from this period reflects the world of those in authority.

Key terms

Magnates: the most powerful noble families.

Marcher Lords: the magnate families who owned huge areas of land and possessed near-regal powers in the south and east of Wales.

The Pale: land around a town that was under English control.

Feudal: a system introduced by the Normans after 1066. The King owned all land and distributed it among loyal servants. They, in return, attended court and Counsel, provided armies, and ran administration at central and local government.

Retained men: men who voluntarily contracted and obliged themselves to provide a certain number of soldiers for their nobleman.

Political nation: those men who were actively involved, at central or local government level, in the administration of the country.

Fig. 3 *The ambitious and destitute flocked to London, hence the city's rapid expansion. This map dates to 1572, but the city was already growing by the end of the 15th century*

The monarch and his capital city – London

London was the only city in England that could, by continental standards, be classed as large. It was favoured by good communications having been, since Roman times and before, the focus of the English road network; and had developed a good port with access across the North Sea to the prosperous Netherlands.

The King held court in London and his great household generated demand for a range of goods from building stone to luxury silks. Magnates, churchmen and some rich merchants invested in magnificent town houses. Other various important buildings added to the architectural splendour of the city including the armouries in the Tower of London, the courts of justice at Westminster, the Guildhall, and London Bridge whose 19 white pillars spanned the River Thames.

The Wars of the Roses

Despite the contemporary understanding that it was a sin against God to overthrow a monarch, civil war had resulted in a series of usurpations in the years 1455 to 1485. The Wars of the Roses started in 1455 at the Battle of St Albans. Traditional historians claim that the civil wars ended in 1485 at the Battle of Bosworth when Henry Tudor, the main Lancastrian claimant, defeated Richard III, a Yorkist king. Other historians, however, argue that **the house of York** was not finally suppressed by **the house of Lancaster** until the Battle of Stoke in 1487, and that Yorkist claimants continued thereafter to threaten the Tudor monarchy.

Cross-reference

The family tree of Edward III's descendants can be found on page 12.

The Battle of Stoke will be described on page 52.

Key terms

The house of York: descendants of Edward III's second and fourth sons whose families intermarried.

The house of Lancaster: descendants of Edward III's third son, John of Gaunt, Duke of Lancaster.

There is no doubt that the Wars of the Roses were a period of domestic upheaval, although historians debate the scale of the turmoil. Certainly Tudor propagandists, such as Edward Hall, presented the civil wars as a period of devastation and carnage, replaced by orderly Tudor rule; a judgement supported by some historians who have found evidence that most nobles and their retained armies were involved in destructive, bloody battles. Other historians have revised this interpretation. They have concluded that most of the conflicts were only short skirmishes, and that the economy continued to grow while culture flourished. J.R. Lander argued in his book *The Wars of the Roses* (1965) that the wars had little or no effect on the development of agrarian and commercial life despite the sporadic, localised disruption. He estimated that more than 30 years of civil war boiled down to as little as 13 weeks of campaigning.

It is important to consider the impact of the Wars of the Roses on the monarchy in England. Contemporaries believed their king, whether Yorkist or Lancastrian, had been appointed by God to defend the kingdom and the people. Any king who failed to preserve public order therefore undermined the purpose of monarchy. In the years before 1471, the authority of the King was diminished by both Henry VI and Edward IV, for both Kings proved to be ineffective and weak. After 1471, however, Edward IV re-established his royal authority and imposed good law and order on his kingdom; in doing so, he strengthened Yorkist monarchy before 1483.

Key profile

Edward IV

Edward, Duke of York, usurped the throne of England from Henry VI after victory at the Battle of Towton in 1461. He owed his success to military support from his cousin Richard Neville, the Earl of Warwick. During the 1460s, the Earl became jealous of the patronage and influence of a rival family, the relatives of the King's wife Elizabeth Woodville, so swapped allegiance to support the Lancastrians. In 1470, Edward IV was temporarily forced into exile by Warwick, Clarence and the Lancastrians. Edward IV returned in 1471 and reclaimed the throne at the decisive Battle of Tewkesbury.

Edward IV made a significant innovation in royal revenue collection. His experience in managing noble estates gave him the confidence and financial expertise to reduce the role of the Exchequer and transfer its functions to his Chamber where he directly supervised its work. This was important because the King had faced insolvency in the first reign that weakened his hold on the throne and left him vulnerable to usurpation. He therefore energetically exploited all sources of royal revenue in his second reign after 1471. He inherited a bankrupt kingdom but left a solvent monarchy in 1483.

One historian, J. R. Green, celebrated Edward IV's second reign as the triumph of 'new monarchy' as Yorkist monarchy crushed the overmighty nobility along with their personal power bases. Subsequent historians have debated the scale of any Yorkist innovations. Some argue that Edward IV was a traditional English king who ruled by the undeniable force of his own personality rather than through new central royal authority. Having been a nobleman, he considered strong nobility to be a mark of strong royal authority, not a threat, and he

Exploring the detail

The red rose and the white rose

The title 'the Wars of the Roses' was invented by Sir Walter Scott but is historically valid. Each house in the wars recognised the red rose as the emblem of Lancaster and the white rose as the emblem of York. This explains why Henry VII later chose the Tudor rose to symbolise the restoration of order. His marriage to Elizabeth of York, the eldest daughter of Edward IV, was another symbol of the reconciliation of Lancaster and York.

Exploring the detail

Edward Hall and J. R. Lander

Edward Hall wrote *The Union of the Two Noble and Illustre Families of Lancaster and York* in 1548 to celebrate the establishment of Tudor kingship.

J. R. Lander wrote *The Wars of the Roses* in 1965, in which he argued that the violence of the civil wars reflected the incompetence of the King, Henry VI, to manage his nobility.

Exploring the detail

J. R. Green

J. R. Green was a late Victorian historian who belonged to a school known as 'the Whig historians'. They had great reverence for the institutions of government, especially parliament, and a disregard for politicians unless they assessed them to be 'statesmanlike'. These historians reflected the values of Victorian England, and this prejudiced their interpretations of the tangled, violent and intensely personal politics of 15th century England. J. R. Green wrote *A History of the English People* in 1880.

■ Key chronology

Timeline of the Wars of the Roses

The period of civil wars has been named 'the Wars of the Roses' because the Yorkist symbol came to be a white rose, while the Lancastrians came to wear a red rose.

1455 A Yorkist army led by Richard, Duke of York, meets Henry VI's army at the Battle of **St Albans**. This is the first battle of the Wars of the Roses.

1459 After four years of relative peace, the wars resume.

1460 The Yorkist army, with Warwick's support, win a victory at the Battle of **Northampton**.

1461 The Lancastrians rally and defeat the Yorkists at the Battle of **Wakefield** where Richard, Duke of York and one of his sons, Edmund, are killed. The bloodiest battle of these civil wars follows at **Towton**. Edward IV wins the day and seizes the throne.

1469 Warwick rebels against Edward IV and defeats him at the Battle of **Edgecote**.

1470 Warwick allies with Lancaster and Edward IV flees to Burgundy. They succeed in the restoration (also known as 'The Re-adeption') of Henry VI.

1471 Warwick is defeated and killed at the Battle of **Barnet**, after which the remaining Lancastrians are crushed at the Battle of **Tewkesbury**. Edward IV is restored to the throne.

1483 Edward IV dies. He is succeeded by Edward V then Richard III.

1485 Henry Tudor, the Lancastrian who united Lancaster and York, seizes the throne at the Battle of **Bosworth**.

1487 The Battle of **Stoke** marks the final struggle of the conflict.

enjoyed noblemen's company. This personal charisma, however, proved to be an ineffective restraint on the rival noble factions after the King's premature death.

In April 1483, England was a peaceful country with a mature and reliable central government machine that administered the King's law and kept the King's peace. This system of government was so mature that it had survived despite the upheavals of the Wars of the Roses. Edward IV had tightened his grip on royal finances and justice, and built a network of loyal nobles with local servants who made royal authority a reality in the regions. Despite these administrative strengths, the catastrophe of usurpation stemmed from the accession of a minor compounded by two key problems left on Edward IV's death: a bitter power struggle at the heart of the politically active section of the nobility; and conflicting wills.

Table 1 *Kings of England during the Wars of the Roses, 1455–87*

	Date	Fate
Henry VI	1422–61	His throne was usurped by Edward, Duke of York, who was crowned Edward IV
Edward IV	1461–70	His throne was usurped by the Lancastrians who restored Henry VI to the throne
Henry VI	1470–1	Edward IV reclaimed the throne. Henry VI was imprisoned in the Tower of London, where he was murdered
Edward IV	1471–83	He died peacefully but prematurely
Edward V	1483	His throne was usurped by his uncle Richard, Duke of Gloucester. Edward V then disappeared, presumed murdered
Richard III	1483–5	He was killed in battle
Henry VII	1485–1509	He died peacefully and passed the throne to his adult heir, Henry VIII

■ Timeline

Britain, 1483–1529

1483	1485	1487	1491	1497	1502	1506

Edward IV (died April 1483)	Edward V (April 1483 to July 1493)	Richard III (1483–

Secure monarchy

The sudden death of Edward IV results in an intense Yorkist family feud that restarts the Wars of the Roses, leads to two usurpations, and the disappearance of two princes.	**After the Battle of Bosworth, Henry VII establishes his reign and the Tudor dynasty. He faces immediate minor plots and defeats his first serious challenger – Lambert Simnel – at the Battle of Stoke, 1487.**	Perkin Warbeck is the figurehead for a series of challenges – on three occasions he attempts to invade England. He is most threatening when taking advantage of domestic discontent in the Cornish rebellion, 1497.	Henry VII appears to have secured his kingship.	**Henry VII's security is threatened by the deaths of Prince Arthur 1502, Elizabeth of York, Isabella of Castile and Philip of Burgundy. He subsequently employs harsh financial penalties to secure his nobles' loyalty.**

Foreign relations

Henry Tudor builds up a court in exile in Brittany and then in France. The King of France supports his invasion in 1485.	Henry VII works to secure international recognition for his kingship, securing the Treaty of Medina del Campo 1489, but failing to reach any agreement with Margaret of Burgundy.	English support for Brittany finally leads to a short Anglo-French war resolved in the Treaty of Etaples 1492.	Henry VII uses his foreign relations and trading agreements to limit overseas support for Perkin Warbeck.

| 1509 | 1513 | 1518 | 1520 | 1525 | 1527 | 1529 |

| Henry VII (1485–1509) | | | Henry VIII (1509–47) | | |

The accession of Henry VIII brings an energetic, popular Renaissance prince to the throne of England. English nobles enjoy the lavish court, generous patronage and military adventures.

Thomas Wolsey's authority as the King's chief minister is not challenged in a decade of relative domestic stability.

The revolt over the Amicable Grant threatens the security of the kingdom.

Henry VIII's desire to annul his marriage to secure the Tudor succession causes intense factional struggle at court.

Henry VII is unable to find a consistent line in foreign relations after the series of deaths. Even his main success, the Treaty of Windsor 1506, is short lived.

Henry VII prepares for, and fights, a war against France. However, English victory over Scotland at the Battle of Flodden, 1513, is much more significant.

Wolsey avoids war, instead he arranges prestigious international events such as the Treaty of Universal Peace 1518 and the Field of the Cloth of Gold 1520.

English foreign relations are hostage to the immense power of the Holy Roman Emperor, Charles V, who defeats the French at the Battle of Pavia, 1525, and seizes control of the Pope after the sack of Rome 1527. Charles V opposes the proposed marriage annulment and prevents any resolution of the King's Great Matter.

The end of the Yorkist monarchy and the triumph of Henry Tudor, 1483–7

1 1483: a year of instability and power struggles

In this chapter you will learn about:

- the instability and power struggles in England in 1483

- the difficulties posed by Edward IV's death

- the reasons why Edward V was never crowned king.

Fig. 1 *William Caxton (c.1422–91) an English printer, presenting to Edward IV what is considered to be the first book printed in England, **Dictes or Sayeings of the Philosophres** in 1477, translated by 2nd Earl Rivers*

Edward IV, King of England, died suddenly and prematurely at Windsor castle – perhaps from a stroke, or peritonitis, or even a chill caught while on a fishing trip – in April 1483 aged only 40 years. He had enjoyed a relatively successful reign, by the standards of the day, restoring peace after the disordered period of Lancastrian rule and providing his subjects with some much needed stability. Edward IV had been a strong king after 1471, able to control the rival noble factions, but his death opened up a destructive, disastrous Yorkist family feud.

■ The Yorkist monarchy at the time of the death of Edward IV

Edward's marriage to the commoner Elizabeth Woodville had offended some of the Yorkist families. The Woodville family was large, and therefore it represented a significant drain on royal patronage. Her father was appointed Treasurer of England, then ennobled as Earl Rivers in 1466, and the next year became Constable of England. Elizabeth had two sons from her first marriage – Thomas Grey, later the Marquis of Dorset, and Richard Grey. She also had seven sisters and five brothers – of whom Anthony was granted the governorship of the Isle of Wight.

On the other hand, the marriage itself was very successful. The royal couple had seven children, including two sons, Edward and Richard. Edward IV had every reason to expect that he would pass his throne smoothly to his adult heir. In April 1483, however, the crown passed to his eldest son, Edward, who was only 12 years old and resident at Ludlow Castle in the Welsh Marches.

Fig. 2 *Edward IV's reputation as king has fluctuated from damning criticism to fulsome praise*

■ Key profile

Edward, the Prince of Wales

In 1473, Edward IV decided his eldest son should take up permanent residence at Ludlow Castle in the Welsh Marches. The Queen's brother Anthony Woodville, Earl Rivers, was appointed 'governor and ruler' of the Prince's household. The power and influence of the prince's Counsel grew, and with it the status of the Woodville family. The young prince grew up under the influence of his maternal family.

Edward V was a minor and, therefore, could not rule alone. His father had made arrangements for a minority on two occasions.

- In 1475, Edward IV made his first written will before he left England to fight the war against France. He arranged for his wife, Queen Elizabeth, to be one of eight counsellors chosen from the bishops and nobles, to rule for the King in a regency Counsel.

- In his final days he amended the will. The detail of these late changes are not known because the will has not survived. Michael Hicks points out (in *Edward IV*, 2004, page 227) that the only thing we know about the second will is that the executors had changed. He comments that it is far from clear whether Edward left the role of Protector to his brother Richard, Duke of Gloucester, and removed Queen Elizabeth's name from the will. If he did amend his will to appoint Richard to rule, it was an obvious decision. Gloucester was the King's only surviving brother and had an outstanding record of loyal royal service.

The power struggle, therefore, revolved around two competing **factions**, Woodville and Gloucester, each of whom feared that the other threatened political exclusion and ruin. There was nothing new about factional rivalry; indeed it was a common feature of every medieval and early modern court. The factional quarrels could threaten the security of the realm if any king was weak, or if the divisions were exceptionally deep and bitter.

On Edward IV's death the strategic advantages lay with the Woodvilles primarily because Prince Edward was with Earl Rivers, the Queen's

Fig. 3 *Edward V was a charming, dignified and precocious youth. He had, however, little goodwill for his uncle Richard, Duke of Gloucester*

■ Key term

Faction: an alliance of powerful courtiers who shared common interests.

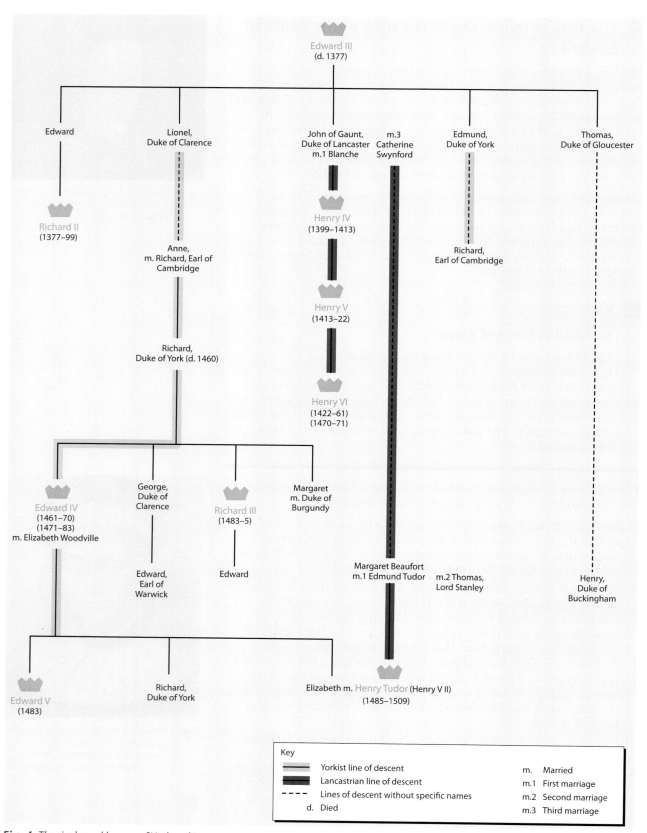

Fig. 4 *The rival royal houses of York and Lancaster*

brother. Rivers had recently been granted the rights to move the Prince guarded by armed retinue and to raise troops in the Welsh Marches. The Queen was centrally placed in London where her husband had mustered arms for a planned war against France. Her son by her previous marriage, the Marquis of Dorset, was Constable of the Tower of London with control over the treasury.

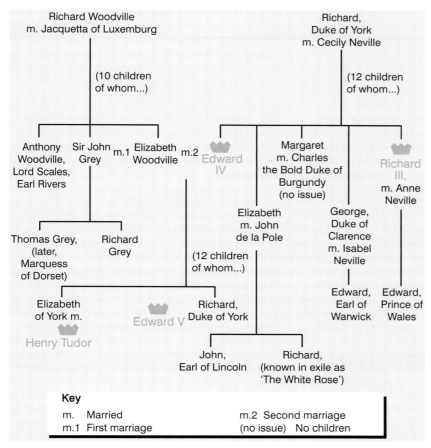

Fig. 5 *The genealogy of the Woodville–York families*

Richard, Duke of Gloucester, was less well placed by being at Middleham Castle in Yorkshire, although he had the active support of two of the greatest magnates, the Duke of Buckingham and Lord Hastings. Hastings, the Lord Chamberlain, was an established enemy of the Woodvilles having competed against Rivers in 1471 for lieutenancy of Calais.

■ **Key profile**

The Duke of Buckingham

Henry Stafford, Duke of Buckingham, was Richard of Gloucester's most powerful ally. Buckingham had a remote claim to the throne being descended from Edward III's youngest son. His power base was his lands in south-east Wales and the south-west Midlands. During the summer of 1483, he achieved a spectacular position in Richard III's government.

Usurpation: the seizure of the throne. In this case Richard, Duke of Gloucester, was to take the throne from the rightful King, Edward V.

■ Key profile

William, Lord Hastings

William, Lord Hastings, managed the east Midlands for Edward IV by developing an extensive network of retainers among the JPs and sheriffs, and by extending his castles at Kirby Muxloe and Ashby de la Zouch. He was loyal to Edward V but opposed the Woodvilles. He played a key role in events during the **usurpation** crisis.

The Counsel met after the King's death. Surviving records of the meeting confirm that the Queen attended. They also reveal that an atmosphere of extraordinary suspicion and fear had already developed. Dominic Mancini, an Italian cleric who visited London during the summer of 1482 and remained until July 1483, reported that one section of the Counsel wanted Gloucester to be Protector but the other section wanted a regency Counsel to include Gloucester. The Crowland chronicler reported that all members of the Counsel wanted a peaceful succession, thereby suggesting that some already feared otherwise.

The Counsel hotly disputed the size of the King's escort to London. Gloucester's allies feared a large escort would strengthen any Woodville plan for a regency Counsel. This appeared to be confirmed when the Counsel heard the Woodvilles hoped for an early coronation on 4 May, for this would represent the end of Edward V's protectorship and therefore undermine Gloucester's position as Protector. Mancini reported that Hastings wrote a curt and urgent message to Gloucester urging him to come to London speedily with a strong band in order to force the issue: 'The King has left all to your possession – goods, heir, realm. Secure the person of our Sovereign Lord Edward the Fifth and get you to London.'

■ Key profile

The Crowland chronicler and Dominic Mancini

The Crowland chronicler: an anonymous source, probably a clerk at court who attended Counsel meetings. He is regarded as being well informed though anti-northern. This influences his judgement of Richard III's reign.

Dominic Mancini was an Italin cleric who was resident in London in the years 1482 to 1483, though he left soon after Richard III's coronation on 6 July 1483. Mancini gathered his information in great detail from men who were well informed about contemporary events.

■ A closer look

Factional rivalry: Richard, Duke of Gloucester (1452–85)

Richard Plantagenet's childhood was dominated by civil war. In 1461, his eldest brother seized the throne and was crowned Edward IV. The new King granted Richard the title Duke of Gloucester.

Edward IV was indebted to Richard Neville, Earl of Warwick, for his success. He rewarded the nobleman by appointing him Gloucester's tutor. Gloucester accompanied Warwick as he travelled around his northern castles of Middleham, Sheriff Hutton, Penrith and Barnard Castle. He learned estate management, was educated in the politics of northern society, and gained experience of war. Meanwhile he met his future wife, Anne Neville, and his lifelong friend Francis, Lord Lovell.

In 1469, Edward IV brought Gloucester back to court in London. Within a few months, Warwick led the north in open rebellion against the King and in 1470, formed an unlikely alliance with Lancaster. Edward IV temporarily lost his throne but was able to recover his crown in 1471, assisted by Gloucester's knowledge of Warwick's fighting methods. Edward gave Gloucester his first military command at the decisive battles of Barnet and Tewkesbury. By 1471, aged only 19 years, Gloucester had proved himself to be a vital and loyal Yorkist.

Sean Cunningham comments on Gloucester's experiences before 1471:

Fig. 6 *Richard of Gloucester. Probably the most infamous of England's monarchs around whom opinion polarises: virtuous king or evil murderer?*

> Richard's character and personality was formed within a period of shocking civil conflict during which the royal family, headed by Edward IV, and its leading kin supporters, the Nevilles, headed by Warwick, turned against each other. To his credit, Richard remained steadfastly loyal to his brother during 1469–71, but the vivid demonstration of squabbling and betrayal, murders and summary executions, and the inconstancy of major nobles, must have left a lasting impression on the adolescent Duke. This is the environment in which Richard was introduced to political life.

 1   *Sean Cunningham, **Richard III, a royal enigma**, 2003*

Gloucester took over Warwick's role as royal lieutenant in the north of England. The northern nobles expected war against Scotland. Therefore, in 1482, Gloucester launched an invasion that captured Edinburgh and Berwick from the Scots. He developed religious patronage, founding collegiate chapels at Middleham and Barnard Castle. He promoted justice through the courts and provided some redress for grievances through his Counsel.

There was nothing to suggest before 9 April 1483 that Richard, Duke of Gloucester, was anything other than a loyal servant of the Yorkist monarchy. However, before 1483, Gloucester was not required to prevent Elizabeth Woodville becoming regent.

A closer look

Factional rivalry: Elizabeth Woodville and the Woodville faction

Edward IV secretly married Elizabeth Woodville in 1464 without even consulting either of his closest advisers, Warwick and Hastings. The marriage created problems throughout Edward's two reigns.

1 It was one factor that led Warwick to rebel against the King in 1469. Warwick was embarrassed by the marriage because it publicly curtailed the diplomatic negotiations for a prestigious royal marriage to Bona of Savoy, a French princess.

2 The Woodville family were seen as social climbers. They were resented by members of the established nobility, especially Gloucester, Hastings and Buckingham.

Fig. 7 *An illuminated manuscript featuring Elizabeth Woodville, majestic and romantic Queen of England, surrounded by carnations*

3 The family appears to have been unpleasant – arrogant, scheming, grasping and vengeful. One notable exception to this rule was Sir Anthony Woodville.

4 Prince Edward, born in 1470, was brought up, almost entirely, by members of the Woodville family. Gloucester feared the prince was more Woodville than York.

In 1483, the Woodville faction knew they were unpopular with many powerful enemies, especially Gloucester and Hastings. They resented Gloucester's huge power base in the north and Hastings' close friendship with the King. They also knew their particular strength – their close relationship with Prince Edward, and, in 1483, they would use this asset to prevent Gloucester from assuming the role of Protector.

The historian C. Ross comments:

> No one knows when Edward first met Elizabeth, still less why he should have chosen to make her his queen. The best explanation may be that it was the impulsive love-match of an impetuous young man. Sir Thomas More commented on the King's reputation as a successful womaniser, 'He was of youth greatly given to fleshly wantonness'.
>
> If Edward's motives for making this remarkable misalliance remain a matter for speculation, its consequences were a matter of high political concern, and ultimately contributed largely to the downfall of the Yorkist dynasty. The immediate disadvantages were obvious to all. Her beauty was not matched by any personal warmth. She was ambitious for her family's interests, quick to take offence and reluctant to forgive. Her personal defects were less important than the political problems arising from her marriage.
>
> Edward could expect trouble on three counts. There were the consequences for the negotiations for a French marriage, he might expect some hostile reaction from his leading nobles, and he had to provide for Elizabeth's horde of relatives. It was unprecedented for a king to make such a marriage.

2

*From Charles Ross, **Edward IV**, 1981*

■ The accession of Edward V and usurpation by Richard III

The hot disputes in Counsel were not reflected in the leisurely arrangements made for the young King to be brought to London. The news of Edward's death did not reach Ludlow Castle until 14 April and the royal party did not leave until 24 April. This delay suggests that the Woodville family surrounding the King did not feel immediate pressure to reach London. Earl Rivers even agreed to meet Gloucester at Northampton so that the two men could move south and enter the capital city together with the new King.

The evening of 30 April proved to be a watershed. Gloucester and his retinue ate at an inn in Stony Stratford where Earl Rivers visited them. Gloucester and Rivers were enjoying a meal and drink together, when Buckingham arrived and joined their company. After Rivers left, to return to the King who was lodging nearby at Grafton Regis, Gloucester and Buckingham agreed their next move. The evening was ironically convivial given Hastings' reports of factional tension in London and the bloodshed to follow.

Gloucester and Buckingham chose to take their first decisive action against the Woodvilles. Early the next day, Gloucester arrested Rivers and his three most trusted attendants Sir Thomas Vaughan, Sir Richard Hawte and Sir Richard Grey. All four men were imprisoned in Gloucester's stronghold – the north of the country. They were held there until their executions at Pontefract Castle on 25 June. Earl Rivers and the Woodville faction had been outwitted and taken by surprise. They had failed to take advantage of their early strategic and military strengths.

These events caused panic in London. Queen Elizabeth fled to **sanctuary** at Westminster Abbey with all her other children, Dorset, and her brother Lionel, Bishop of Salisbury. There they remained when, on 4 May, Edward V, Gloucester and Buckingham entered the city and the Counsel confirmed Gloucester as Protector.

There was little to suggest even in early May 1483 that Gloucester would ruthlessly usurp the throne; indeed the political tension seemed to relax. The Protector ruled, apparently harmoniously, for several weeks during which time he and the Counsel rearranged Edward V's coronation for 22 June and called parliament to meet on 25 June.

The Gloucester faction, however, began to fragment as Hastings took exception to Gloucester's behaviour towards Buckingham and Queen Elizabeth. Hastings, along with other members of the Counsel, distrusted the rewards that Gloucester heaped on Buckingham. They remembered Edward IV's judgement that Buckingham should be excluded from any serious role in government. Gloucester now gave Buckingham great power in the West country and Welsh marshes, including the right to raise troops in five western counties, the titles Chief Justice and Chamberlain in both North and South Wales, and stewardship of certain manors and constableship of castles as they became available.

Hastings had been a great personal friend of Edward IV and he disliked Gloucester's continuing intolerance of the widow, Queen Elizabeth. His suspicions were aroused on 10 June when Gloucester wrote to the authorities in the city of York asking them to send armed men to assist him and Buckingham

■ Activity

Talking point

'Richard Duke of Gloucester was determined to seize the throne from the time he heard of his brother's death.' Do you agree or disagree with this statement?

■ Key term

Sanctuary: a place of safety in a church. In this case, Queen Elizabeth took refuge in Westminster Abbey.

Fig. 8 *Dressed in blue velvet and surrounded by his uncles, Edward V entered the city of London on 4 May accompanied by his uncle Richard, Duke of Gloucester. He processed to the Bishop of London's Palace at St Paul's where he was safely lodged, but was moved to the Tower of London by 19 May*

against the Woodvilles. Hastings, devoted to the interests of all Edward IV's children, came to believe that the Protector harboured sinister ambitions. In early June, Hastings met several members of the Counsel privately including Thomas Rotherham, Archbishop of York and John Morton, Bishop of Ely.

■ Key profile

Thomas Rotherham and John Morton

Thomas Rotherham was a loyal servant of Edward IV who combined the role of Archbishop of York with that of Lord Chancellor of England. As Lord Chancellor, he was the Keeper of the Great Seal, the chief royal chaplain and advisor to the King in both spiritual and worldly matters.

John Morton also combined his church appointment, Bishop of Ely, with the role of Master of the Rolls. This title was an abbreviation of the full 'Keeper or Master of the Rolls and Records of the Chancery of England'. Morton was responsible for keeping the judicial records of the Court of Chancery.

■ Key term

Summary execution: put to death without a time-consuming trial. This was illegal – the right to trial, established long before 1483, is a core feature of the English system of justice.

Convinced that Hastings was scheming against him, Gloucester moved against his former ally. As a set-up he called a Counsel meeting in the White Tower on 13 June to be attended by Buckingham, John Howard and all the suspected conspirators. Suddenly, during the Counsel meeting, he accused Hastings, Lord Stanley, Morton and Rotherham of plotting with the Woodvilles, and added an additional charge of treason against Hastings. Armed men were waiting to escort Hastings first to church confession, then to **summary execution** on Tower Hill. The indictment for treason was read afterwards over the dead man's body.

Fig. 9 *Richard, Duke of Gloucester, orders the arrest of his erstwhile friend William Hastings, a dramatic scene familiar to readers of Shakespeare's play* Richard III. *Hastings had urged Gloucester to speed to London after the death of Edward IV*

The other Counsellors were treated less brutally. Morton and Rotherham were imprisoned in the Tower briefly before Morton was sent to Buckingham's castle at Brecon in south Wales where he was well looked after, and Rotherham was released. Stanley was temporarily detained in his own home.

After this brutality, on 16 June, Gloucester's desire to secure the crown for himself accelerated. He sent a deputation to Westminster Abbey to request that Richard, Duke of York should leave sanctuary and join Edward V in the Tower to help him prepare for the coronation; although preparations for the coronation actually stopped around this time. Queen Elizabeth agreed, possibly reassured by the removal of Hastings who was a long-term enemy of the Woodville family, though probably because she had no choice but to allow her son to go. Once the two Princes were together, Gloucester made his intentions clear. He planned to denounce their legitimacy and put himself forward as the rightful king.

▮ **Key profile**

Richard, Duke of York

Richard was the second son of Edward IV and Queen Elizabeth Woodville. His older brother became king on April 9 1483, and Richard was his heir-presumptive. Richard joined his elder brother in the Tower of London but the two princes soon disappeared. In the 1490s Perkin Warbeck claimed to be Richard, Duke of York, but was proved to be an imposter.

Gloucester therefore raked up an old, dubious scandal that Edward IV had contracted to marry Lady Elizabeth Butler before he actually wed Elizabeth Woodville. This meant that all Edward IV's children were declared illegitimate. The source of this scandal might have been Robert Stillington, Bishop of Bath and Wells. When the armed men had arrived from York and the planned Parliament had been cancelled, Buckingham presented this scandalous story to a select assembly of Lords. They agreed that Gloucester should claim his right to the throne. The Lord Protector was moving into a position of unquestionable authority.

On 22 June, Friar Ralph Shaw delivered a sermon at St Paul's Cross in London during which he praised Gloucester's virtues and told of the pre-contract, concluding that the Protector was entitled to rule; and other churchmen preached the same message. Shaw's sermon was flawed because it did not legitimise Gloucester's right to rule. If the children of Edward of York and Queen Elizabeth were illegitimate, the rightful king would have been the son of Gloucester's older brother George, the Duke of Clarence. That child, Edward, Earl of Warwick, was already in Gloucester's custody.

The preparations for usurpation were almost complete. Richard needed to permanently remove any future threat from the Woodville family, therefore Earl Rivers, Grey, Hawte and Vaughn were taken to the execution block at Pontefract Castle. These executions were overseen by Sir Richard Ratcliffe, and witnessed by the men of York and the rest of the army that was about to depart for London.

Richard made his final moves in the usurpation drama.

▮ On 25 June, an assembly of the Lords and most of the Commons gathered at Westminster. Buckingham presented a roll of parchment, a petition, to the assembly. It detailed the evils of the Woodville family through their deception of Edward IV. It alleged that Edward was snared by Woodville sorcery to marry when he was already under contract to another woman. The petition begged Gloucester to take the crown.

▮ The next day Buckingham read the petition to a large crowd that included many London notables at Baynard's Castle. Gloucester appeared on a battlement and acknowledged the crowd, whereupon he was hailed as Richard III. He rode by horse to Westminster Hall and ceremoniously sat in the royal seat in the Court of the King's Bench.

▮ From this seat Richard, Duke of Gloucester formally declared that his accession to the throne should be dated from 26 June 1483.

Richard III had usurped the throne of England without using military force, after apparently claiming the title 'King of England' through legitimate inheritance, and at the request of the Lords and Commons of the realm. He could make preparations for his own coronation.

■ Activity

Research exercise

Edward IV has been blamed for the events after his death in several ways. Using the table below, find evidence to support each, then judge whether Edward IV should be held accountable on all, some or none of these charges. Was one factor more significant than any of the others?

	Evidence	Was Edward IV to blame?
He failed to contract a valid marriage		
He left behind factional divisions		
He did not leave clear guidance about the succession		
He gave the Woodville family too much power		

Fig. 10 *The story of the disappearance of the princes is so emotive that it has generated amazing stories of miraculous escape and secret survival, along with endless speculation about the identity of those responsible*

The princes in the Tower

Richard had seized the crown speedily and ruthlessly. However, in the months following his accession, rumours and suspicions grew that he had murdered his two nephews. Medieval society was brutal. It was an act of political folly to keep a dangerous rival alive, especially a deposed king. Edward IV was allegedly responsible for the murder in the Tower of London of the feeble Henry VI, after his defeat at the Battle of Tewkesbury in 1471, and had ordered the judicial murder of his own brother George, Duke of Clarence.

The historical precedent for murder, of either a previous king or a family member, was established. Richard clearly had both a strong motive and an opportunity to remove his rival, the deposed Edward V, and his younger brother. Most contemporaries seem to have believed that the two princes were dead within a few weeks of Richard III's accession to the throne. By autumn 1483, Elizabeth Woodville was apparently prepared to support a challenge to Richard III by Henry Tudor, the leading Lancastrian claimant to the throne who was currently in exile in Brittany: a plan she would not have backed without excellent reason to believe her sons were already dead.

■ Key profile

Henry Tudor

Henry Tudor was born in Pembroke Castle in 1457, the only son of Edmund Tudor, Earl of Richmond and Margaret Beaufort. His claim to the throne as a Lancastrian was through his mother's line back to Edward III, although it was a weak bastard line of descent. Tudor was left as the main Lancastrian claimant after the overwhelming Yorkist victories in 1471 at the battles of Barnet and Tewkesbury. He and his uncle Jasper Tudor fled to the relative safety of Brittany. The chance that Tudor would ever claim his inheritance looked increasingly hopeless as Edward IV fathered a family and consolidated his rule, but this changed following the usurpation of the throne by Richard III.

The disappearance of the princes played a large part in building support for the rebels later in 1483 from the southern and western counties of England; however the rest of the country was less affected. The northerners, both nobility and gentry, remained loyal to Richard.

■ A closer look

The fate of the two princes

The fate of the two princes, Edward V and his younger brother Richard, Duke of York, is the great unsolved mystery of Richard III's reign. The boys were last seen alive while practising archery and playing in the garden of the Tower of London.

The traditional story of their death is based on Thomas More's book *History of King Richard III* (*c*.1513). In his account, the two princes were confined to their room in the Tower of London. Meanwhile, Richard III set off on his coronation **progress** but on the road to Gloucester decided to act against his nephews. The King passed the responsibility for this grisly task to Sir James Tyrell, Master of the Horse, who, assisted by Miles Forest and John Dighton, smothered the two boys in their beds. The bodies were buried at the foot of a flight of stairs in the Tower.

■ Key term

Progress: a king's journey around the country to meet his subjects.

■ Key profile

Thomas More

Thomas More, a Renaissance scholar and politician, is profiled in much more detail in Chapter 6. His *History of King Richard III* reflects his anti-Richard judgement based mainly on evidence from contemporary witnesses. It is written in the new Renaissance style that favoured a dramatic turn of phrase compared to the more mundane medieval chronicle. The history was intended to be a meditation on power and corruption, rather than an accurately researched history.

Sir James Tyrell devised that they should be murdered in their beds. To the execution wherof, he appointed Miles Forest, a fellow fleshed in murder before-time. To him he joined John Dighton, his own horse-keeper, a big, broad, square knave. Then, when all the other servants had left, this Miles Forest and John Dighton, about midnight came in to the chamber and suddenly lapped them up among the clothes, so bewrapped and entangled them, keeping down by force the feather bed and pillows hard unto their mouths, that within a while, they gave up to God their innocent souls into the joys of heaven, leaving their tormentors their bodies dead in the bed.

3   *Extract from Thomas More,* **The History of England***, c.1513*

Who were the main suspects?

■ **Richard III** remains the prime suspect for the murder. He failed to produce the two princes alive when politically damaging rumours began before the Buckingham rebellion, in October 1483. There is no evidence that Richard would sanction the killing of his brother's sons.

■ A second suspect is **Henry Tudor**. He had a clear motive to ensure the princes were permanently removed. No contemporary charges were ever made, however, either at home or abroad, against Tudor.

■ Another suspect is **Henry Stafford, Duke of Buckingham**. Buckingham remained in London for several days after Richard set out on the 1483 progress. Richard did not take advantage of Buckingham's failed rebellion in October 1483 to blame him for the murders.

How important is this mystery?

The two child victims of this historical 'Whodunnit?' are historically insignificant. Their fate, however, is important, both because it sheds light on the intense uncertainty in London during the summer and autumn of 1483, and because their disappearance was catastrophic for Richard III. The general acceptance in the southern and western counties of England that Richard had disposed of his nephews may have been a cause of the Buckingham rebellion. The King's policies after the revolt explain Richard III's loss of southern support before Bosworth. However, this judgement needs to be kept in context. The only contemporary chronicler, the Crowland chronicler, reported that the Buckingham rebellion was to put Edward V back on the throne, suggesting that there was no general acceptance that the princes were already dead. The chronicler later changed his account after it was reported the princes were dead.

Cross-reference

The Buckingham rebellion is explained later on pages 25–27.

The Crowland chronicler is introduced on page 14.

Activity

Research exercise

This mystery is the focus of detailed commentary. Take one of these three main suspects and find out more about the evidence that either incriminates or absolves them of responsibility for the deaths.

Activity

Revision exercise

List all the people you have read about in this section in a table. Place them in one of three columns: Yorkist, Lancastrian or other. Highlight those you think played key roles in events between April and July 1483 and explain why.

Summary questions

1 Explain why Edward IV's death opened up such a bitter family feud in the weeks from 9 April 1483 to 26 June 1483.

2 Explain why Richard III was able to usurp the throne of England in June 1483.

2 The reign of Richard III

In this chapter you will learn about:

- how Richard III never recovered from the popular assumption that he was implicated in the murder of his two nephews
- the causes, events and consequences of the Buckingham rebellion in October 1483
- the evidence that Richard III was a capable administrator.

Fig. 1 *Richard III fought under the banner of the white boar. This commemorative charter plaque is now displayed on the wall of St Michael's Tower in Gloucester*

The Cat, the Rat, and Lovell our dog
Rule all England under an hog

1

■ Cross-reference

Richard's leading nobles are discussed later in this chapter on page 37.

William Collingbourne's rhyme, written in 1484, referred to the nobles Ratcliffe, Catesby, Lovell and Richard III whose banner was a boar. The rhyme was found pinned to the door of St Paul's Cathedral in London! Collingbourne was charged with treason, not so much for this libellous jibe on the King and his chief advisers, but because he was in communication with Henry Tudor.

■ Activity

Source analysis

Explain the political allusions in Collingbourne's rhyme (Source 1). Do you think it was simply an absurd piece of doggerel or was it a serious affront to the King?

■ Instability in the reign of Richard III

The early months – 26 June to 11 October, 1483

Once he had assumed the crown, Richard III set about establishing his own government.

- ■ He arranged his coronation for 6 July.
- ■ He appointed his chief officers of state: the Bishop of Lincoln, John Russell, as Chancellor; John Gunthorpe as Keeper of the Privy Seal; and William Catesby as Chancellor of the Exchequer.
- ■ He rewarded his loyal servants: John Howard was elevated to the Dukedom of Norfolk and his son, Thomas Howard, was titled Earl of Surrey.
- ■ He empowered his three greatest magnates, Buckingham, Norfolk and Northumberland virtually as his lieutenants in Wales, East Anglia and the North respectively.
- ■ He deployed his army from the North as additional forces to keep law and order over the coronation, although afterwards he allowed them to return home.

The coronation was a glorious occasion. Buckingham and Norfolk stood on either side of the King, while the queen was attended by the Duchess of Suffolk and the Countess of Richmond. Almost the entire peerage of England was present in Westminster Abbey, along with over 70 knights, yet only London and the nobility had any real understanding of the events that had led to the coronation of Richard III during which he had promised to nourish peace and govern justly. He needed to show himself to the rest of his kingdom.

He set out on a progress by mid-July. He wound his way through the south-west Midlands, including Gloucester and Worcester, to the central counties where he stayed in Warwick and Nottingham among other places, to the North via Pontefract Castle where he was reunited with his son, Edward, whom he formally created Prince of Wales. As he travelled, so he met foreign envoys. He agreed a treaty of friendship with the envoy sent by Queen Isabella of Castile in the hope that it would bring him international recognition. He was unable, however, to come to any arrangement with Louis XII, the King of France, which was a concern as France traditionally supported the house of Lancaster. Richard III's relations with the Duke of Brittany became increasingly important to the security of his kingship.

The progress moved through Yorkshire to the city of York. The royal family made a state entry into the city accompanied by a splendid retinue of bishops, members of the nobility and officers of the Royal Household. They were led through the city by the Mayor and Aldermen who were wearing scarlet robes, and cheered by a mass of citizens as they passed from gate to gate. After a welcoming speech, the Mayor presented the King with a hundred marks in a golden cup and the Queen with a hundred pounds on a golden plate. Richard III hastily arranged for a great ceremony of investiture of Edward, Prince of Wales, in the grandeur of York Minster. This was the happiest period of the whole reign.

In the middle of September the royal family separated. Queen Anne accompanied her son and his cousin Edward, Earl of Warwick, to Middleham Castle, while the King went south to London. He knew that he had serious and growing opposition that needed to be suppressed. Richard had left his Counsel at Westminster to carry out the business of government during his absence on progress. On 29 July he had followed Chancellor Russell's advice to set up a commission of '**oyer and terminer**' for the capital city. This commission was to try unnamed men for an 'enterprise'. The historian Rosemary Horrox concludes that the 'enterprise' was probably an attempt to rescue the princes from the Tower by starting fires all over the City of London, so creating confusion as cover for the rescue. Richard later had to set up a similar commission, to be overseen by Buckingham, for the south-eastern counties on 28 August. Such commissions were necessary to keep law and order – Richard clearly faced gathering trouble.

Richard had also heard rumours from his contacts in Brittany that the King of France had offered safe custody to Henry Tudor. This threat was compounded by his distrust of Tudor's relatives who were still in England. On 13 August, Richard placed all the lands held by John Welles, described as a king's rebel, in the control of John Lord Scrope of Bolton. Welles was the half-brother of Henry Tudor's mother, Lady Margaret Beaufort, so he fled and joined Tudor in exile.

The Buckingham rebellion, October 1483

Richard's hold on power was far from secure, despite appearances in York, and was soon revealed to be fragile. He learned in October that he could not rely on his closest ally or his brother's powerful network of local support. The opposition, that grew in the south-eastern counties during July and August 1483, became stronger and more widespread, culminating in a series of rebellions across southern England during the autumn of 1483. These rebellions are known as 'the Duke of Buckingham's rebellion' although the name is misleading. The rebellions were planned, and had even started in the Kentish Weald, before the Duke of Buckingham defected to the rebels.

On the face of it, Buckingham's defection was unlikely. He had been well rewarded for his central role in the usurpation. In July, he was granted **constableship** of all castles and **stewardship** of all lands in Shropshire and Herefordshire as they became available. He was given additional land in the East Midlands and southern England. It is unclear why he chose to rebel, though one possible explanation is that he developed an insatiable appetite for reward and was offended when he was denied it. Richard promised him half the earldom of Hereford, though this would have to be confirmed by parliament. It seems the **letters patent** for this title were never issued, suggesting that the King changed his mind.

Key terms

Oyer and terminer: the two words are used to describe the work of a commission set up to 'hear' the evidence that a serious crime had been committed and to 'finish' by giving the verdict and carrying out justice.

Constableship: a post given by a king to a loyal servant who was trusted to supervise a castle.

Stewardship: another reward for loyal service – to manage crown lands.

Letters patent: Royal order granted under the Great Seal – in this case to confirm the grant of a title.

Activity

Revision exercise

Draw a spider diagram to summarise the details about the Buckingham Revolt under the headings 'Causes', 'Events' and 'Results'.

■ **Cross-reference**

The executions of leading nobles at Pontefract Castle in June 1483, and the imprisonment of John Morton, are outlined on page 18.

To recap on the conflict between Yorkists and Lancastrians, see page 4.

Henry Tudor is introduced on page 21.

Fig. 2 *Henry VII: the first Tudor King of England whose dynasty ruled until 1603*

Other explanations have been put forward.

■ The Crowland chronicler reported that Buckingham was driven by personal conscience after the assumed death of the two princes. This was the chronicler's second explanation for the rebellion.

■ Thomas More linked the rebellion to conversations between Buckingham and John Morton, who had been placed in his custody in Brecon Castle, which inflamed the Duke's grudges against the King.

■ Some argue, though it is improbable, that Buckingham planned to remove Richard III and become king himself, for he too was descended from Edward III.

■ Buckingham perceived himself to be a kingmaker. He wanted to lead the rebellion that would place Henry Tudor on the throne of England. This is the outcome that Edward IV's loyal servants increasingly desired. Such loyal servants included Sir Thomas Bourchier of Surrey, Sir William Hawte of Kent whose brother had been executed at Pontefract Castle, Sir John Harcourt of Oxfordshire and Sir William Norreys of Berkshire.

The rebellion was not one event, nor did it have one leader. It was a series of household revolts by Yorkists who were loyal to Edward IV and his sons. During Richard's coronation progress, the Edwardian loyalists had plotted to rescue the princes from the Tower. Once rumours spread that the princes had disappeared, presumed murdered, Edward IV's loyal servants were stirred into action.

These loyal servants intended to exploit persisting support for the house of Lancaster to remove Richard III. Henry Tudor, the leading Lancastrian claimant, was in exile in Brittany. Their rallying cry intriguingly linked the 'Buckingham rebellion' to the Lancastrians, although it was not a Lancastrian rising. The vital link in this story is John Morton, Bishop of Ely, who was still a prisoner at Brecon Castle. He was able to put Buckingham in contact with Margaret Beaufort, Henry Tudor's mother. She contacted her son in Brittany.

Henry Tudor took the opportunity to launch his claim for the throne on the back of the popular uprisings. His preparations had been underway from mid-September but historians are not certain about his date of departure across the Channel. Polydore Vergil gave the possible dates as 6 or 10 October, but that seems too early, and Tudor would have been caught by appalling autumn storms in the Channel. A modern historian, Louise Gill, who has written a specialist study of the Buckingham rebellion, claims he was still moored in Brittany on 30 October, and did not reach Plymouth until the first week of November.

■ The rebellion started in south-east England on 11 October with uprisings in **Kent**, followed by **Sussex** and **Surrey** during the next 10 days. Prompt action by the King's loyal lieutenant in the south, the Duke of Norfolk, contained these rebels. Norfolk seized control of the bridge over the River Thames at Gravesend.

■ By 18 October further rebel armies had formed in the south-west counties of **Cornwall** and **Devon** led by Thomas Grey, Marquis of Dorset, and two members of the Courtenay family, Edward and Walter Courtenay.

■ Another rebel army gathered in the central-southern counties at two centres – Newbury, **Berkshire** and Salisbury, **Wiltshire**. Giles Daubeney was one of the leaders in this sector. Historians, however, know very little about these rebels' activities.

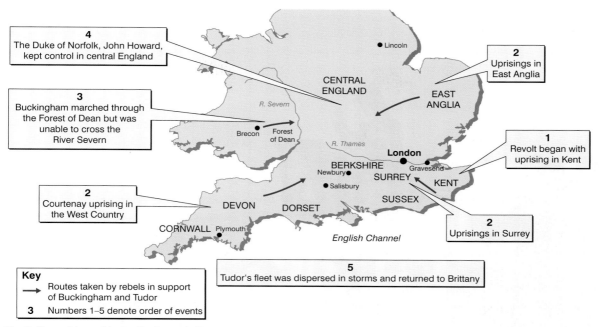

Fig. 3 *The uprisings of the Buckingham rebellion*

■ Buckingham planned for another rising from his own power base in **south Wales**, but this proved unrealistic. He departed from his castle in Brecon and marched through the Forest of Dean hoping to join the Courtenays in the West Country. As soon as he left, Ricardian loyalists torched his castle. He was unable to cross the River Severn because it flooded during heavy rainfall, and because Sir Humphrey Stafford of Grafton in Worcestershire, who remained loyal to the King, destroyed any bridges. Drenched by the rains, harrassed by Ricardians, and in the face of mounting desertions from his unwilling and demoralised troops, Buckingham hid and Morton fled to Flanders. Buckingham was betrayed to the sheriff of Shropshire, tried and then executed in Salisbury market place on 2 November.

Richard had contained the rebels in the south east, and subdued the Welsh uprising. He could now turn his full attention to the south west and central-south. His army marched into Wiltshire, where the rebels scattered into sanctuary or fled. Dorset and Daubeney both chose to escape to Tudor's court. Richard III entered Salisbury unopposed on 28 October.

It is not clear whether Buckingham intended to claim the throne in his own right or whether he planned to declare for Tudor, and install Henry VII on the throne of England. Tudor was moored off the coast at Plymouth waiting for a signal to land from Buckingham or Dorset. He heard of the Duke's execution on 8 or 9 November and sailed back to Brittany.

The outcomes of the rebellion were disastrous for Richard III despite his success in suppressing it. Henry Tudor had now emerged as a credible rival, because he was seen as the Yorkist household's replacement for Edward IV's sons. That is why, on Christmas Day 1483, Henry Tudor made a public promise to marry Edward's daughter, Elizabeth of York, if he was crowned King of England.

■ **Key chronology**

The Buckingham rebellion

Please note that the dates are approximate as few records survive.

1483

11 October	Richard III, in Lincoln, learns that Buckingham backs the rebels in Kent.
15 October	An unusually heavy storm blows over England causing rivers to flood.
By 18 October	The south-west rebels gather in Exeter.
18 October	Buckingham invites Henry Tudor to invade.
28 October	The King secures Salisbury.
2 November	Buckingham is executed for treason.
By 8 November	Most of the rebel leaders flee from England.

Fig. 4 *The English weather helped Richard to crush a serious challenge to his kingship from the Duke of Buckingham in the autumn of 1483. In this picture, Buckingham attempts to cross the River Severn at Gloucester but 10 days of storms and rains swelled the waters so it became impassable*

Richard was clearly unable to depend on his leading gentry so now had to build his own base of support. He developed two main policies to build his royal authority:

1 He tried, where possible, to develop existing power structures by handing more land and local responsibilities to his established loyal gentry. He rewarded Viscount Lovell by extending the lands he already held in the Thames Valley.

2 His usual, and much more controversial, policy however was to plant loyal northerners in the Midlands and south. Sir Richard Brackenbury from Durham, Constable of the Tower, and deeply implicated in the princes' murder was appointed sheriff of Kent and Constable of Tonbridge Castle. Sir Richard Ratcliffe, an eminent northerner, was given extensive lands in Devon that immediately made him a great landowner. Such plantations caused deep resentment and in 1485 would prove to be politically disruptive.

After the rebellion, 97 people were **attainted** and lost their lands and their heirs were disinherited. Most of those attainted were southern gentry, while 40 northerners benefitted after being granted new lands, offices and annuities. In 1485, Tudor would be able to rely on the support of southern gentry in his bid to usurp the throne.

Richard III – increasing instability

Richard's short reign was dominated by the consequences of his usurpation, the popular assumption that he had murdered his nephews and the political fall-out from the Buckingham rebellion.

In his coronation oath the new King had declared a commendable interest in justice for all. During his reign, parliament passed legislation concerned with minor reforms of legal procedures. It is not, however, clear whether these were driven through by Richard or individual parliamentarians. Richard also made unusual efforts to provide legal remedies for the less well off by establishing some **conciliar** measures that would evolve into the Court of Requests under the Tudors. Contemporaries, however, remembered only the summary execution of Hastings.

The new King's main problem was that he was only ever seen as a usurper by the majority of his subjects, and so faced growing public disaffection, which made his hold on power tense and uncertain. He sent instructions to Southampton, Windsor and York that the city authorities should repress and punish those who repeated slanderous rumours that he had murdered the princes, as well as poisoning his wife.

Richard avoided relying on the great magnates, fearing that they might use their power to usurp the throne, following his own example. He was not generous with ennoblement. Instead, Richard chose to rule through minor nobles such as Scrope of Bolton, Dacre, Greystoke and Fitzhugh. The lower tiers of royal administration adapted to the new rule but even gentry like Sir Richard Ratcliffe and William Catesby, who were awarded land and offices, did not get titles.

Richard set up an independent royal Counsel to keep law and order in the north. He named his son, Edward, as the leader of the Counsel but intended to run it himself. The north, however, was always less troublesome than the south so he handed the Counsel of the North to his nephew John de la Pole, Earl of Lincoln. In doing so, he overrode the interests of the two great northern magnates the Earls of Westmorland and Northumberland making it no surprise that Northumberland had little reason to back him at Bosworth.

As King, Richard did his best to continue the Yorkist tradition of active supervision of the royal purse. He had inherited a small surplus from his brother, which was quickly reduced by Edward's lavish funeral. Evidence survives that Richard closely administered the crown estates, his main source of ordinary revenue. He involved himself closely in the running of these estates, giving instructions to local officials and making determined efforts to secure payments from tenants and officers. He also passed an Act of Parliament outlawing the unpopular 'benevolences' Edward had relied on, though he increasingly depended on forced loans, also very unpopular, to meet his growing commitments. He had to pay for the suppression of the Buckingham rebellion, to wage war in Scotland, and then to defend himself against Tudor's impending invasion.

Richard's reign was so short that he only had time to call one parliament, and that was delayed until January 1484 by the Buckingham rebellion. It was dominated by Richard's right to rule; passing *Titulus Regius* proclaiming the princes' illegitimacy, voting the king customs revenues for life, then passing Acts of Attainder against those implicated in the rebellion. Some minor acts were passed but nothing of lasting significance for, in 1484, Richard's attention was drawn firstly to foreign policy and secondly to family tragedy with the deaths of his son, Edward, in 1484 and his wife, Anne, in 1485.

In a desperate, ill-judged attempt to appear a worthy king of England, Richard chose to continue Edward's war against Scotland despite James III's desire for peace. He was required to fund an expensive campaign that

Key term

Conciliar: in this period, kings started to create small counsels to deal with particular problems.

Cross-reference

You can learn about the Battle of Bosworth on page 34.

■ Cross-reference

Henry Tudor and his activities to date are discussed on page 33.

Relationships between England, Brittany and France are described on page 61.

■ Key term

Renaissance: a rebirth of interest in Europe in arts and sciences, often patronised by lavish royal and ducal courts.

resulted in defeat at Lochmaben in July, followed by a three-year truce. By this time, however, his main problem was not the border dispute – his main problem was Henry Tudor.

Henry Tudor, the leading Lancastrian claimant, had been sheltered at the court of the Duke of Brittany since 1471. Richard negotiated secretly for Duke Francis II of Brittany to surrender Tudor in return for the annual revenues from the earldom of Richmond. His plans were foiled when Bishop Morton, in exile in Flanders, sent a warning to Tudor who promptly fled to France.

Despite all this turmoil, Richard found some time to become acquainted with his countrymen by going on progresses around the country. At court, probably to placate Lancastrians, he developed a cult of Henry VI by arranging for the dead King to be exhumed and reburied in the newly-built St George's Chapel, Windsor. He also presented himself as a legitimate, genuine **Renaissance** king by supporting Henry VI's foundation at King's College, Cambridge. Henry VI had drawn up detailed instructions for the chapel, going to great lengths to ensure that it would be equal in size and beauty.

Richard gave the impression that he was reconciled with Edward IV's family. In March 1484, he won over Elizabeth Woodville by guaranteeing her safety if she and her daughters came out of sanctuary and attended court, even agreeing an annuity of 700 marks per annum. The reality, however, was that Richard had seized the throne violently, was never able to escape from the shadow of suspicion, and never had the chance to effectively demonstrate whether he had the capacity for kingship.

Fig. 5 *Richard III gave instructions that the chapel of King's College, that had been started by Henry VI and continued by Edward IV, should be completed speedily. The chapel is one of the best examples of perpendicular architecture in England with ornate and intricate fan vaulting*

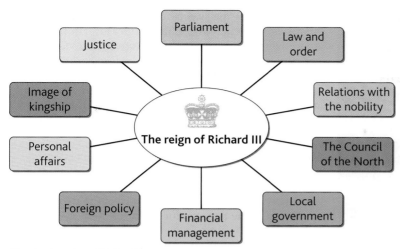

Fig. 6 *The reign of Richard III*

Activity

Research exercise

'Richard III needed time to prove he had the capacity for kingship.' Using the table below, find evidence to support or counter this statement. What do you think were the most important qualities for a king in the late 15th century?

Evidence that Richard III had the capacity to rule	Evidence that Richard III did not have the capacity to rule

A closer look

Richard III

In William Shakespeare's history play *Richard III,* the King is portrayed as a scheming, cold-hearted murderer. The melodramatic tragedy presents Richard as an ambitious and malicious villain.

> But I, – that am not shaped for sportive tricks,
> Nor made to court an amorous looking-glass,
> I, that am rudely stamp'd, and want love's majesty
> To strut before a wanton ambling nymph;
> I, that am curtail'd of this fair proportion,
> Cheated of feature by dissembling nature,
> Deform'd, unfinish'd, sent before my time
> Into this breathing world scarce half made up,
> And that so lamely and unfashionable,
> That dogs bark at me as I halt by them; -
> Why I, in this weak piping time of peace,
> Have no delight to pass away the time,
> Unless to spy my shadow in the sun,
> And descant on mine own deformity:
> And therefore, - since I cannot prove a lover,
> To entertain these fair well-spoken days, -
> I am determined to prove the villain

2

*William Shakespeare, **Richard III**, Act 1, Scene 2*

Questions

1 Explain why Richard III faced opposition during his short reign.

2 Did Richard rule with scant regard for the laws of the land?

Fig. 7 *Laurence Olivier plays the eponymous villain in Shakespeare's play. Shakespeare presented the King as a deformed and scheming monster*

This interpretation was common to all Tudor histories, especially those written by Sir Thomas More and Edward Hall. History is written by the victors, so the Tudors wrote the history of the last Yorkist King. One contemporary historian, John Rous, originally described Richard III as a model king who was loved by his subjects and famed for his justice; however, Rous revised his comments after Tudor was crowned, and instead he described the King as cruel.

Richard has his defenders, especially members of the Richard III Society, who wish to revise the historical interpretation. They stress his deep religious convictions, his innocence over the disappearance of the two princes, and his genuine concern for impartial justice.

The Rous Roll is one of England's late medieval treasures. The section of the Roll was written during the reign of Richard III before the death of Edward, Prince of Wales, in 1484. The Roll has pencil drawings, heraldic crests, coats of arms to present Richard and the true heir of Richard, Duke of York.

The most mighty prince Richard by the grace of God King of England and of France and Lord of Ireland; by very matrimony without discontinuance of any defiling in the law by male heir lineally descending from King Henry the second; all avarice set aside, ruled his subjects in his realm full commendably, punishing offenders of his laws, especially extortioners and oppressors of his commons, and cherishing those that were virtuous, by which guiding he got great thanks of God and love of all his subjects, rich and poor, and great laud [praise] of the people of all other lands about him.

3 *Sean Cunningham, **Richard III, a royal enigma**, 2003*

Thomas More wrote *The History of King Richard III*. The book was never finished, only covering the few months from the death of Edward IV to the imprisonment of Archbishop John Morton at Brecon Castle. More's opening description of the King sets the tone for the whole work.

little of stature, ill-featured of limbs, crook backed, his left shoulder much higher than his right, hard favoured of visage... he was malicious, wrathful, envious, and from afore his birth, ever forward. It is for truth reported that the Duchess his mother had so much ado in her travail, that she could not be delivered of him uncut; and that he came into the world with his feet forward... and (as the fame runneth) also not untoothed... He was close and secret, a deep dissembler, lowly of countenance, arrogant of heart, outwardly companionable where he inwardly hated, not letting to kiss whom he thought to kill; dispiteous and cruel, not for evil will always, but after for ambition, and either for the surety or increase of his estate.

4 *Paul Murray Kendall, **Richard III**, 1973*

A. F. Pollard wrote *Richard III and the Princes* in 1991, in which he reached a balanced assessment of the King.

> Richard III was a man of considerable ability, energy and attractiveness. His chivalry, in particular, in an age which highly valued such martial qualities in a young nobleman warmly commended him to his contemporaries... It was his tragedy that his ambition, and his sense of his own worth and importance, led him to disregard all law and right in the pursuit of his own interests. He did not hesitate to kill to make himself king. What he did in 1483 both surprised and horrified contemporaries not only because it was unexpected of him, but because it went beyond the bounds of contemporary ethics.
>
> ...he was not one-dimensional. He was neither a hateful child-murderer, nor a paragon of contemporary virtue. He was a man who lived up to several of the ideas of contemporary nobility, yet one who when tested was found wanting. It is possible that he himself came to understand this and that the realisation was the cause of great anguish.

5 *A. F. Pollard, **Richard III** and the Princes, 1991*

Activity

Source analysis

Read Sources 2–5. How useful are these extracts as evidence about the appearance and personality of Richard III?

The gathering storm – the threat from Henry Tudor

The political upheavals in 1483, following Edward's death, lifted Henry Tudor from obscurity and placed him at the heart of events. The abortive Buckingham rebellion taught him valuable lessons about the need for careful preparations and the dangers of misplaced optimism. Tudor set about planning his second invasion with great political, military and diplomatic care. His public promise that he would marry Elizabeth of York was clever public relations, winning support from disaffected royal servants in England.

Some of these royal servants left England to join the growing court in exile including Sir Giles Daubeney and Sir Robert Willoughby – both of whom had been loyal to Edward IV. Sir James Blount, lieutenant of Hammes Castle, who had kept the Earl of Oxford in custody for 10 years, chose to release the Earl and fled with him to Tudor. During 1484 and 1485, Tudor's agents frequently crossed the Channel to assess and build his level of public support. They were encouraged by continuing sporadic uprisings that destabilised Richard's rule, such as the disorder in Essex at the end of 1484, led by Sir William Brandon who exploited latent loyalties to the Earl of Oxford. These agents reported that support was strongest in Wales. Tudor heard from a lawyer called Morgan Kidwelly that Rhys ap Thomas and Sir John Savage, one of Lord Stanley's nephews, would back him.

Henry Tudor's mother, Margaret Beaufort, was a key contact in England promoting her son's interests. Her marriage to Lord Stanley, one of the most powerful noblemen, put her in a strong position to influence opinions. Her family connections to the Courtenays, traditional Lancastrian loyalists, drew support from Sir Edward Courtenay. In all, Tudor knew he was building a satisfactory level of support, although no great magnate had declared for him.

Cross-reference

The Buckingham rebellion, and Henry Tudor's part in it, are discussed on pages 26–27.

Giles Daubeney is discussed in more detail on page 80.

Key chronology

Tudor's moves to Bosworth

1485

1 August   Sets sail from France.

7 August   Lands at Mill Bay in Milford Haven.

8 August   Sets out for Haverfordwest.

10 August   Reaches Cardigan.

11 August   Turns east at Machynlleth.

12 August   Rhys ap Thomas declares for Tudor at Newtown in mid-Wales.

15 August   Enters Shrewsbury.

16 August   Arrives at Newport.

17 August   Camps at Stafford.

19 August   Reaches Lichfield.

20 August   Tudor meets both Lord Stanley and Sir William Stanley at Atherstone.

21 August   Both armies are camped between the villages of Sutton Cheney and Shenton on Redmore plain.

22 August   The Battle of Bosworth.

Tudor's planning, though, was not always straightforward. He was forced by Richard's diplomacy to flee from exile in Brittany to the court of the King of France, Charles VIII. This move, ironically, made him a much greater threat to Richard because the French King lent him 60,000 francs and 1,800 mercenaries led by Philibert de Chandée, later the Earl of Bath. As Tudor's position strengthened, so Richard lost confidence. He spent huge sums of money commissioning a fleet based at Southampton commanded by Viscount Lovell and made elaborate preparations to defend west Wales, putting a beacon network in place to warn of Tudor's invasion. He sent out instructions to reinforce his position. One such order was to Sir Marmaduke Constable, his steward at Tutbury, who was told to take an oath from all his inhabitants that they would not be retained by any lord except the King.

By the summer of 1485, Richard knew that he would have to fight to defend his kingship. He spent most of his time at Nottingham Castle, centrally placed in the Midlands, so he was ready wherever and whenever Tudor chose to invade.

The Battle of Bosworth

The Battle of Bosworth is one of the most decisive battles in English history and yet details about the preceding events, the location of the battle and the actual contest are obscure because contemporaries did not record their experiences. Modern historians are not certain that the battle even took place on Ambien Hill. The following account is one scenario, based on the very incomplete records.

Tudor's advance towards Bosworth

Henry Tudor set sail from France having been in touch with various friends and sympathisers, but without any guarantees of support. This adventure was a huge gamble with untold risks. He felt so uncertain of success that he chose to land at Mill Bay out of sight of Dale Castle and village, both of which he feared would be occupied as part of Richard's chain of coastal defences. After the invasion force had successfully landed, he knighted 11 of his loyal followers.

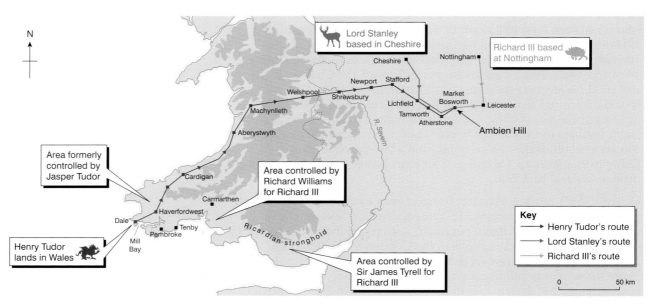

Fig. 8 *The advance to Bosworth*

The army's move to Haverfordwest was important because Tudor needed to hold a significant town; however, he was very conscious that key men – the Stanleys, Rhys ap Thomas and John Savage – still had not openly declared for him. Tudor showed strategic intelligence choosing to move north into central Wales where the Duke of Buckingham had landed, and away from the Yorkist loyalists in South Wales and near Brecon. At Cardigan he was joined by Richard Griffiths and John Morgan; both men were friendly with Rhys ap Thomas.

Key profile

Rhys ap Thomas and Sir John Savage

Rhys ap Thomas was a prominent Welshman who had been favoured by Richard III. The King relied on Rhys and other Welshmen to block Tudor's progress but Rhys ap Thomas was aspirational, and was promised further influence if he betrayed his King.

Sir John Savage was a leading man in South Wales. He had secretly promised to betray Richard and back Tudor. He suvived the Battle of Bosworth and prospered under Henry VII.

Tudor moved up the coast to Machynlleth at a moderate pace, taking time to send messengers to potential allies. As he turned east to cross difficult mountainous terrain, he was encouraged by Rhys ap Thomas' declaration. Having been promised the lieutenancy of Wales under Tudor, Rhys ap Thomas brought an additional 1,800–2,000 men to swell Tudor's army.

The army advanced to Shrewsbury, where they faced their first real opposition when the bailiffs of the town refused to open the gates. The situation might have been ugly; however, Sir William Stanley, who was shadowing every move, sent a messenger to advise the bailiffs to yield. They did, and then Sir Richard Corbet joined Tudor with 800 men. It is unsurprising to learn that Corbet was Sir William Stanley's stepson.

The numbers in the rebel army again increased at Newport when Sir Gilbert Talbot and 500 men joined; however, Tudor still did not have the crucial support of one of the great English noble families, the Stanleys, nor that of the Duke of Norfolk nor of the Earl of Northumberland. He met Sir William Stanley at Stafford but still did not secure his support.

Cross-reference
For more information on the life of Sir William Stanley, see page 75.

Richard III was acutely conscious that he could not rely on Stanley's loyalty, not least because Lord Stanley was married to Tudor's mother. He held Lord Stanley's eldest son, Lord Strange, as a hostage to guarantee continued support. Lord Stanley belatedly responded to Richard III's muster, leaving his estates in Cheshire with his army to reach Lichfield. He moved on to Atherstone leaving Lichfield just before Tudor arrived. This may have been a coincidence or was possibly tacit assistance, enabling Tudor to billet his men in the city.

At Atherstone, Tudor met both Lord Stanley and his brother William Stanley. Historians assume that they discussed battle tactics; however, neither Stanley openly committed to engage with Tudor although Lord Stanley did send four knights (Sir Robert Tunstall, Sir John Savage, Sir Hugh Persall and Sir Humphrey Stanley) and their retinues to reinforce his vanguard.

Activity

Thinking point

Explain why Richard III was so anxious about the loyalty and wherabouts of the Stanley family in the days before the Battle of Bosworth.

Richard III's actions before Bosworth

From mid-June, Richard III set up quarters in Nottingham anticipating the challenge from Tudor, and from here he sent out commissions of array to many shires to muster their troops. He was in Nottingham when he learned on 11 August that Tudor had landed.

He immediately summoned Norfolk, Northumberland, Lovell, Sir Richard Brackenbury and others to join him at Leicester. It seems that he did not rush because he believed the pretender would be crushed in Wales either by Rhys ap Thomas or by Lord Stanley. He became less complacent after he learned that Rhys ap Thomas had defected to Tudor; and then Lord Stanley made excuses for not returning immediately to the King.

Lord Strange was interrogated and revealed that Sir William Stanley and John Savage planned to join Tudor, though Lord Stanley would remain loyal to the King. Richard III declared the two men traitors and on 19 August moved his army to Leicester. Two days later, both armies were camped near to Ambien Hill making the final preparations for battle the next day.

Fig. 9 *King Richard III and the Earl of Richmond at the Battle of Bosworth. Richard III rides a charge but the last Plantagenet king is killed leaving a new Tudor dynasty. Historians have serious difficulties when explaining the outcome of this controversial and mysterious battle. There is not one surviving eyewitness contemporary account*

The Battle of Bosworth, 22 August 1485

Richard's army of some 10,000 Englishmen was assembled on the top of Ambien (sometimes known as Ambion) Hill with archers in front commanded by the Duke of Norfolk, Richard himself in charge of the troops towards the rear, and the Duke of Northumberland at the rear with the reserve. Tudor had a maximum of 5,000 men of various nationalities. The vanguard, under the command of the Earl of Oxford, was strengthened by the highly-professional French mercenaries under Philibert de Chandée. Sir Gilbert Talbot commanded Tudor's right wing and John Savage the left wing. The most important strategic placings were the Stanleys. Sir William was probably on Tudor's left flank with about 3,000 men, while Lord Stanley was on the right flank, though he actually played no part in the battle.

The battle was inconclusive until Richard chose to personally end Henry Tudor's challenge. He led a charge towards Tudor before Stanley and Percy's inaction became open rebellion. The gamble almost succeeded because in the close-quarter fighting Tudor's standard bearer, William Brandon, was killed holding the red dragon banner; and the formidable John Cheney, a mighty Tudor loyalist, was forced from his horse to the ground.

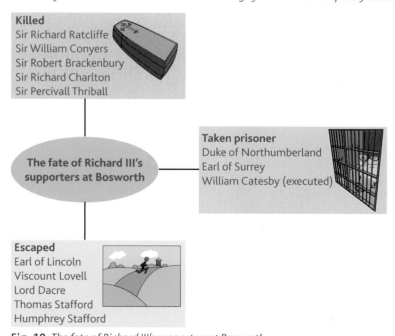

Killed
Sir Richard Ratcliffe
Sir William Conyers
Sir Robert Brackenbury
Sir Richard Charlton
Sir Percivall Thriball

The fate of Richard III's supporters at Bosworth

Taken prisoner
Duke of Northumberland
Earl of Surrey
William Catesby (executed)

Escaped
Earl of Lincoln
Viscount Lovell
Lord Dacre
Thomas Stafford
Humphrey Stafford

Fig. 10 *The fate of Richard III's supporters at Bosworth*

Philibert de Chandée proved crucial in this decisive phase of the battle. His pikemen executed a complex manoeuvre to protect Tudor himself from the Ricardian charge. This particular manoeuvre had been used by the Swiss, who had trained Chandée's mercenaries, but had never previously been seen in England. Another decisive factor was Sir William Stanley who intervened with his retinue to save Tudor from disaster. Richard III was killed and his army put to flight.

Richard's body was treated shamefully after the battle. He was slung naked across a horse's back and taken to Leicester Abbey, where for two days he was on public display, still naked but for a small black cloth, then was buried unceremoniously.

■ A closer look

The Battle of Bosworth

Richard III's charge towards Henry Tudor was fatal and decisive. It has been presented as impetuous and foolhardy despite Richard's reputation as an experienced and cautious commander. Many of the historical records written after the battle were written by contemporaries, whose vested interest was to denigrate the Yorkist King.

Recently, Michael Jones, in his book *Bosworth: Psychology of a Battle*, 2002, has written about the battle trying to explain Richard III's apparently rash attack. He does not see it as a desperate gamble but as the final act of Richard's ritual affirmation that he was the rightful king and his desire for a personal confrontation with Tudor. For that final fateful charge he wore a loose-fitting robe depicting the royal coat of arms sending a decisive message, according to chivalric tradition, that he was fighting for victory or death.

In all this, Michael Jones presents Richard as courageous and supremely confident, even heroic. He explains that in medieval times these qualities were promoted through the immensely popular stories of the Trojan Wars. According to Michael Jones, Richard III had a copy of the history of Troy.

In 1460, Richard's father died in a cavalry charge leading his men from high ground at Sandal Castle into fierce hand-to hand fighting. After the battle, the Duke's body was mutilated and his decapitated head displayed on a pike outside the city of York. As a child, Richard learned to honour the memory of his father. Richard III's charge at Bosworth is, therefore, interpreted by Michael Jones as the restoration of family honour.

■ A closer look

History and psychology

Michael Jones has attempted to revise the story of Bosworth by putting Richard back into his family traditions and contemporary society's values. He has reconstructed what might have been going through Richard's mind as he launched his final charge. This is not based on fantasy but medieval knowledge, real and romantic, about how battles should be fought.

Psychohistory is a contentious area of historical investigation.

■ Activity

Challenge your thinking

Do you think that the study of psychology is a useful activity for historians?

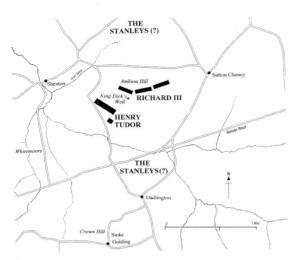

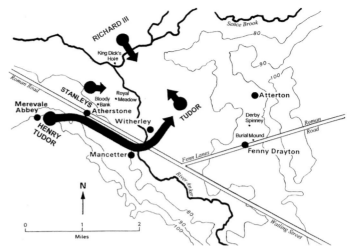

Fig. 11 *This map illustrates the traditional battle site with Richard III on Ambion Hill and Henry Tudor advancing from the west. Historians do not know the position of Lord Stanley's army. Recent historical research has raised questions about the exact site of this battle*

Fig. 12 *This map illustrates an alternative site for the battle and a revised battle plan. Tudor's flanking manoeuvre meant that he finally advanced from the south-east. This new interpretation of the battle suggests the fighting took place further to the east than the traditional account*

Consciously or unconsciously historians have always dabbled amateurishly and haphazardly in other subject areas. In their discussions and analyses of the motives and actions of men and societies they have had to venture into the realm of psychology. Later commentators have rightly remarked that so long as the historian continued to back his own psychological insights without reference to the discoveries of modern psychology he was producing fiction.

Social psychology is of the utmost value to a historian. When we look back over the human past, one obvious feature stands out: the amount of time, energy and human life that has been given over to war; which leads itself to analysis in the light of important studies in human aggression produced by social psychologists. An understanding of the significance of group psychology for the historian emphasises the study of *mentalités* – the world view, the perceptions, the attitudes of mind of past people.

6 *Quoted from Arthur Marwick,* **The Nature of History***, 1989*

Summary questions

1 Explain why Richard III was defeated at the Battle of Bosworth.

2 What do you learn about the nature of late medieval land warfare from events at Bosworth in 1485?

The consolidation of Henry VII's position, 1485–7

In this chapter you will learn about:

- how Henry Tudor moved from being King of Bosworth to King of England

- how he began to enforce his personal rule over the kingdom.

Fig. 2 *A stained-glass window showing a Tudor rose. Henry VII was the first King to realise the potential of windows for political propaganda, a practice continued by Henry VIII. The two English Kings exploited technological advances in glass making in Renaissance Europe – for the French made the best coloured glass, and the most skilled glaziers were Flemish*

On 3 September 1485, Henry Tudor processed into London. The new monarch was met at Shoreditch by the mayor and aldermen of the city of London who were wearing scarlet robes. They proceeded to St Paul's accompanied by crowds of sword-bearers and sergeants. The citizens of London provided processions and pageants along the route to demonstrate their goodwill towards the new King. At the huge cathedral Henry heard prayers and a *Te Deum* after having presented his three standards – the banner of St George, the red fiery dragon of Cadwaladr, and a dun cow. In depositing his banners in this way he was consciously copying Edward IV's conduct after the Battle of Barnet, 1471.

Fig. 1 *Henry VII: the King constantly needed to secure his kingship and the new Tudor dynasty, and to defend the peace of the realm*

Establishing power

From Bosworth to London

Henry Tudor was proclaimed King of England by Lord Stanley on the battlefield at Bosworth. He knew little about his kingdom, and even less about kingship, yet he behaved like a king from the start. It was clear that the new King would be wise, prudent and rely heavily on the friendship and loyalty of his companions from exile.

He immediately declared that his reign started on 21 August. This was a politically astute announcement because it enabled him to consider any men who fought for King Richard III on the battlefield at Bosworth as traitors to King Henry VII. The punishment for treason among noblemen was attainment by an Act of Attainder.

He also publicly rewarded some of his loyal servants, knighting 11 men on the actual battlefield. He then took action to start the consolidation of his kingship. He sent Sir Richard Willoughby to Sheriff Hutton in Yorkshire to secure Elizabeth of York, and Edward, Earl of Warwick, and bring them both to London. He showed similar decisiveness in sending out a Proclamation soon after the battle making it clear to all Englishmen across the kingdom that Richard III was dead, and Henry Tudor on the throne by the grace of God.

Cross-reference

Acts of Attainder are discussed in more detail on page 28.

To refresh your knowledge of Elizabeth of York see page 43.

Activity

Thinking point

Explain why Henry VII was so keen to knight his supporters, to secure Elizabeth of York and to get to London.

Key terms

Counsel: a group of advisers chosen by the King. This was the central administrative and decision-making body. Different sized groups of the Counsel were known by different names: the Counsel, the King's Counsel, the Great Counsel, the Royal Counsel or the Privy Counsel.

Chancellor of England: one of the most important ministers of state, also known as Lord Chancellor, with particular responsibility for legal matters.

Treasurer at the Exchequer: another key minister with particular responsibility for royal finances.

Keeper of the (or Lord) Privy Seal: another important minister. The Privy Seal was used for the correspondence of the Counsel.

Royal household: personal advisers and companions to the King. These men travelled with the King wherever he went and also attended Court.

Lord Chamberlain: the noble who ran the King's household at court. This man was usually one of the King's closest personal friends and advisers.

Cross-reference

Positions within the royal household are discussed in more detail on page 102.

More information on Reginald Bray and Giles Daubeney is also provided on pages 73 and 80.

Henry, by the grace of God, king of England and of France, prince of Wales and lord of Ireland, strictly chargeth and commandeth, upon pain of death, that no manner of man rob or spoil no manner of commons coming from the field; but suffer them to pass home to their countries and dwelling places, with their horses and harness.

And moreover, the king ascertaineth you, that Richard Duke of Gloucester, lately called King Richard, was lately slain at a place called Sandeford, within the shire of Leicester, and there was laid openly, that every man might see and look upon him.

 Extract from the proclamation of Henry Tudor

Henry slowly made his way towards the capital city, taking care to avoid hasty decisions. He paused for a few days at St Albans. This gave his royal servants time to prepare the triumphant entry into London. It also gave Henry a chance to reflect on the appointments to his new Counsel and the structure of his government. He realised that it was vital to put both in place, for the early weeks of his reign might prove very difficult.

In the **Counsel** he appointed Thomas Rotherham, Archbishop of York, first to be Chancellor of England and then moved him to temporary Treasurer at the Exchequer. Rotherham was an elderly, experienced churchman who had served within Yorkist government and was a recognised expert in public affairs. This stop-gap appointment bought Henry VII time before he could bring in John Morton, Bishop of Ely, to be **Chancellor of England** and the Yorkist Lord Dynham to be the permanent **Treasurer at the Exchequer**. He extended his reliance on able clerics by appointing Bishop Peter Courtenay to be **Keeper of the Privy Seal** with responsibility for ensuring continuity of administration in the early stages of the reign, although this post was later given to a friend from exile, Richard Fox.

Henry exercised his prerogative right to distribute patronage very carefully. In many ways he was fortunate because he had few family demands for positions or titles. Tudor was an only child, so had no siblings to recognise, in contrast to the demands made by the extensive Woodville family on Edward IV's patronage. There was also little chance of immediate rebellion. The previous king, Richard III, had been widely disliked and died without an heir. Henry VII was related by his mother's second marriage to the Stanleys, the noble family that had gained most from events at Bosworth. This made it unlikely that Lord Stanley would rebel. Besides, there was genuine goodwill towards the new monarch. Many Englishmen and women warmly anticipated the promised marriage to Elizabeth of York as the restoration of the regime of Edward IV.

Henry VII had to make a lot of important decisions in the days after Bosworth. He was required to take Counsel on these matters but was not obliged to follow that Counsel. Many of these early decisions were made by the new King in consultation with his close intimate group of friends and family – his mother, Lady Margaret Beaufort; his uncle, Jasper Tudor; his stepfather, Lord Stanley; and John de Vere, the Earl of Oxford.

He also considered his **royal household**. Sir William Stanley became **Lord Chamberlain** but most senior posts were granted to men who had shared the King's exile including Reginald Bray, Giles Daubeney, Richard Guildford, Thomas Lovell and John Risely. These men were personal friends, courtiers, and also members of the King's Counsel. Contemporaries regarded them as the most influential politicians in the kingdom.

The confirmation of kingship and promise of dynasty

The coronation was an immense display of Henry VII's kingship designed to impress both Englishmen and foreigners, and to confirm Tudor's undeniable God-given right to rule.

Coronation

The detailed royal financial accounts reveal two characteristics of this new reign, both grandeur and prudence. Henry was very conscious of the need to appear regal – the purple velvet for his robe cost 40 shillings per yard and he spent lavishly on ermine, ostrich feathers and saddles. The accounts are evidence that the King paid different prices for separate orders of scarlet cloth, suggesting he was shopping around for the best price.

The series of events leading up to the coronation were prescribed by tradition and Henry deliberately followed them to the letter. On 27 October, Henry dined at Lambeth Palace with Thomas Bourchier, the Archbishop of Canterbury, then went in procession to the Tower of London, the traditional lodging for a sovereign before the coronation. The next day, Henry granted titles to loyal servants including the Dukedom of Bedford for Jasper Tudor, then dined with them at one table in the King's great Chamber before overseeing the installation ceremonies. On 29 October, he took part in another great procession to Westminster Hall wearing a long purple robe, but bare-headed, and accompanied by his heralds, nobles, household and the Mayor of London.

The coronation took place on Sunday 30 October. The service was almost identical to that used for Richard III. The Archbishop of Canterbury anointed and crowned the new King, Bedford had the honour of bearing the crown, Derby carried the sword of state, and Oxford bore the King's train. Afterwards, Henry showed himself to the people and returned to the Tower for a banquet.

The first parliament

Henry had **issued writs** for parliament on 15 September but it did not meet until after the coronation on 7 November. Henry called his first parliament to carry out some specific duties. Some of these tasks were customary at the start of any new reign, but others reflected the nature of Henry's accession to the throne. Henry required parliament to declare and confirm his kingship, to reverse and enact attainders, to make some financial arrangements, and to pass laws.

The business of the new parliament included the following:

1 **The declaration of the King's title:** this was a statement that Henry was King by just hereditary title as well as the grace of God revealed through battlefield victory (Source 2).

2 **Attainders:** some previous Acts of Attainder had been passed during the reign of Richard III so now needed to be reversed, and other new acts needed to be passed against those who fought against Tudor at Bosworth.

Activity

Thinking point

How accurate is the view that 'Henry VII behaved like a king from the start'?

Key term

Issued writs: parliament was not permanent. Issuing writs was the process by which a monarch summoned both the Commons and the Lords to attend parliament.

Fig. 3 *This picture of Henry VII's first Act of parliament includes a portrait of the King. The border is decorated with flora and fauna*

3 **Financial matters: tunnage and poundage** was granted for the King's life, and an Act of Resumption enabled Henry to reclaim all lands held by Henry VI before the outbreak of the Wars of the Roses, although this act did include substantial provisos.

4 **Legislation:** the new King secured the passage of several acts to ensure the maintenance of public peace and the enforcement of law and order across the realm. Parliament approved a new oath of loyalty to be sworn by the royal household, the Commons and the Lords, both temporal and spiritual. The chancellor stressed the importance of this oath to men who were Justices of the Peace. Another important measure was the nullification of Richard III's act that declared the children of Edward IV illegitimate.

Parliament remained in session for only five weeks, during which it sat on various occasions. Its final action before **prorogation** on 10 December was to formally and publically request the King to marry Elizabeth of York as he had promised in Rennes Cathedral on Christmas Day 1483. Historians have argued that the decision to delay the marriage until after the coronation and first parliament was political but it seems equally likely that the new King needed time to attend to the urgent business of government, then to meet and court his intended bride. Henry and Elizabeth shared a blood relationship and therefore required dispensation to get married. It was approved initially on 16 January 1486 by eight English bishops, then subsequently confirmed by the Pope on 2 March.

> To the pleasure of Almighty God, the wealth, prosperity and surety of this realm of England, to the singular comfort of all the king's subjects of the same, and in avoiding all ambiguities and questions, be it ordained, established and enacted, by authority of this present parliament, that the inheritance of the crowns of the realms of England and of France, with all the pre-eminence and dignity royal to the same pertaining, and all other seignories to the king belonging beyond the sea, with the appurtenances thereto in any wise due or pertaining, be, rest, remain and abide in the most royal person of our now soveriegn lord king Harry the VIIth and in their heirs of his body lawfully come, perpetually with the grace of God so to endure, and in none other.

2   *Act for the Confirmation of Henry VII (1485)*

■ Cross-reference

The imposture of Lambert Simnel is covered on pages 48–49.

Marriage of Henry VII and Elizabeth of York

The marriage was celebrated by Archbishop Bourchier on 18 January. The details of the service are less significant than the symbol of union between the two warring houses of Lancaster and York, and the promise of legitimate heirs to secure the Tudor dynasty.

Queen Elizabeth was described by contemporaries as being a very good-looking and able woman. She certainly proved very successful at her primary task – giving birth to heirs for the new King. She gave birth to eight children; however, only four reached adulthood.

The Queen's coronation was delayed until Henry had faced the first really serious challenge to his kingship, Lambert Simnel, and until Prince Arthur had been born.

■ A closer look

Elizabeth of York

Elizabeth of York was the eldest daughter of a king. She was destined to marry to her father's political advantage, therefore she was well educated, being taught to read, write and speak French and Spanish well.

Edward IV's death threw Elizabeth's life into turmoil. She fled into sanctuary at Westminster Abbey with her mother, four sisters and the younger prince, Richard; it is unknown how she coped with her two brothers' disappearance though the human tragedy cannot be understated. She faced further traumas when Richard III's soldiers surrounded the sanctuary, and later when she was forced to accept her illegitimacy.

Fig. 4 *The marble effigy of Elizabeth of York is a very important resource for historians because no original portrait of the Queen survives*

Richard III's fortunes deteriorated with the death of his wife. This opened up the possibility that he might marry his niece, Elizabeth of York, especially after she was received at court during the Christmas festivities of 1484. The precise nature of the King's romantic intentions is unclear, but the rumours provoked such public angst that he was forced into public denial, and he sent Elizabeth to Sheriff Hutton in Yorkshire with Edward of Warwick.

Her coronation at the age of 22 was magnificent. Elizabeth was elegant, majestically fair, and tall – her alabaster effigy in Lady Chapel of Westminster Abbey indicates she had inherited the formidable Yorkist height. She wore a kirtle of white cloth of gold, damasked, and a mantle of the same furred with ermine and finished with gold. On her loose red-gold hair, she wore a crest of gems and a rich crown.

It is difficult for historians to piece together Elizabeth's life but one very good source is the Privy Purse Expense accounts for her court. These reveal that she enjoyed hunting and kept a pack of greyhounds and a goshawk. She supported the arts by sponsoring William Caxton's printing of *The Fifteen Oes*. She loved her four sisters, who had been left destitute, and provided for their private expenses. She closely oversaw the expenses of the royal nursery where, intentionally, Tudor and Yorkist cousins grew up together in a close family unit. On the other hand, she was prudent with her own money, for her gowns were mended and refashioned, yet she was generous towards her servants, providing rewards such as cherries and bunches of flowers.

Life was not easy. Elizabeth suffered the pains of childbirth and the loss of children, especially the death of her son Arthur in 1502. It appears that Elizabeth may have been overshadowed by her mother-in-law who was largely responsible for her son winning the throne. There were rumours that Tudor was repelled by Elizabeth because

■ Exploring the detail

Women in history

Historians play an important role in broadening and extending historical study, raising awareness of issues and achievements sidelined by previous generations of historians. Good gender history opens up investigations into areas where women did have influence and roles, so adding to our knowledge and understanding of the past. It is often very challenging because surviving sources tend to be very limited, as indeed this case study illustrates.

■ Activity

What role did Elizabeth of York play in both the political history of England during the late 15th century and the private sphere of the royal family?

Fig. 5 *A second example of Tudor propaganda through stained-glass windows. In this window Arthur, Prince of Wales, is shown to be at prayer*

Activity

Research exercise

Define the word 'propaganda'. It is a word most commonly associated with the 20th century, but as you read the section below, you will discover ways in which Henry VII understood the value of propaganda and used it to his advantage. Make a list of examples of such propaganda.

of his aversion to the house of York, although this aversion did not prevent the Queen conceiving eight children, or the King being heartbroken on her premature death.

On Candlemas Day, 2 February 1503, Elizabeth gave birth to a short-lived daughter. The Queen died on her 38th birthday, 11 February 1503. Twelve days later, her coffin was buried in Westminster Abbey. Six years later her husband, who never remarried, was laid beside her.

Tudor propaganda

Henry VII wanted English men and women to believe that Tudor had a legitimate claim to the throne. He used the symbol of the red rose of Lancaster counter-balanced with the white rose of York to make the double Tudor rose, the symbol of reconciliation between two warring houses.

King Arthur was the legendary protector of the British. Henry deliberately exploited this ancient symbol of honourable kingship in choosing to name his son Arthur, and also by ensuring the baby was born in Winchester Castle, a place rich in Arthurian links and where the allegedly original round table was displayed.

Henry also presented himself as a reputable king through his Welsh ancestry; not his recent family history, but his descent from the ancient kings who fought against the Saxon invaders in the Dark Ages. At Bosworth, he fought under the banner of the red dragon of the Welsh kings who defeated the Saxons, while their emblem was a white dragon. The red dragon became one of the two supporters of the royal arms of the Tudor monarchs.

Cadwaladr was the last, and most revered, of the Welsh kings. At the coronation banquet, the King's champion rode in to issue the customary challenge to any man who disputed Henry's right to rule. The champion's horse was bedecked in a back cloth embroidered with Cadwaladr's supposed arms. In 1486, Henry was welcomed as the rightful King into the city of Worcester with this speech (Source 3):

> Cadwaladr's blood lineally descending,
> Long hath be told of such a Prince coming,
> Wherefore Friends, if that I shall not lie,
> This same is the Fulfiller of the Prophecy.

3

The Beaufort family emblem, the portcullis, was also used frequently to represent Tudor legitimacy since Henry's mother, Margaret Beaufort, was a direct descendant from Edward III. The first parliament 1485–6 re-enacted an act from 1397 that declared the Beaufort family legitimate, although it omitted the subsequent 1407 act that barred any Beaufort from the throne. Henry VII's chapel in Westminster Abbey is richly decorated with portcullises. Margaret Beaufort was an influential and honoured figure at court throughout her son's reign; her status was reflected in her official title 'Full noble Princess Margaret, Countess of Richmond and mother of our sovereign lord the King'.

Henry VII also played on his Lancastrian lineage by naming his second son after Henry VI. He presented his murdered ancestor as a martyr and campaigned for the Pope to canonise him, making Henry VI's tomb at St George's Chapel, Windsor a place of pilgrimage. Henry VII meanwhile arranged for a new stained-glass window to be installed in King's College Chapel, Cambridge in honour of his uncle, the founder of the college. In all this Lancastrianism, however, Henry VII had to be careful because Henry VI had failed in the art of government – a reputation he did not want.

Tudor propaganda appears to have been very powerful. For, although the Wars of the Roses could be said to have continued beyond 1485, and even after the Battle of Stoke in 1487, through the activities of Yorkist sympathisers such as Lambert Simnel and Perkin Warbeck, it is a lasting achievement of Henry VII and his propagandists that these have gone down in history as 'pretenders' or 'imposters'.

Learning outcomes

From this section you should have developed a good understanding of the reasons for the instability of the monarchy after the death of Edward IV in 1483. You have seen how Richard III was able to usurp the throne, only to face a reign beset by rebellion and threats from the all-powerful nobility. You have also seen how Henry Tudor succeeded in winning sufficient support to overcome Richard III in battle and establish a new Tudor dynasty.

Cross-reference

Lambert Simnel and Perkin Warbeck are discussed on pages 48 and 54.

Activity

Research exercise

Margaret was the senior surviving Beaufort so her claim to the throne was stronger than her son's. Find out why contemporaries did not believe a woman could rule England.

AQA Examination-style questions

(a) Explain why Richard, Duke of Gloucester, made himself King of England in 1483. *(12 marks)*

(b) How important was foreign support for Henry Tudor in explaining Richard III's defeat at Bosworth? *(24 marks)*

Examiner's tip

The answer to this question needs to demonstrate good detailed understanding about the importance of foreign support. Henry Tudor spent 14 years in exile in both Brittany and France. The foreign rulers allowed him to build a court in exile, especially after the failure of the Buckingham rebellion in 1483. He required assistance from the King of France in 1485, both ships and men, before he could even contemplate any invasion to claim his throne.

You will need to balance the importance of foreign support with other factors that explain Henry Tudor's victory. Richard III's position weakened as he alienated the southern nobles and suffered bankruptcy. Henry Tudor gained support as he marched through Wales but still was outnumbered at the start of the battle. You will need to examine the events of 22 August, in particular the loyalties of the magnate families and the military decisions, to decide on your response to the question. You should reach a clear judgement about the relative importance of the range of factors under consideration.

In this chapter you will learn about:

- how Henry VII faced continued challenges to his throne

- how seriously Henry VII felt threatened by both the impostures of Lambert Simnel and Perkin Warbeck, and the challenges to internal law and order, and how he dealt with them

- how he used domestic policies and foreign relations to strengthen his royal authority.

Lambert Simnel was like a puppet in a shadow-play. Dancing before the lighted screen, his silhouette assumed the proportions of greatness, and his movements seemed portentous. In the flickering light he took the shape of a boy-king, and it seemed, however momentarily, that the fate of nations hung on his life. Of course, the illusion could never be entirely concealed. The machinations of the puppeteers were soon thwarted, and the whole charade destroyed.

1
*From Michael Bennett, **Lambert Simnel and the Battle of Stoke**, 1987*

Henry's great purpose was to establish himself and his family on the throne of England. In 1486, he faced numerous minor plots and conspiracies that developed into serious security threats after foreign powers intervened. To make matters worse, Henry had to rely on some undependable noble families to maintain law and order across the realm, and he was personally unprepared for the royal financial management that was necessary to maintain his authority.

Dealing with threats to the dynasty

Surviving Yorkists

Elizabeth of York had five sisters, three brothers and numerous cousins and, although some had died or disappeared by 1485, there were surviving Yorkists who could be expected to resist the new King. The most serious immediate threat was John de la Pole, Earl of Lincoln, who had been named heir by Richard III after the death of Edward, Prince of Wales. In 1485, Lincoln had made his peace and was amicably received, with his brother Edmund, at Henry's court. This apparent reconciliation, however, was an empty gesture for both brothers would commit treason.

The Lovell rebellion, Easter 1486

Three minor noblemen, who had prospered under Richard III, led the first unsuccessful Yorkist challenge to Tudor – Francis, Viscount Lovell and the Stafford brothers, Humphrey and Thomas. All three men had fought for Richard at Bosworth then fled into sanctuary, but broke out in 1486 to lead insurrections. The Staffords were arrested, and Humphrey executed, although Thomas was pardoned and spared. Lovell, crushed by Jasper Tudor now Duke of Bedford, fled into Cumbria to the home of Sir Thomas Broughton before escaping to Flanders.

The most important outcomes of this rebellion were that, firstly, the rules of sanctuary were altered, making it impossible to plead sanctuary in treason cases, and, secondly, that the Yorkists learned they needed a Yorkist prince to stand against Henry.

The rebellion also made clear the importance of protecting the security of the dynasty on several fronts. Firstly, Henry was in a very weak position on the international scene, facing several committed foreign opponents and fearing the awesome power of France. He anticipated that one country or more from France, Scotland, the Holy Roman Empire, Burgundy, Ireland and Spain might profit from supporting the Yorkists in reclaiming the throne of England; therefore he worked to prevent such anti-Tudor co-operation.

Within England, Henry relied on his close family and his small group of capable, faithful friends from France. He did reward English noblemen with titles and land; however, he also introduced measures to control them through varied means such as acts of attainder, bonds and acts of resumption.

All these precautions, however, were not enough to prevent the first serious challenge to Tudor emerging by the end of 1486.

■ Cross-reference

The foreign policies implemented by Henry VII to secure his kingship are discussed on page 58.

The measures that Henry took to ensure loyalty among his noblemen are outlined on page 74.

Henry's financial arrangements are explained on page 87.

■ Key chronology

Lambert Simnel

1486

November Rumours of an imposture reach the King in London.

1487

February The King calls his Counsel to agree pre-emptive action against a Yorkist imposture.

Spring The Earl of Lincoln and Lord Lovell are reunited at the court of Margaret, Duchess of Burgundy.

5 May Lincoln, Lovell and Yorkists arrive at Dublin.

24 May Coronation of Lambert Simnel as Edward VI in Dublin.

4 June 'Edward VI' and his Yorkist army land in Cumbria.

16 June The Battle of Stoke.

HENRY sentencing LAMBERT SIMNEL and his TUTOR

Fig. 1 *Lambert Simnel and his tutor, on trial before Henry VII*

The challenge from Lambert Simnel 1486–7

The failure of the earlier Lovell rebellion taught the Yorkists that they must have a Yorkist prince to head any serious challenge to Henry VII. Their problem was that no Yorkist prince was available, since Edward IV's two sons had disappeared and Edward, Earl of Warwick was confined in the Tower of London. Their solution was to find and train two young men who could be **imposters** – pretend to be one or other of the Yorkist princes. The first was Lambert Simnel and the second was Perkin Warbeck.

Key profile

Lambert Simnel

In the 15th century, Oxford was a town full of ambitious men. The university provided routes for advancement and promotion in both the Church and the state. It was a growing town with new colleges, and other educational establishments such as grammar schools, being built. Many scholars and students supplemented their income by tutoring young boys. One such scholar was a priest, Richard Simons, who tutored a 10-year-old boy named Lambert Simnel.

Polydore Vergil wrote about Simons, presenting him as a crafty and ambitious man who groomed Simnel to impersonate one of the Yorkist princes. Simons planned that once the imposture was accepted, he would be rewarded with a high church post, possibly a bishopric. He had to teach the boy a great deal: the lessons included basic Latin grammar, polite French, the practical and social skills of an aristocratic household, details of Yorkist family life, and the self-assurance of a king. Simons taught well, for the boy impressed the Anglo-Irish nobles in Dublin with his grace.

It was also very clear to the Yorkists that they needed foreign assistance to support their challenge. During the spring of 1487, the Earl of Lincoln fled from England to the court of Margaret, Duchess of Burgundy, where he was reunited with Viscount Lovell. They persuaded the Duchess to sponsor the Lambert Simnel imposture both with financial aid and the military assistance of 2,000 German mercenaries led by Martin Schwarz.

The Yorkists also planned to win support from Ireland. With Yorkist acquiescence, the Anglo-Irish nobles had, in effect, ruled Ireland despite the presence of the King's lieutenant. The dominant earls of Kildare had a choice to make after the Battle of Bosworth: either to abandon their Yorkist allies and support Tudor, or to remain loyal to the Yorkists, possibly even trying to overthrow the new King.

On 5 May, Lincoln, Lovell and the Yorkist army arrived in Dublin, forcing the Anglo-Irish nobles to make a decision. Seeing the situation as an opportunity to continue building autonomy, they chose the latter course of action, and recognised Simnel as King.

The coronation of Lambert Simnel as Edward VI, in Christchurch Cathedral, Dublin

Gerald Fitzgerald, Earl of Kildare, presided over the ceremony on 24 May 1487. The boy king wore splendid robes and magnificent rich gowns. He was surrounded by the great men of the lordship of Ireland and the Anglo-Irish nobles, as well as the Archbishop of Dublin and four other Irish bishops. John de la Pole, Earl of Lincoln and Francis, Viscount Lovell, sat in the congregation. John Payne, Bishop of Meath, gave the sermon outlining the King's indisputable claim to the throne. Despite the customary ritual, there was however some evident improvisation since Edward VI was crowned with a circlet of gold taken from a nearby statue of the Virgin Mary.

Henry VII's early response to the imposture

Henry knew of the threatened imposture long before the coronation in Dublin. It is likely that rumours of such a conspiracy were circulating by November 1486, and these may explain the King's decision to issue a summons to attend Royal Counsel in February 1487. There is no official record of the King's response to the imposture until the Great Counsel resolved to parade the real Earl of Warwick in London. Given that the Earl of Lincoln was a member of this Counsel, it appears the King had not yet realised that a leading Yorkist at the heart of his government was implicated.

The same Counsel deprived Elizabeth Woodville of her estates and confined her to a nunnery. These pre-emptive actions were possibly to prevent her conspiring against Tudor or supporting an imposter, for this was a period of great uncertainty. Many people were under suspicion, yet managed to escape, such as Sir Edward Brampton, a godson of Edward IV and a notable Yorkist, who fled into exile in Burgundy.

Margaret of Burgundy interpreted Tudor's seizure of the throne in 1485 as a French-backed coup. She won Burgundian hearts by allowing Burgundy to be a haven for those Englishmen inconvenienced by regime change in England. Burgundy became a home for dissidents including Yorkist nobles such as Viscount Lovell, Yorkist merchants like John Cabot, and some Yorkist churchmen. Once the Earl of Lincoln arrived, he became the undisputed leader.

After Henry VII learned of Lincoln's departure for Burgundy and the court of the Duchess of Burgundy, he had to deal with open rebellion.

◼ A closer look

Margaret, Duchess of Burgundy (1446–1503)

Margaret of York was one of the most important women in late 15th century north-west European politics. As the third daughter and sixth child of Richard, Duke of York and his wife Cecily Neville, she was sister to both Edward IV and Richard III. Her marriage to Charles the Bold, Duke of Burgundy ensured she was the pivot of the Anglo-Burgundian alliance. Tudor historians presented her as an implacable opponent of Henry VII and the mainspring of all plots against the King, an interpretation supported by Maximilian and Philip who were both willing to allow Margaret to front their conspiracies.

Historians still acknowledge her sympathetic support for both Lambert Simnel and Perkin Warbeck. She certainly maintained Yorkist exiles at her court and partly financed the imposters' invasion fleets. Margaret's support for the Yorkist pretenders has been interpreted as stemming from her unremitting obsession with securing Yorkist revenge on Tudor.

Recent historians have, however, stressed the limitations to her financial and military help, which amounted to only 5,000 men and two small fleets. These were only minor expenses to Margaret, a very wealthy woman, who maintained a luxurious household, patronised building works, gave generously to charities, and collected magnificent books. Historians also consider her

Fig. 2 *An image of Margaret, Duchess of Burgundy, kneeling in her chamber before the resurrected Christ. The original illumination had a beautiful border depicting flowers, birds and an angel. Margaret commissioned this image shortly after her marriage to Charles the Bold*

dependence on the consent of Maximilian in supporting both the imposters. Margaret was not a free agent conducting a personal vendetta, but an accomplished European politician primarily concerned with preserving her reputation in the Low Countries. She was widowed for 26 years. Throughout this time she depended on either Maximilian or Philip, but she never signalled any intention to leave Burgundy or to remarry.

Open rebellion

Henry VII knew he faced open revolt from the Earl of Lincoln, the Earl of Warwick (albeit through other people) and various Ricardians. Lincoln did not have a secure power base because his father, the Duke of Suffolk, still held estates in eastern England; however, Warwick had formidable links to estates in Calais, the Welsh borders and the Scottish marches, thus making this a very serious rebellion. Henry VII took action to undermine Ricardian support among the great magnates by promising favours to the Earl of Northumberland in return for loyalty, while ascertaining that the Howard family was reluctant to reinstate the Yorkist dynasty. He was already a shrewd king.

Henry spent Easter 1487 at Norwich where he oversaw the repair of the eastern coastal beacons and commissioned a fleet at Harwich. In doing so, he effectively set up an operational headquarters should he face invasion from the east. He then moved to Kenilworth where he received news through his efficient intelligence network that the rebels had landed on 4 June on the north-west coast of Cumbria. This rebel beach-head was predictable – a remote and inaccessible spot with known allies in the region to secure the landing, and a real prospect of recruiting support from loyal Ricardians in the north of England.

The rebels passed through a Ricardian heartland on the route to York. Sir Thomas Broughton who owned lands in Wensleydale had fought for Richard III at Bosworth, and Broughton Tower had sheltered Viscount

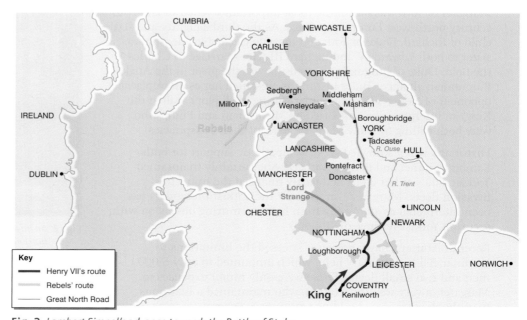

Fig. 3 *Lambert Simnel's advance towards the Battle of Stoke*

Lovell after the 1486 revolt. The nominal Edward VI was also welcomed by Sir Thomas' brother, John Broughton, and the Huddleston family of Millom. From here, they moved into Lonsdale after being received by Sir Thomas Harrington at Masham in Hornby Castle. From Masham, the rebels wrote letters to potential allies in Yorkshire including John, Lord Scrope of Bolton and Thomas, Lord Scrope of Masham. Both these Lords were old, experienced and powerful but did not commit their families immediately to the rebellion. All these families were opponents of the Tudor dynasty and tenants of the lordship of Middleham.

The King sent out orders for mobilisation summoning the nobles to meet him with their retinues at Coventry or Nottingham. He decided his strategy and battle formations in advance, relying on the Duke of Bedford to command the King's battalion and the experienced cavalry leader, the Earl of Oxford, to command the vanguard. Oxford would command key nobles such as the Earl of Shrewsbury, the Earl of Devon, Lord Hastings and Edward Grey, Viscount Lisle. Henry VII sent one cavalry wing northwards under the command of Sir Edward Woodville, Lord Scales, to hinder recruitment in Yorkshire and another cavalry wing under the Stanleys to hinder recruitment in Lancashire. The Stanleys' motives and loyalties were not clear, for the Earl of Derby was with the King but Lord Strange was absent – a chilling reminder of Bosworth. Henry's need for tight control is reflected in his insistence on public order and discipline by passing measures similar to martial laws.

Fig. 4 *Lambert Simnel landed on this remote coastland in the Furness area of Lancashire on 5 June 1487. The choice of such a remote spot is similar to Henry Tudor's decision in 1485 to land at Mill Bay near Dale in western Pembrokeshire*

The Earl of Lincoln also had a clear strategy. He aimed to keep the rebel army moving, to keep the rebels' morale high and to avoid creating local resentment – hence his decision not to move into the city of York but to by-pass it, and head south towards Boroughbridge. This strategy left him little time for rebel recruitment, yet he scored a notable victory at Tadcaster over the Lancastrian Henry, Lord Clifford. The exact route taken by the rebel army is not clear but it seems they followed the Great North Road southwards taking care to avoid hostile towns like Pontefract. After three days of running battles with Lord Scales' cavalry, Scales fled to Nottingham. When news of this defeat reached York, the city proclaimed for Edward VI – it seemed the advantage lay with Simnel and Lincoln.

By the time the King reached Nottingham, he had regrouped his army into battle order. Three great columns made up of the peers most closely associated with the Tudor dynasty (Bedford, Oxford, Derby, Lisle and Scales) supported by a group of younger peers (Shrewsbury, Devon, Wiltshire, Strange, Hastings and Grey) with a large number of knights (Sir John Cheney and Sir James Blount), some of whom were experienced soldiers. His recruitment had been extensive and was particularly successful in the north Midlands. The royal army, completed by tough billmen and skilful archers, moved northwards towards Newark and the Battle of Stoke.

Cross-reference

To recap on the actions and loyalties of the Stanleys, including Lord Strange, look back to page 35.

Sir William Stanley is also profiled on page 75.

It is clear that both armies were moving speedily despite their cumbersome artillery and baggage trains and were crossing major rivers. They were both using the network of major roads. Nottingham was of crucial strategic importance because it controlled one major bridge over the River Trent, and was only 16 miles from another bridge at Newark.

The rebel army reached Newark then followed the south bank of the river towards East Stoke along the Fosse Way, another major road. It appears Lincoln was deliberately drawing the royal army towards a carefully chosen site that would favour his smaller army. He was hoping that his small army could win against a larger force, as Henry VII had won at Bosworth.

The Battle of Stoke, 16 June 1487

Fig. 5 *Martin Schwarz and his forces at the Battle of Stoke, 16 June 1487. The mercenaries proved unable to turn the battle in favour of Lambert Simnel and the Yorkist challenge to Henry VII*

To Henry VII this battle was a real threat – he did not know the size, the power nor the route of the rebel army and, above all, he was acutely aware that battles were unpredictable. Tudor was not confident and feared either that Lincoln might have made a secret deal with other, apparently loyal, nobles; or that the royal reserve led by Stanley might turn from Tudor to York.

In reality, the rebel army had failed to win enough support during their march through England and numbered approximately 8,000 on the day of the battle. Many of the rebels, especially the Irish troops, were poorly armed and equipped; although some German mercenaries, who were employed for their reputed military skills and were accustomed to a higher standard of conflict abroad, were using new pike tactics.

Lincoln arrayed his army on the top of a ridge with his German mercenaries at the front, while the royal host of approximately 15,000 massed below. At the start of the battle, the Earl of Oxford marched his vanguard forward as a disciplined unit of men-at-arms and billmen interspersed with longbow archers.

Schwarz and his crossbowmen held them up temporarily with a volley of bolts, but could not sustain their resistance since they needed time to reload. When the English longbowmen came into range they fired their steel-tipped arrows at the rebel army crammed tightly together on the top of the ridge. The unprotected Irish suffered huge casualties, which demoralised the rebels so Lincoln decided to launch a fierce attack on the King's army by charging downhill. For a short while the outcome may have swung in the balance; however, Oxford had withstood a similar attack at Bosworth and, after three hours, his experience counted. Lincoln and Fitzgerald were killed, while Lovell and Broughton were assumed dead though their bodies were never identified. Lambert Simnel was taken alive by Robert Bellingham.

The King returned to Newark in the early afternoon, and moved from there to Lincoln to celebrate and give thanks for his victory. He ordered any captured German mercenaries ignominiously out of the country, and hung some socially insignificant English rebels along with all the surviving Irishmen. He spared the lives of all notable English rebels, although they were required to make confessions and recognise good behaviour **bonds**, and some had to pay fines.

Key term

Bonds: a bond was a lump sum of money. The person who gave the bond recognised himself as owing the lump sum stated. The sum did not have to be paid provided the condition (usually good behaviour) was observed. If the condition was broken, the sum had to be paid in penalty.

Activity

Thinking point

Compare Henry Tudor's successful rebellion in 1485 with Lambert Simnel's failure in 1487. Use this to draw up a list of five essential ingredients for a successful rebellion, then prioritise them.

The significance of 1487

After the months of tension and the grim bloodshed of battle, Henry VII was able to review his hold on royal authority in England. The Battle of Stoke would prove to be the last engagement of the Wars of the Roses and, therefore, a real watershed in the nation's history. The experience of the rebellion and the manner of its suppression shaped the character of the early Tudor dynasty.

Henry had been pre-occupied with the imposture from the middle of February 1487, and after the battle had to deal with continuing uprisings in Yorkshire and Northumberland. He did not return to London until October. Henry walked a tightrope in this year of crisis for he had to deal firmly with the rebels, yet he could not risk alienating whole districts or creating entrenched resistance as Richard III had after the Buckingham rebellion. By August, Henry was beginning to issue pardons and, in November, he called parliament to pass an Act of Attainder against 28 rebels, but he only took action against one major landowner – the Earl of Lincoln. There was no repeat of the massive land-transfer of 1483.

Cross-reference

The land-transfer of 1483 is discussed on page 28.

Henry knew he faced continued challenges from conspiracy and rebellion, and that there were Yorkist agents at the heart of his government. It was clear that some regions threatened to support any challenge to the King, and the problem of Ireland remained unresolved. He had good reason to fear foreign attack, especially with assistance from Burgundy.

Despite this, Henry was actually in a much more secure position by the end of 1487. Meeting the Simnel challenge had enabled him to assess the real quality of his ministers and servants and to understand the supreme importance of cultivating a network of loyal knights in the counties of England. The cost of the campaign and his acute shortage of ready money drove him to improve the crown's financial position through the enterprising financial management of men like Sir Reginald Bray. He was also made aware of the problem of inadequate law making and enforcement, so the Star Chamber was used to strengthen that aspect of personal monarchy. Henry also began to address the problem of rebellious nobles by extending the use of bonds that meant financial ruin if the noble stepped out of line.

Cross-reference

Sir Reginald Bray is profiled on page 73.

The Star Chamber is described more fully on page 74.

Henry VII was able to end the year on a positive note with the coronation of Elizabeth. The list of those attending the ceremony, reception and associated tournaments is proof that Henry's hold on the political nation was broadening. It was becoming more difficult to challenge princely powers, although this did not prevent three serious domestic challenges: rebellion in Yorkshire in 1489; Perkin Warbeck's imposture during 1491–7; and a further rebellion in Cornwall in 1497.

The Yorkshire rebellion, 1489

In 1489, parliament voted subsidy for the war to defend Brittany, and one of the King's men responsible for collecting it was Henry Percy, the Earl of Northumberland. Many men in Northumberland and Yorkshire believed they already paid for the defence of the realm through local taxes to maintain the Marcher borders; so a rebellion broke out in April 1489. The earl met the rebels and their leader, John à Chambre, at Thirsk but tempers were soon frayed and a scuffle broke out. The earl found himself isolated and was murdered, an event recorded by the poet John Skelton entitled 'Doulourus dethe and much lamentable chaunce of the most honourable Erle of Northumberlande'.

The rebels asked in vain for a pardon but this was denied by the King. Since the Earl of Northumberland had represented royal authority in the Northern Marches, Henry needed to firmly re-establish royal control, therefore he sent a large army to the north led by the Earl of Surrey who had John à Chambre hanged for treason at York. The rebels found another leader from their ranks, Sir John Egremont, who was an illegitimate member of the Percy family and a Yorkist sympathiser. He, however, proved to be unreliable for he soon fled for his life to the court of Margaret, Duchess of Burgundy.

After this débâcle, Henry did not attempt to raise tax again from Northumberland and Yorkshire.

Perkin Warbeck

Perkin Warbeck was Henry VII's most persistent rival, able to carry off his imposture for eight years. His imposture started in Cork, Ireland. Here, the Yorkist rebel John Taylor and the ex-mayor of Cork, John Atawater, confirmed his identity as Richard, Duke of York, the younger brother of Edward V. This was a crisis point for Henry VII as it coincided with the unfolding Breton crisis and its attendant threat from the Auld Alliance. Taylor and Atawater realised the possibility that the Warbeck imposture might win support from anti-Tudor foreign rulers.

■ Key profile

Perkin Warbeck

Perkin Warbeck was born and raised in Tournai, Flanders where his family was already well-established and ambitious for further success. They ensured their son was well educated in various languages and also in account keeping, as preparation for a career in the lucrative cloth trade. Warbeck served several masters, including the Yorkist trader Sir Edward Brampton, whilst trading across Europe from Antwerp and Bruges to Lisbon.

Henry VII immediately sent a small army to Ireland. Warbeck had won insufficient support after failing to receive the great Irish acclaim given to Simnel in 1487. He was unable to resist and, in 1492, was forced to flee to France.

Charles VIII, King of France, was at war with England over Brittany, so received Warbeck as a prince showing him appropriate honours. Henry, however, outmanoeuvred Warbeck by negotiating the Treaty of Etaples, forcing the imposter to flee again, this time to the Burgundian court where he was sheltered by Duchess Margaret. She trained him as a Yorkist prince.

Henry was so worried by Warbeck's presence in Burgundy that he adopted new, desperate tactics. In 1493, he introduced economic warfare by placing an embargo on the English woollen cloth trade with Burgundy, realising this might destabilise domestic peace as the embargo caused anguish.

By 1494, Warbeck had found another backer in the Holy Roman Emperor, Maximilian, who felt betrayed by the Anglo-French agreement made in the Treaty of Etaples. He recognised Warbeck though, fortunately for Henry VII, he lacked sufficient military resources to back him in the field. Henry rode his luck further when Charles VIII decided to wage war in Italy and withdrew his support for Warbeck to secure the northern borders of France.

■ Cross-reference

The crisis in Brittany and the Auld Alliance, and the Treaty of Etaples are detailed on page 64.

More information on Margaret of Burgundy can be found on page 49.

■ Key chronology

Perkin Warbeck

1491 Perkin Warbeck begins his imposture in Cork, Ireland. He claims to be Richard, Duke of York, the younger Prince in the Tower.

1492 Warbeck flees to France, where he is received by Charles VIII.

1493 Embargo on woollen cloth trade with Burgundy.

1494 Warbeck secures the backing of the Holy Roman Emperor.

1495 Warbeck attempts to invade England for the first time.

1496 Warbeck's second invasion of England, backed by the Scots army.

1497 Third attempt to invade England; Warbeck surrenders.

1498 Warbeck imprisoned in the Tower of London.

1499 Warbeck and the Earl of Warwick executed for treason.

■ Cross-reference

Henry VII's foreign policy is discussed in more detail on page 59.

The proposed marriage between Henry's son Arthur and the Spanish Princess Catherine of Aragon is covered on page 67.

Warbeck attempted his first invasion of England in 1495, when he sailed from the Netherlands and landed at Deal in Kent. English local authorities easily dealt with the imposter's small force because Henry VII had been forewarned of the attempted invasion by Sir Robert Clifford, a royal agent among Warbeck's supporters. Clifford implicated Sir William Stanley in the plot so the nobleman was arrested, charged with treason and executed. In acting swiftly and decisively, Henry lopped off the English branch of the Warbeck conspiracy before it could develop into a significant threat. Warbeck himself never even disembarked in England but stayed on his ship before setting sail for Ireland. After 11 days, the imposter had failed even to land in Waterford due to lack of support, so he set sail to Scotland.

James IV welcomed Warbeck, providing shelter, a pension and a royal wife – his cousin Lady Catherine Gordon. These anti-Tudor gestures put the proposed Anglo-Spanish marriage in serious doubt.

In the following year, Warbeck was involved in a second border raid on England, this time with the Scots army, but once again failed to rally support once he had crossed the border into England. Henry pursued him with diplomatic warfare, opening negotiations for Princess Margaret to marry James IV, who judged the time was right for more amicable Anglo-Scottish relations, and Warbeck was no longer welcome in Scotland. The imposter was once again on the move.

In 1497, Warbeck returned to Ireland where Kildare proved loyal to Henry VII, thus driving out the last desperate, opportunist bid for the throne of England. Warbeck landed in Cornwall hoping to exploit the Cornish tax rebellion. Several thousand Cornishmen joined his army but it not only proved to be disorganised, poorly led and under-equipped, it also exposed Warbeck's own inadequacies as military leader. Henry had again been forewarned about the invasion, so sent Sir Giles Daubeney to crush the rebellion at Exeter. Warbeck and some close companions fled to sanctuary at Beaulieu Abbey near Southampton, where he soon gave himself up to the King, and made a full confession.

Henry initially showed remarkable leniency, allowing Warbeck to remain with his wife at court. However, he tried to escape again in 1498 and this time Warbeck was humiliated and sent to the Tower of London. Once there, he was soon plotting to escape with Edward, Earl of Warwick.

Henry learned of the plotting, which may, in fact, have been set up by agents to kill two birds with one stone. In 1499, both men were put on trial for treason, after which Warwick was beheaded and Warbeck hung.

Fig. 6 *There are no surviving contemporary images of Perkin Warbeck admitting his imposture. This is a later interpretation of the dramatic climax to the six-year pretence*

■ Cross-reference

Sir Giles Daubeney is profiled on page 80.

The Cornish rebellion is described on page 56.

A closer look

Perkin Warbeck – ingenuity and skill

The continuing fascination of the Perkin Warbeck story lies in 'How did he do it?' Even when he was unmasked by Henry VII's diplomats in summer 1493, the impersonation continued. It seemed that because Warbeck was so good at being Richard, Duke of York it hardly mattered that he was not the real thing. The portrait

■ Activity

Revision exercise

Read the account of the Perkin Warbeck imposture on pages 54–55. Make notes on the following issues: strengths and weaknesses of the rebellion; strengths and weaknesses of the King; range of foreign involvement; and extent of domestic Yorkist support.

of Warbeck as a fat young boy reveals him plausibly like Edward IV. But not every fat young boy with a passing resemblance to Edward IV could have done what Warbeck did.

Warbeck's masters were men of trade and the sea. Bruges, cloth capital, banking capital of the world, was a swirling mass of energy – host to every nation that traded. Sir Edward Brampton had a place there, and introduced him to the Portugese court, and placed him in the service of Vaz da Cunha, an adventurer who was frequently employed in exploration.

Warbeck existed for a year in this atmosphere of court exploration-mania and enterprise before moving on. He lived by his wits, accommodating himself to new masters.

Before Warbeck was accepted as Richard, Duke of York by Margaret of Burgundy, she subjected him to an intense questioning on the household and personalities of the court of Edward IV. His desire to serve and his method of service – his repeated reinvention of himself – took him to the point where he stepped into the shoes of a prince.

Activity

Revision exercise

Complete the following table, comparing the nature and extent of the threat to Henry VII from Lambert Simnel and Perkin Warbeck.

	Lambert Simnel	Perkin Warbeck
Duration of the threat		
Extent of domestic support		
Foreign intervention		
Henry VII's responses		
Other comparisons		

The 1497 Cornish rebellion

The 1497 rebellion followed attempts to raise tax in Cornwall for a war against Scotland in retaliation for the Scots' support for Perkin Warbeck. The unpopular tax was apparently collected aggressively in Cornwall with many examples of maladministration and corruption. Parliament had attempted to protect the poorest subjects from paying this tax by stipulating that no one should pay unless he had an income of over 20 shillings a year from land, but this was not applied in Cornwall. Many Cornishmen were poor, just scraping a living as tin miners or farmers, and they resented paying tax for a border raid against the Scots. Cornwall's remote geographic location and vigorous regional identity, sparked by poverty, fuelled rebellion.

The rebels were led by Thomas Flamanck, a lawyer, and Michael Joseph, a blacksmith. The rebel army, of about 6,000 ill-armed peasants, planned to march peacefully to London and present their grievances to the King. The rebellion was temporarily hijacked by Perkin Warbeck, who saw it as a springboard for his own challenge to the King. He joined the rebel army in Cornwall. Despite Warbeck's presence, the rebels clearly lacked any real menace for they failed to enter Exeter on 17 September, had gained few supporters by the time they reached Somerset, and Warbeck deserted their cause. At this point Lord Audley joined their ranks. He had different motives for rebellion against the King. Lord Audley had financial difficulties and was out of royal favour. The rebels reached Blackheath outside London before they were suppressed, with many rebels killed, and their leaders captured and executed.

There are two possible interpretations for the fact that this rebellion reached the capital city. Some historians suggest that there was widespread resentment against the taxes, because nothing seemed to stand in its way. The people either joined or sympathised with the rebel army, and the local nobles, who would have been expected to act immediately to re-establish law and order for the King, seem to have stood aside. The King sent Lord Daubeney to defeat the rebels but he too was somewhat slow in carrying out this task, possibly biding his time to see how the rebellion developed, and subsequently found himself under bonds. Similarly, many wealthy families from southern England and the West Country were severely fined.

Another interpretation is that Henry VII made a deliberate decision to ride out the rebellion and that this is evidence of his increasing strength as a monarch. Francis Bacon explained the King's delay before attacking the rebels as a measured response by a secure monarch who, facing several challenges, chose to keep his armed strength close to the capital city.

> But for the course he held towards the rebels, it was utterly differing from his former course and practice; which was ever full of forwardness and celerity (speed) to make head against them, or to set upon them as soon as ever they were in action. But now, besides that he was attempered by years and less in love with dangers, by the continued fruition of a crown; it was a time when the various appearances to his thoughts of perils of several natures, and from divers parts, did make him judge his best and surest way, to keep his strength together in the seat and centre of his kingdom.

2

Henry did learn one lesson from the 1497 rebellion – he had to avoid expensive wars and needed to negotiate with James IV of Scotland rather than fight him. Foreign wars were very expensive so forced the King to raise extra revenue by asking parliament to vote taxation. Taxation was unpopular and risked provoking rebellion, which was expensive to suppress. Foreign wars also interrupted trade, so caused economic decline, unemployment and falling profits. Henry was, by nature, cautious and defensive, personal qualities that were reinforced by his experiences in 1497.

Cross-reference

More information on the imposition of bonds and its impact on certain nobles can be found on page 89.

Activity

Thinking point

'Tudor monarchs most feared the breakdown of law and order.'

1 Consider the strengths and weaknesses of the resources at Henry VII's disposal to maintain law and order.

2 Examine the interrelationship between Perkin Warbeck, taxation, regionalism and noble disaffection in provoking rebellion in 1497.

Summary questions

1 How important was the threat posed by the Earl of Suffolk, the 'White Rose', to the throne of England?

2 Explain why remote counties, rather than central counties, were so often the source of rebellion during this period of English history.

Henry VII and the countries of Europe

Fig. 1 *King Ferdinand of Aragon and Queen Isabella of Castile supported Christopher Columbus' voyage to discover America. Henry VII emulated their exploration but was less successful; and his son, Henry VIII, did not sponsor subsequent voyages*

In this chapter you will learn about:

■ the nature of foreign relations under Henry VII

■ how Henry VII's relations with foreign powers fluctuated over the reign.

A true friendship and alliance shall be observed henceforth between Ferdinand and Isabella, their heirs and subjects, on the one part, and Henry, his heirs and subjects, on the other part. They promise to assist one another in defending their present and future dominions against any enemy whatsoever.

1 *From D. O'Sullivan and R. Lockyer, **Tudor England**, 1993*

The Treaty of Medina del Campo marked the acceptance of Henry VII's claim to the English throne by the rulers of Spain, one of the major states in western Europe.

Protecting the security of the dynasty through relations with foreign powers

Henry VII, along with other Tudor monarchs, would not have recognised the modern historians' practice of separating foreign from domestic policy. This was mainly because he did not think in terms of structured policies, but constantly reacted to events – rebellions, conspiracies and pretenders. The example of Perkin Warbeck illustrates the intricate

Cross-reference

Perkin Warbeck's story is told on page 54.

interweaving of royal governance with financial and foreign policies throughout this period.

Henry would not have recognised the modern term 'national interest'. What we call 'foreign policy' was not dictated by political values, but by changing *personal* relations between princes in Europe. Each ruler had objectives that guided their actions in Europe. Henry's priorities were:

1 To secure his throne.

Henry was fully aware that during the Wars of the Roses three English kings had been defeated and deposed by rivals supported by France or Burgundy, and he did not intend to become the fourth.

2 To achieve international recognition of his kingship and his dynasty's legitimate succession.

The most obvious way to achieve this was through marriage alliances with foreign royal families. Royal intermarriage was very common and could establish strong alliances between powerful families.

3 To promote prosperity in England.

England was already an established trading nation whose prosperity depended on internal peace and advantageous commercial terms. Economic prosperity generated increasing employment and personal wealth, circumstances that would deter rebellion. Social stability was, therefore, encouraged by economic security.

4 To maintain prestige while keeping the costs down.

Foreign entanglements were always very expensive and risky. The King would have to fund such adventures through extraordinary revenue, usually unpopular taxation. Henry realised that the treasury was far more secure when England functioned as a useful ally for one of the main powers in Europe, than when financing an independent foreign policy. England had ceased to be a major European power after defeat in the Hundred Years' War in 1453, and was now a second ranking European power.

Europe during the reign of Henry VII

In 1485, the most important countries in Europe comprised:

- France: the kingdom of France was ruled by Charles VIII, a member of the house of Valois. The French monarch was the strongest power in Europe and he used that power to annexe other provinces including Brittany, Navarre and Burgundy. This brought France into conflict with many European countries.

- Spain: Ferdinand of Aragon and Isabella of Castile married in 1469 and they held both kingdoms from 1479. This created the appearance of a unified country. Aragon was, however, a far less significant state than Castile. The Spanish rulers fought wars to expand their territories against both the Muslims in the south and the French over Navarre.

- The Holy Roman Empire: the Empire was a loose federation of German, Italian and French-speaking cantons. The Emperor was elected by three archbishops and four secular princes and commanded no central government, therefore his power and resources were in his own lands. The Empire was dominated by the Hapsburg dynasty who ruled territories in modern-day Austria, as well as inherited lands in Spain, Italy and the Netherlands including Burgundy. Conflicts

Exploring the detail

Table 1 *Kings of England who were defeated by rivals who were assisted by France or Burgundy during the Wars of the Roses*

Henry VI	1461 and 1471	Defeated by Edward, Duke of York who was backed by the Duke of Burgundy
Edward IV	1470	Defeated by Henry VI who was backed by the King of France
Richard III	1485	Defeated by Henry Tudor who was backed by the King of France

Exploring the detail
Royal intermarriage

One instance of this is Margaret, sister of Edward IV, who was married to Charles the Bold, Duke of Burgundy. On his death in 1477, the Dukedom passed to Maximilian of Hapsburg who became Holy Roman Emperor in 1493. Maximilian meanwhile married Charles the Bold's daughter from a previous marriage.

Fig. 2 *Europe in 1487*

Fig. 3 *This is a contemporary manuscript depicting cloth dyers at work. They are immersing the bolt of cloth in a vat of dye over a fire. At the bottom right you can see a pile of faggots (sticks) to be added to the fire. The export of cloth was England's major export in the late 15th and early 16th centuries*

between the Holy Roman Empire and the King of France are known as the Hapsburg-Valois conflicts.

■ The Duchy of Burgundy: The duchy passed to the Hapsburgs in 1477 after the death of Duke Charles the Bold. However, the French King aimed to annexe the duchy making it a point of Franco-Hapsburg contention. It consisted mainly of the commercially-important areas now known as Belgium and the Netherlands.

■ The Italian states including the Papal States: Italy was made up of small states. The Papal States dominated the centre of the country, while the north had city states, the main ones being Florence, Milan and Venice. These states were at the focus of European trade and wealth, making them irresistible to foreign rulers seeking glory or territory.

Henry's relations with foreign powers

Henry's foreign policies were an extension of his personal monarchy in that they reflected his cautious preference for peace over war. It was, of necessity, a defensive policy. England was a middle-ranking power in late 15th century Europe, considerably overwhelmed by the

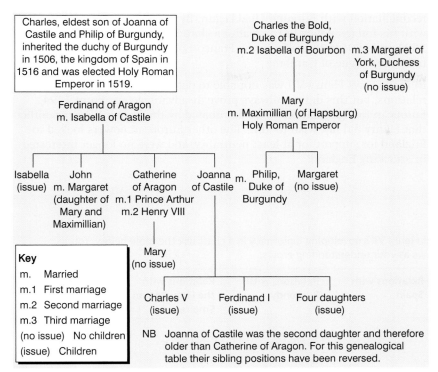

Fig. 4 *The royal families of Spain, Burgundy and the Holy Roman Empire 1477–1519*

■ **Key chronology**

Deaths that rocked English foreign policy, 1502–6

1502 Prince Arthur
1503 Queen Elizabeth
1505 Isabella of Castile
1506 Philip of Burgundy

■ **Exploring the detail**

The Italian Wars, 1494–1515

Italy was a collection of states of which Milan, Venice, Florence, the Papal States and Naples were the most important. After decades of internal stability and prosperity, each of these important states looked to extend its influence at the expense of its neighbours. Charles VIII of France had a dynastic claim to the state of Naples, wished to tap into Italian wealth, and planned to extend French trade in the Italian states. He took the opportunity of Italian disunity and invaded Milan, Florence and entered Rome in 1494.

His astounding success provoked hostility from the Italian states, and intervention from Spain and the Holy Roman Empire. Italy became the battleground of Europe during the Italian Wars, a conflict that effectively spilled into the Hapsburg-Valois wars from 1521.

established might of France, the emergence of united Spain, and the unpredictable Hapsburg dynasty. Henry lacked the power to dictate events so was forced into increasingly reactive policy concerning the developing crises over Brittany, the succession to Castile, the outbreak of the lengthy Italian wars, various pretenders, and the accession of an Anglophobic king in Scotland. It is not surprising that Henry's responses tended to be defensive and short term, nor that this arch-survivor proved to be good at changing course, avoiding major conflict, and seizing any opportunities that came his way.

Another complication Henry faced was the quality of the information available upon which to base decisions about foreign policy. The English king did not yet employ career diplomats to reside in foreign courts and report events accurately. As a result, diplomatic reports were compiled by amateurs, often noblemen, who frequently misinterpreted both foreign languages and procedures, and who were vulnerable to the slow pace of communications.

Henry's inheritance was weak for, in 1485, he was a newly-crowned usurper with little credibility among the European princes. The previous Yorkist kings were pro-Burgundy and pro-Brittany (Figure 4) while remaining anti-French, and therefore had wanted to keep both Burgundy and Brittany independent of the growing might of France. Tudor, on the other hand, owed a debt of loyalty to France for providing shelter after 1484 and supporting his usurpation, and also was indebted to the Duke of Brittany who had sheltered him from 1471. Brittany would be the focus of his first significant foray into European diplomacy.

As with governance and financial management, Henry changed the direction of his foreign policy throughout his reign. By the turn of the century, he had become a much stronger king; being at peace with France, an ally of Spain, with support from the Holy Roman Emperor; and his

■ Cross-reference

Henry Tudor's time in exile in France and Burgundy is outlined on page 30.

reconciliation with Burgundy had begun. By 1509, Henry was weak again with his foreign policy in ruins after a shattering series of deaths between 1502 and 1506, vulnerable to the Franco-Spanish alliance and excluded from the League of Cambrai.

In many ways Henry VII was not able to determine English foreign relations, but this did not always prove disadvantageous. From 1494, European foreign relations were dominated by the Italian Wars, a conflict that Henry did not wish to join. The other European powers looked to England for support, or at least neutrality, and were no longer interested in attacking England.

■ Activity

Revision exercise

As you study this chapter, keep a record of Henry VII's developing diplomacy in a chart like the table below. You may wish to add additional columns or rows as your understanding grows.

Period of foreign policy	Relations with France	Relations with Spain	Relations with Burgundy	Relations with the Holy Roman Empire	Relations with Scotland
Establishing 1485–7					
Consolidating 1487–1501					
Recovering 1501–09					

■ Exploring the detail

Brittany

The Duke of Brittany swore feudal overlordship to the King of France. Duke Francis of Brittany died in 1488 leaving a minor, his daughter Anne, who became a ward of the King of France. The King of France, Charles VIII, was also a minor but the regent Anne of Beaujeu planned to marry Charles VIII to Anne of Brittany. Duke Francis had anticipated this outcome but the arrangement for his daughter to marry Maximilian of Hapsburg, and his plots with the Regent's enemies in France, failed to prevent the marriage.

■ Cross-reference

More information on Maximilian and Ferdinand can be found in the sections on Burgundy (page 65) and Spain (page 67).

To recap on Perkin Warbeck, look back to page 54.

France

France was the dominant power in Europe so this was the most challenging foreign relationship for Henry VII to manage. This relationship was strained from the start of Tudor's reign, because the kingdom of France aimed to completely absorb the semi-independent state of Brittany.

The expansion of French influence into Brittany was a significant concern for Henry VII. On a personal basis, he owed the Duke of Brittany a debt of loyalty for the shelter he had received in the years 1471 to 1484. He also knew that additional territory made the King of France even wealthier, therefore reducing the likelihood that the King of England could lay legitimate claim to the throne of France. Besides, French expansion raised security issues to the English south coast, and particularly threatened England's last continental possession, Calais. French presence in Brittany might also threaten English trade in the English Channel. Throughout the crisis, Henry realised he could not appear weak in his first major test on the European diplomatic stage.

Henry clearly could not stand back and let France take Brittany unopposed; however, he was militarily and financially weak so looked for allies. Maximilian of Burgundy and Ferdinand of Spain were also anxious about the absorption of Brittany and the consequent strengthening of their enemy, France. They both sent troops to Brittany in 1487 as a show of opposition, but were then distracted by other wars, Maximilian against Hungary, Ferdinand against the Moors, leaving Henry VII in 1488 to act alone.

Brittany
Henry owed Duke Francis II of Brittany a debt of gratitude for providing shelter during his exile to 1483. A commercial treaty was signed between England and Brittany in July 1486.

Scotland
Initially, Henry VII feared the Scots might capitalise on his accession and invade. He raised a loan from the City of London but this proved both unpopular and unnecessary. King James III was pleased to end years of Yorkist–Scottish hostility. A three-year truce was signed between England and Scotland in July 1486.

Ireland
Eastern Ireland beyond the Pale was under the control of Gerald Fitzgerald, Earl of Kildare. He, like Burgundy and the Holy Roman Empire, had prospered under the Yorkists and was a source of rebellion against Tudor. He was not able to make any pre-emptive agreement with Kildare.

France
The king of France, Charles VIII, had also sheltered Tudor in exile. This created a conflict of interest for Henry VII as France was looking to absorb Brittany. Despite this, a one-year truce was signed between England and France in October 1485 that was subsequently extended to 1489.

Burgundy
Margaret, Duchess of Burgundy, was an implacable enemy of Henry VII. He was never able to make any diplomatic arrangements with Burgundy. This complicated foreign affairs because Burgundy had been acquired by the Holy Roman Empire in 1477 when Maximilian married Mary, the daughter and heiress of Charles the Bold of Burgundy.

Spain
The marriage between Ferdinand of Aragon and Isabella of Castile in 1479 had formed another power in Europe. Henry VII feared a Franco-Spanish alliance against England but that proved unlikely as Spanish ambitions to reclaim Roussillon and Cerdagne, and to absorb Navarre, brought them into conflict with France.

Holy Roman Empire
Maximilian was alarmed by Tudor's invasion of England because it was sponsored by his enemy, France. Tudor wanted to use Maximilian as an ally in preventing an agreement between France and Spain. All that Henry could achieve was a one-year extension to Edward IV's existing treaty from January 1487.

Pope Innocent
The pope gave Henry support from the start of the reign. He formally recognised his title to the kingdom in a Bull that was printed and circulated by Henry – the first clear use of printed political propaganda in England. In 1486, Humphrey Stafford appealed to the pope claiming he had been removed from sanctuary, but the pope did not oppose the execution nor the revised law on sanctuary.

Fig. 5 *Henry VII's foreign relations in 1487*

Cross-reference

Henry's relationships with the papacy are outlined on page 81.

In 1489, Henry signed the Treaty of Redon, promising to assist Brittany in defying French ambitions, and sending 3,000 English troops, paid for by Anne of Brittany. Henry made it clear to the King of France that he intended to defend Brittany, not to assert England's claim to the French throne. These actions have usually been interpreted by historians as a minimal and defensive response by Henry, but more recently it has been suggested that he was actually more assertive; and it was the Bretons who restricted the size of the English army and so blocked any English reconquest of former territories, Normandy and Guyenne.

Henry showed diplomatic skill and gave himself time for thorough preparations by avoiding a rush into armed conflict with France. He opened negotiations with Spain that culminated in the Treaty of Medina del Campo. Meanwhile, Tudor looked for support or neutrality from the Pope, and the rulers of the Netherlands and some German states. Despite Henry's opposition, France ploughed on with the absorption of Brittany when Charles married Anne in December 1491. The French also showed their displeasure with Henry VII by receiving Perkin Warbeck at court and pouring more troops into Brittany.

■ A closer look

The Breton Crisis, 1487–92

The main conflicting interests were as follows:

- Brittany: to maintain independence from France.
- France: to absorb Brittany into the kingdom of France.
- England: to honour Tudor's obligation to Brittany, while avoiding conflict with France.
- Spain and the Holy Roman Empire: to prevent France absorbing Brittany.

In 1487, the French regent declared the plan for Charles VIII to marry Anne of Brittany.

In 1489, the Treaty of Redon was signed. Henry made agreements with Ferdinand and Maximilian to build an anti-French alliance, while the Bretons agreed to cover the costs of the 3,000 strong English army.

In 1491, France took control of Brittany when Charles VIII married Anne. Henry reasserted his ancient claim to France and besieged Boulogne.

In 1492, the Treaty of Etaples was negotiated, with the following terms:

1 The French would pay an annual pension of 50,000 crowns (£5,000), as agreed in 1495.
2 Charles VIII would not support any imposters.
3 Henry would withdraw his English troops from Brittany.

Henry summoned parliament to grant a subsidy to fight the war against France with an army of 12,000. He launched a short campaign late in the fighting season in the knowledge – gleaned by his spies in the French court – that France wanted a war in the lucrative Italian peninsular, and would be disinclined to waste revenue on a conflict with England. The short siege of Boulogne ended with the Treaty of Etaples. Henry had asserted his strength, avoided a major campaign, and secured his international reputation.

Over the next two decades, Anglo-French relations were relatively good, although they deteriorated again after 1506 when France was drawn into a closer entente with Spain and became a signatory of the Treaty of Cambrai.

Burgundy

Under the Yorkist kings, England had good relations with Burgundy because:

- Burgundy had achieved independence from France so was naturally anti-French.
- England's major exports, wool and woollen cloth, went through Burgundian markets so both countries' commercial prosperity depended on good relations.

Anglo-Burgundian relations under Tudor were difficult. Margaret of Burgundy was Tudor's implacable opponent; she constantly conspired against Henry, and Maximilian also plotted against Henry when it suited him.

Cross-reference

Margaret of Burgundy is profiled on page 49.

Key profile

Maximilian of Burgundy, King of the Romans

Maximilian married Mary of Burgundy, who was the daughter of Charles the Bold, the Duke of Burgundy. It was through this marriage that he inherited lands in Burgundy. In 1493, Maximilian was elected to be the Holy Roman Emperor, a position he held until his death in 1519. As Holy Roman Emperor, Maximilian was immensely powerful, being first in rank in Europe.

Henry learned an early lesson from Maximilian about the dangers of alliances. In 1489, both men signed the Treaty of Dordrecht. In this, Maximilian agreed to send troops to Brittany to help Henry resist French expansion, while Henry would send 3,000 troops to assist Maximilian who was being besieged by French and Flemish troops.

Maximilian did not send troops. Instead, he concentrated on his interests in Hungary before making peace with Charles VIII.

Fig. 6 *Maximilian of Burgundy. Through wars and marriage, Maximilian extended the influence of the Holy Roman Empire and so earned the name 'The Last Knight'*

In 1493, Anglo-Burgundian relations deteriorated further when Philip took over direct rule of Burgundy while Maximilian inherited the title Holy Roman Emperor. Henry wrote to Philip protesting about Margaret's continued support for Perkin Warbeck but Philip ignored his letter. Henry retaliated by banishing Burgundian merchants from England and put an embargo on English trade with Burgundy that lasted until 1496.

Key profile

Philip of Burgundy

Philip, the son of Maximilian of Hapsburg and Mary of Burgundy, was also known as Philip the Fair. He married Joanna of Castile with whom he had a son, Charles, born in 1500. Philip succeeded to the Dukedom of Burgundy in 1493 after Maximilian was elected Holy Roman Emperor. Isabella's death in 1504 provoked a succession struggle for Castile between Ferdinand and Philip; however, Philip died in September 1506 and his wife retired into insane obscurity, so Ferdinand triumphed.

■ Cross-reference

Ferdinand and Isabella of Spain, and the struggle of the Castilian succession, are further discussed in the section on Spain on page 67.

■ Exploring the detail

Terms of the secret Treaty of Windsor, 1506

■ Henry secured more advantageous trading terms than those agreed in the *Intercursus Magnus*. This new settlement was known as the *Intercursus Malus*, ('malus' meaning 'evil') because it was loaded towards the English merchants.
■ Philip would ensure Suffolk was handed over, provided Henry VII guaranteed his life.
■ Henry recognised Philip and Joanna as the rulers of Castile.
■ Henry would marry Philip's sister, Margaret of Savoy.

■ Cross-reference

The *Intercursus Malus* is discussed on page 93.

After 1495, diplomatic relations began to improve when Warbeck left Burgundy. Maximilian wanted English support for his campaign against France and forced Margaret to back down. Besides, Henry and Philip had both suffered from the commercial restrictions of the embargo and agreed in *Intercursus Magnus* (the Great Settlement) in 1496 to remove trade barriers. Relations were better but not easy because Philip continued to harbour Yorkists, and Henry had no intention of backing Hapsburg in their bitter conflict against Valois.

The next significant crisis in Anglo-Burgundian relations arose after the death of Isabella of Castile in 1504. Henry had to make a difficult decision – whether to back Philip or Ferdinand's claims in the disputed succession to Castile. He gambled and chose to back Philip for several reasons:

1 Henry wanted to protect English trade with Burgundy.
2 Henry saw an opportunity to negotiate an advantageous marriage for Prince Henry to Philip's daughter Eleanor.
3 Maximilian was sheltering the leading Yorkist pretender Edmund de la Pole, Duke of Suffolk. Henry hoped to gain custody of Suffolk by backing Philip.

Ferdinand moved to secure his own claim to Castile. Philip was determined to go to Castile with Joanna to pre-empt Ferdinand. During the voyage from the Netherlands to Spain, they were caught in a storm in the Channel and forced to seek shelter in England. Henry VII showed great opportunism, lavishly entertaining his unexpected visitors, before capitalising on this lucky break to force the profitable secret Treaty of Windsor.

Philip and Joanna arrived in Castile to a rapturous welcome and Ferdinand retreated to Aragon, apparently now only King of insignificant Aragon. Henry's gamble appeared to have paid off. Later that year, however, his diplomatic house of cards collapsed. Philip died unexpectedly, Joanna allegedly went mad, Ferdinand resumed control of Castile, and Maximilian assumed regency of Burgundy for his young grandson Charles. The Treaty of Windsor was abandoned. Margaret of Savoy refused to marry Prince Henry. Henry was now isolated in Europe with the only benefit being that Suffolk was already in his custody.

There was some diplomatic consolation. Henry's relations with Maximilian remained good because both continued to fear the power of France, especially after the French reconciliation with Spain. He abandoned the controversial *Intercursus Malus*, reverting to traditional English foreign policy – safeguarding good relations with the natural ally Burgundy. Discussions of a proposed marriage between Princess Mary and Maximilian's grandson, Charles, were further evidence of this policy reversal. In this, Henry demonstrated foresight, because the Archduke Charles would soon be the most powerful ruler in Europe.

At the end of the reign, Anglo-Burgundian relations were still not entirely secure. Henry was never confident that he had Maximilian's continued support. This was made clear in 1508 when Maximilian chose to sign the Treaty of Cambrai with the Kings of France and Spain. The Treaty was a military alliance against Venice, part of the continuing Italian Wars, and therefore did not involve Henry. It can be argued that the distraction of war against Venice gave Henry some respite at the end; however, there was danger that the focus of the alliance might move to an anti-Tudor position. England's security depended on strong allies in Europe and these were conspicuously absent in the years 1508 to 1509.

Spain

Henry was determined to strengthen his links with the new power in Europe and worked hard to secure the Treaty of Medina del Campo in 1489. It provided Henry with recognition on the international stage and valuable security. Its terms included that:

■ Ferdinand and Henry VII agreed mutual support to defend their countries against any enemy, and assurance that neither king would make any peace, alliance or treaty with France without the other's agreement

■ neither country would assist or harbour rebels or pretenders

■ Princess Catherine of Aragon would marry Prince Arthur of England.

Anglo-Spanish relations were generally good after this, although there were fluctuations.

1   The Spanish did not honour their commitment to provide assistance in Brittany because Ferdinand and Isabella were preparing for their final attack on the Moors in Granada.

2   The on-going Perkin Warbeck saga threatened the Spanish marriage. The Spanish princess would not marry into a politically-unstable royal family.

3   There were endless arguments between Ferdinand and Henry about the size and payment schedules for Catherine's dowry.

Fig. 7 *Ferdinand of Spain. Ferdinand was a very able monarch – a cunning negotiator, a capable soldier and a ruthless statesman*

The Spanish marriage was finally agreed in a marriage treaty in 1499. Catherine and Prince Arthur were married in 1501, but the latter's death in 1502 immediately endangered the Anglo-Spanish alliance. Henry proposed that, instead, Catherine should marry Prince Henry. Ferdinand resisted, holding out for better terms because he did not need the English alliance at a time when Spanish relations with France were improving. By 1503, however, Franco-Spanish relations had again deteriorated and so Ferdinand accepted the proposal. Catherine and Prince Henry were betrothed. This betrothal required papal dispensation from Pope Julius II, dispensation that would later prove to be the source of great controversy.

The alliance with Spain foundered after 1504. The death of Isabella opened up the Castilian succession question. Henry realised that Ferdinand was no longer the immense European power he had been as King of united Spain. He tried to retract Prince Henry's betrothal to Catherine, claiming that the prince was aged under 12 years at the time of the papal dispensation, therefore it was not valid. Furthermore, Tudor then chose to back Philip against Ferdinand's claim in the Castilian succession crisis.

As a result of such diplomatic fluctuation, Ferdinand signed the Treaty of Blois with France in 1505 and, the next year, married Louis XII's niece. After Philip's death in 1506, Ferdinand reclaimed the upper hand, emerging as the sole ruler of united Spain and strong with his French alliance. Spain no longer needed English support.

■ **Exploring the detail**

Ferdinand of Aragon and Isabella of Castile

The Iberian peninsular was made up of various Christian kingdoms and the emirate of Granada. The two largest and most powerful kingdoms, Aragon and Castile, were brought together by the marriage of Ferdinand and Isabella in 1469, but were not united; hence the uncertainty after Isabella's death in 1504. Ferdinand and Isabella's two daughters, Joanna of Castile and Catherine of Aragon, married into the royal families of Burgundy and England.

■ Cross-reference

Details of the controversy surrounding the King's Great Matter are given on page 132.

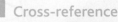 Activity

Thinking point

Consider the deaths of the following. What impact did they have on English foreign relations?

	Death	Impact of the deaths on English foreign relations
1502	Prince Arthur	
1503	Queen Elizabeth	
1505	Isabella of Castile	
1506	Philip of Burgundy	

Scotland

Relations between England and Scotland were traditionally difficult, with frequent border warfare, and complicated by the persistent danger of a Franco-Scottish alliance. Henry was relatively fortunate because the problems took a while to develop. James IV was a minor and his regent, the Earl of Angus, was an anglophile Scot. In 1495, however, glory-hunting James came of age and proved to be a formidable foe. He was a dedicated warrior who spent huge sums on weaponry, building a significant arsenal, with his particular enthusiasm being artillery.

Henry watched developments in Scotland carefully. This caution proved wise when events came to a head with James IV recognising Perkin Warbeck. He gave the imposter a royal welcome, sheltered him for two years, paid him a pension and agreed to Warbeck's marriage to his cousin, the Lady Catherine Gordon. Most controversially, in 1496, Warbeck launched an abortive invasion of England with James IV's support. In retaliation, Henry built the largest army of his reign. In 1497, the Earl of Surrey marshalled English troops on the Scottish border but James IV was saved from invasion by the start of the Cornish rebellion. The rebellion was ironically provoked by the subsidy raised to pay for the war against Scotland.

All the indications had suggested Henry would have scored a notable victory over the Scots but the Cornish rebellion had taken him by surprise. James IV was left isolated by Warbeck's departure and faced growing discontent from his chief lords. It suited both Kings to make peace at the Truce of Ayton in 1497. This established Anglo-Scottish harmony for the remainder of the reign and matured into a formal peace treaty in 1502. Its long-term strength was symbolised by Henry's agreement in 1501 for his daughter Princess Margaret to marry James IV, with the actual marriage taking place in 1503.

Ireland

Ireland was part of the kingdom of England and so policy towards Ireland is not technically foreign policy. It makes logical sense to consider Irish policy here, however, because the Anglo-Irish lords played their part in the relations between princes that determined European diplomacy.

Henry showed remarkable leniency in dealing with those in Ireland who promoted the failed Simnel imposture. He forced the Earl of Kildare and the other Anglo-Irish nobles to swear an oath of allegiance to the English monarchy. In 1491, the King's patience was strained and he showed less tolerance after Perkin Warbeck appeared in Dublin. Tudor dismissed Kildare and sent a small English army to Ireland. Warbeck fled to France.

Cross-reference

The impostures of Perkin Warbeck and Lambert Simnel and the events of the Cornish rebellion are discussed in chapter 4.

Fig. 8 *This beautiful document is the Treaty of Perpetual Peace, concluded between England and Scotland in 1502 and cemented by the marriage of James IV of Scotland to Princess Margaret, Henry VII's eldest child. English craftsmen wrote and illuminated the treaty with many images, including roses and thistles*

In 1494, Henry sent Sir Edward Poynings to Ireland as Lord Deputy. Poynings:

- undermined the autonomy of the Anglo-Irish nobles through 'Poynings' Laws'. The most important law prevented them holding parliamentary sessions or legislating without the English government's approval.
- restored order, crushing the continuing troubles and a major rebellion organised by Kildare's brother.
- prevented Warbeck returning to Ireland.
- arrested Kildare, and sent him to England as a prisoner. Kildare's lands were attainted by the Irish parliament meeting at Drogheda in the Pale.

In 1496, however, Henry reverted to ruling Ireland through the Anglo-Irish nobles rather than an imposed governor. He reinstated Kildare as Lord Deputy and reversed the attainder, although he took the precaution of keeping Kildare's son at the court in England to guarantee loyal conduct.

Historians debate the success of Poynings' governorship and the reasons for Kildare's reinstatement. Elton argued that the decision was taken by a strong and confident king who judged the crisis had passed, and so chose to revert to the Yorkist policy of maintaining only a bridgehead of direct royal control in Ireland, in the Pale around Dublin. Elton saw Poynings' expedition as a success. S. G. Ellis argued that the reinstatement of Kildare was a failure because it marked the end of English control in Ireland. He wrote the decision was pragmatic as Henry did not face a threat from Ireland. It was, however, an admission that direct rule had proved expensive and futile in Ireland.

Poynings had succeeded, albeit temporarily, in reducing support for Warbeck, and preventing the imposter from threatening Tudor rule from Ireland.

Activity

Thinking point

Using the table below, decide how successful Henry VII was in his conduct of foreign policy.

Aim	Policy	Evidence of success	Evidence of failure
1 To secure his throne			
2 To achieve international recognition of his kingship and his dynasty's legitimate succession			
3 To promote prosperity in England			
4 To maintain prestige while keeping costs down			

Activity

Revision exercise

Draw a fortune graph showing the fluctuations of Henry's relations with the other princes in Europe in the years 1485 to 1509. The graph has been started for you below.

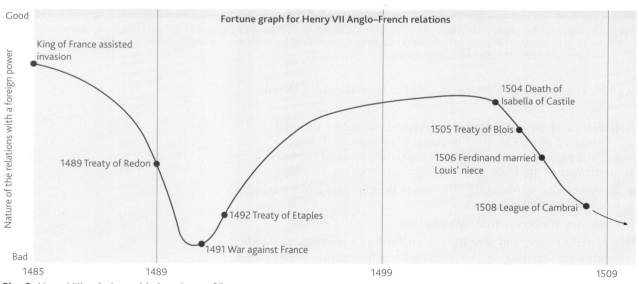

Fig. 9 *Henry VII's relations with the princes of Europe*

Summary questions

1 How far was Henry VII's foreign policy merely defensive in the years between 1487 and 1509?

2 In what ways was dynastic marriage important in Henry VII's relations with foreign powers in the years 1487 to 1509?

6 Establishing royal authority

In this chapter you will learn about:

- the concept of personal monarchy
- central and local government under Henry VII.

Key chronology

Henry Tudor

1457 Born to the Lancastrian Edmund Tudor and Margaret Beaufort. Edmund Tudor dies before his son's birth, so Henry is born to the earldom of Richmond. His mother then marries Sir Henry Stafford, and brings her son up at Bourne in Lincolnshire.

1461 After the political revolution, Henry is separated from his mother and brought up in Raglan and Chepstow Castle by the Yorkist William Herbert, Earl of Pembroke.

1470 When Henry VI is restored to the throne, Tudor returns to his mother and uncle.

1471 After the disastrous battle of Tewkesbury, Tudor is the leading Lancastrian claimant so flees with his uncle to Brittany.

1483 Tudor tries to use the Buckingham rebellions as a springboard to challenge Richard III but is unable to land, so returns to Brittany. On Christmas Day, he publicly promises to marry Elizabeth of York if he is ever crowned King of England.

1484 The Duke of Brittany does a deal to hand Tudor over to Richard III. Tudor flees to the court of the King of France.

1485 Tudor claims the title King of England.

Most kings have an unreal education. They have been princes, or at any rate great noblemen, never treated quite naturally by those they meet. In Brittany, Henry was nothing much. He must have learned a lot about courts in all that time hanging about waiting for the Duke to get ready to go hunting or sitting through interminable meals; in gossip, in getting to know what people really thought behind the flattery they used to the powerful, in joining in the hollow laughter at the ducal jokes; in watching the intrigues, the gossip campaign to put down this minister, the deals to bring somebody else to power. The Breton court had a weak ruler, a lot of intrigue and occasional blood-letting. The conclusion Henry appears to have drawn was that rulers should never let themselves go, should maintain their dignity at all times, should always remain in control, never become indebted to a party or group. Behind-the-scenes wheeling and dealing, followed by his own wheeling and dealing at the French court, must have taught Henry a vast amount about how politics really worked. No wonder that as king he was careful, always wanting to double check every bit of information, always determined to keep up a front, to prevent the mask slipping, never behaving as 'one of the lads' in the way Edward IV or Henry VIII often did.

 C. Davies, 'The Making of Henry VII', 2001

Activity

Talking point

How effectively was Henry VII prepared for his role as King of England? Compare his experiences with those of Edward IV and Richard III.

Henry VII's personality and mode of governing would undoubtedly have been shaped by his early experiences.

Personal strengths:

- He spoke and understood several languages, being particularly comfortable with French culture.
- He knew the dangers of imposters lurking in foreign courts seeking aid.
- He had built a close group of loyal and trusted colleagues while in exile.

Personal disadvantages:

- He had no formal experience of estate financial management.
- He had not attended the English court.
- He had not developed effective relationships with the political nation in England.
- He knew little of the country and was virtually unknown to the English people.

Activity

Revision exercise

In a period of personal monarchy, the personality of the King was the vital determinant of the nature of royal rule. Write a curriculum vitae for Henry Tudor for the post of King of England.

Cross-reference

Information on the Marcher Lords can be found on page 3.

Key terms

Government: is the mechanism of government, in other words the institutions that enabled the King to govern the realm.

Governance: the process of ruling, both formal and informal or, in this case, the ways that Henry ruled the country through his ministers, parliament, the nobles and the gentry.

Central government: decision-making bodies who ran the country including the court, Counsel and parliament.

Local government: administration, revenue collection and law enforcement carried out at county level by JPs and sheriffs, and in parishes by churchwardens, constables and overseers of the poor.

Relations with the nobility

Fig. 1 *The Tower of London served as the main royal palace in London during the reign of Henry VII. In this picture the king is shown greeting a guest, looking out of a window and signing a document in the White Tower. In the background is the Old London Bridge across the River Thames*

The English magnate remained a significant force in English **government** and **governance** towards the end of the 15th century, although the number of noble families had fallen during the Wars of the Roses to about 60.

Over the course of Henry VII's reign there was a significant change in the relationship between the crown and nobles who came to act less as free agents of the crown. Instead, they were increasingly drawn more into the work of **central** and **local government** as the King extended his network of control across the realm. The only exceptions to this trend were the Marcher Lords, who continued to exercise considerable independence. Henry allowed his stepfather, Lord Stanley, later titled the Earl of Derby, to exercise considerable control in Lancashire and Cheshire.

The system of government was becoming more active and centralised under Henry VII. These changes were driven by the gentry, often aspirational social climbers, some of whom chose to educate their sons in Law at the Inns of Court rather than in a noble household. Royal service was the most effective way to move up the social ladder, for there were significant opportunities to benefit from royal patronage. Sir Reginald Bray is a good example of a royal servant who made a small fortune – in his will he left £1,000 a year in lands.

Key profile

Sir Reginald Bray

Sir Reginald Bray was a faithful servant of Henry Tudor. He had joined the Buckingham rebellion in 1483 then fled into exile. He helped Tudor to raise funds before the Bosworth campaign, then used his administrative and financial skills in government as a member of the Counsel. He held many important posts including chancellor and was a leading member of the Counsel Learned.

Their legal training meant the gentry became skilled administrators, able to function as the lynchpins both of crown control of the shires and of the increasing bureaucracy of central government, especially the emerging specialised committees overseen by the Counsel. The King's reliance on service and Counsel from such socially low-born ministers, rather than the noble class, has been interpreted as evidence of Henry's anti-noble attitudes. There may be some truth in these interpretations, but there is more to it. Henry VII trusted men with legal training who shared his crown-centred view that royal authority needed to be centralised not devolved.

M. Condon wrote about the growing importance of the gentry in Counsel:

> Few men had any real influence with Henry VII. He was a strong king who was master of his own policy. There is remarkable unanimity amongst contemporary observers and chroniclers emphasising the King's independence and naming those few men who could command influence. Morton, Fox, Bray, Lovell, Daubeney and, latterly, Dudley were most frequently mentioned. The one factor common to them all was membership of the King's Counsel.

2   *M. Condon, in John Guy (ed.),* **The Tudor Monarchy***, 1997*

So power within the Counsel became concentrated in the hands of fewer men, mostly lawyers, underlining the peripheral status of those men who attended only occasionally and diminishing the importance of the nobility as a group. From the mid-1490s these counsellors acted in conciliar committees auditing lands and revenue, leasing lands, granting offices, collecting fines, organising collection of benevolence and, thus, investigating local prosperity and influence. Most significant of all was the Counsel Learned in the Law, which became increasingly prominent in the administration and enforcement of that system of **recognisances** which are the hallmark of Henry VII's policy of control.

Henry VII turned to a conciliar solution for every administrative problem. The result was that domestic government was increasingly dominated by legal processes, fed by a system of information and enquiry, and governed by astute and searching legal minds with a steady tenacity of purpose.

Historians have examined the relationship between Henry VII and his nobility in great detail as it was integral to the smooth governing of the kingdom. Some historians such as J. R. Green and A. F. Pollard interpreted his policies as being anti-noble and reliant on the use of coercion because he saw them as a danger, pointing to the King's:

- reluctance to grant titles and land as rewards, instead he preferred to award the ancient honour of the Order of the Garter

Key term

Recognisance: this was when a person formally acknowledged a debt or obligation. It was not a new means of royal control but they were used efficiently by Henry VII from 1485 and, arguably, punitively after 1502.

Cross-reference

The Counsel Learned in the Law is detailed on page 78.

■ readiness to use attainder and financial sanctions on the nobility

■ close surveillance of the noble families so that he claimed his full feudal rights.

More recently, historians such as P. Williams have refuted this and have presented a revised interpretation that Henry was not 'anti-noble' but his instinct was to not trust nobles with their local power bases, and he was intolerant of those nobles who abused their position.

■ He used Acts of Attainder to punish any nobleman who proved treacherous. Besides individual attainders, he used other legislation to strengthen his control over the nobles.

■ In 1487, he secured the Star Chamber Act, which established a tribunal headed by the three primary officers of state, to hear charges against noblemen who broke laws over maintenance and retaining.

■ Another effective control measure was financial surveillance to ensure obedience and loyalty through measures such as bonds and recognisances.

■ Exploring the detail

The court of the Star Chamber

The Star Chamber was a court of law in the royal Palace of Westminster that heard political conspiracy, libel, perjury and treason cases. The court was named after the 'Starred Chamber', a room built by Edward II for the meetings of his Counsel, due to the stars painted against the navy-blue ceiling.

Table 1 *Penalties used by Henry VII on his nobles*

Penalty	Detail on penalty	Comment on penalty
Acts of Attainder *These were not new but dated back to the 14th century*	Parliament passed the act to declare a nobleman guilty of a crime against the Crown, usually treason. The noble might be imprisoned, and the attainted family lost the right to inherit lands and titles. These acts were reversible.	Thomas Howard lost the title Duke of Norfolk and his family estates after Bosworth. He was released from prison and restored to the earldom of Surrey in 1489 to suppress uprising in Northumberland. Henry VII passed an Act of Attainder when he had faced a crisis. Each act attainted a different number of people: 1485–6: 28 people were attainted 1487: 28 people were attainted 1495: 24 people were attainted
Acts against illegal retaining and maintenance *Previous kings had also tried to control retaining and maintenance but, like Henry, they needed retained armies for defence*	Noblemen kept retained men who served them as accountants and land agents, but who also fought in their private army. These retained men wore their nobleman's badge, known as livery, to confirm their loyal service. Noblemen sometimes used their retained men to bring unlawful influence on others in a court case, e.g. controlled juries. This was called maintenance. There was a considerable amount of legal retaining and maintenance, which Henry VII permitted to continue.	Parliament passed laws against retaining. In 1485, the Lords and Commons were required to swear that they would not retain illegally. In 1504, nobles had to obtain special licences to retain from the King. Both acts gave the King, rather than his nobles, the power to decide whether retaining was illegal. In 1506, Lord Burgavenny was set a £70,000 fine for retaining over 471 men.
Bonds and recognisances *These became the King's most important method of magnate control*	A bond recognised that the person involved recognised himself as owing the lump sum stated, which was not payable if the condition (usually good behaviour) was observed. If the condition was not observed, the sum stated was paid. A person did not have to do anything wrong to give a bond. Most givers of bonds did not pay. A recognisance was when a person formally acknowledged a debt or obligation. The recognisance was often enforced by a bond.	The Marquis of Dorset had to give a bond after his suspected involvement in the Simnel plot. The bond guaranteed future loyal conduct. Lump sums payable from bonds: 1493–4: £3,000 1504–05: £75,000 (These figures are not revenues paid to the King but the amount that would have been paid to him if the bond was forfeited.)

Another historian has recently written about Henry's relationship with his nobility. Christine Carpenter is very critical of the King who, she believes, had a negative attitude to the nobles. In her assessment, Henry VII came to a strong throne in 1485 because he replaced a king (Richard III) who was thoroughly disliked and he did not face a powerful rival house. According to Carpenter, Henry VII's persistent internal rebellions were fuelled by noble opposition because he did not appreciate the nature of kingship in England and the mutual trust between king and the nobility.

These penalties were often applied in combinations. Lord Burgavenny clearly could not pay the massive fine imposed in 1506. Instead, he paid a reduced fine of £5,000 over a 10-year period and took on two recognisances: one valued at £3,200 that he would remain law-abiding, and another that he would not enter Kent, Surrey, Sussex or Hampshire without the King's permission.

The most significant measure applied at this time was the 1485 Act against **retaining**. All members of the Lords and Commons had to swear that they would not retain or be retained illegally. This act sounds like the end of retaining in England; however, it was not clear what retaining was 'legal' and what was not; besides the act left it to the Crown to prosecute, or not, as the King chose. The King wanted to end retaining that threatened his authority or corrupted public order; however, he needed his noblemen to keep their retained armies for suppressing rebellion and maintaining his law. This balancing act meant that application of the 1485 Act was not consistent.

A closer look

An English nobleman – Sir William Stanley

Sir William Stanley played an absolutely crucial role in events leading up to, and during, Bosworth. He was generously rewarded, being appointed to the overtly prestigious post as chamberlain of the royal household, and he acquired great personal wealth. This loyal servant of the Tudor monarchy was, however, found guilty of concealment (i.e. secret communications) in 1495, and subsequently executed, for having conspired with Margaret, Duchess of Burgundy over the imposter Perkin Warbeck. His alleged crime was uncovered and reported by Sir Richard Clifford, working as an agent for Tudor.

He was found to have been communicating secretly with Warbeck from 1493. In addition, it was rumoured that Sir William Stanley would not fight against Warbeck if the imposter proved to be a son of Edward IV. His execution was an act of judicial severity, prompted by the King's alarm that disaffection might be so close to his person, making Stanley a high-profile victim intended to deter any other challengers while the Warbeck conspiracy dragged on.

The Act of Attainder passed by parliament against Sir William Stanley brought the King an immediate income of £9,000 from the fine and £1,000pa thereafter from all estates surrendered to the crown. It was accompanied by a commission empowered to complete a massive security operation in 26 counties rooting out sedition across the realm. Finally, the King embarked on a royal progress in the west and north-east to impress his permanence and authority on Stanley's tenants and retainers.

Cross-reference

More information on the work of Christine Carpenter is given on page 96.

Key term

Retaining: noblemen's practice of recruiting members of the gentry to serve as administrators, often accountants, and also expect them to fight in their private army.

Exploring the detail
Looking ahead

The nobles would enjoy a brief period of resurgence in the first five years of Henry VIII's reign. The new King granted lands and relaxed controls but his income fell by £19,000 pa compared with 1509. Then he appointed Wolsey and the nobles were once again on the back foot.

Activity
Revision exercise

'The relationship between the King and nobles was one of mutual dependency.' Draw a spider diagram that illustrates aspects of this mutual dependency.

Government and the Church

Henry VII was determined to establish his rule and to secure his dynasty, but to achieve these aims he had to strengthen royal rule. Despite the years in exile, Henry VII was closely involved and informed about the government and governance of his realm.

Management of central and local government

Henry VII was not innovative. Instead, he developed existing institutions and relationships. Indeed the nature of royal rule was already changing before 1485 under Edward IV's new style of kingship.

- From 1471, the crown regarded the nobles less as independent local power-brokers but more as local agents with specific responsibility to transmit royal authority.
- The King increasingly managed his own finances, especially the crown lands and his feudal dues, to enhance royal authority.
- There was greater emphasis on the dignity of the monarch with the court being reformed to project royal majesty in the fashion of continental Renaissance courts.

The English court

Since wealth was power, the King's court had to be magnificent and generous. In this, he consciously copied continental examples, especially the royal courts of Burgundy and France.

The most spectacular assets of Renaissance monarchy were the person and the image of the ruler. Henry VII deliberately cultivated his personal image to command subjects' obedience and to strengthen his authority by giving the impression it was permanent. His propaganda was aimed at the general population. Widespread contemporary illiteracy gave political significance to the construction of magnificent royal palaces, and the presentation of elaborate ceremonies and public spectacles. In the great hall at Richmond Palace, Henry displayed statues of previous English monarchs, many dressed as noble warriors with swords in their hands, and also rich Burgundian tapestries from Arras.

Court was also the source of patronage, so it grew in size and importance as the King's bureaucracy expanded and the power of local magnates was reduced. The King lived at court surrounded by those who served him from nobles to minor servants. These courtiers enjoyed paid positions or the right to receive free food. There were several levels to the court.

1 The least political were the service departments, such as the scullery and buttery where catering requirements were supervised by the Lord Steward.

2 There were two politically important sections of the court: the Privy Chamber set up by Henry VII in the 1490s to provide a place for his personal servants; and the Chamber. The latter section, overseen by **the Chamberlain**, was the centre of patronage and communication between the King, his ministers and all the gentry at court.

Places at court, especially in the Chamber, were valued because they gave access to the powerful and therefore opportunities to promote family and local interests.

Key term

The Chamberlain: also known as the Lord Chamberlain, he was an experienced nobleman and member of the Counsel, also a personal friend of the King. He had administrative and political functions for he often spoke for the monarch in Counsel or in parliament, and he was responsible for organising court ceremonies.

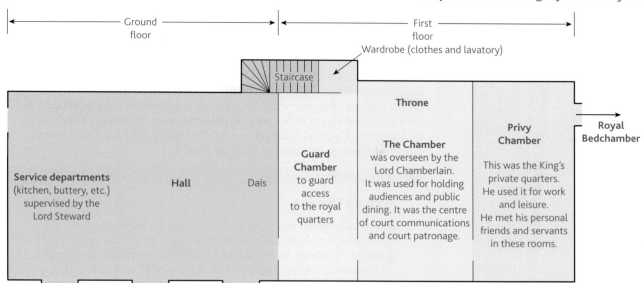

Fig. 2 *The court of Henry VII*

Patronage

The personality of the King was central to the governance of the country but he clearly could not rule alone. He relied on all his **royal servants** to carry out central and local government, and to represent him at the European courts. In return, they expected patronage: to be rewarded by the King with lucrative favours such as land grants, titles, offices, salaries, fees and commissions.

The Counsel

The Counsel was the nerve centre of Henry's government since he ruled through his Counsel by issuing decrees and proclamations. The Counsel advised the King and acted as a court of law. Despite this importance, the Counsel was a flexible body with few procedures or formal rules – when the King went on progress he designated some counsellors to travel with him while others stayed at Westminster to manage the ordinary business of government.

During the reign, some 227 men were recorded attending Counsel, though in fact Henry normally consulted only an inner core of six or seven trusted and close advisers; most were named as counsellors primarily to give status, then sent to foreign embassies or outlying parts of the region.

Another important function of the Counsel was to act as the link between the King and central government on the one hand, and his subjects and local government on the other. A constant stream of messages, orders and reports flowed from the Counsel to the Justices of the Peace (described on page 79) who controlled the localities.

Specialised committees of the Counsel

During Henry's reign some of the specialist work of the Counsel was devolved to specialised committees known as conciliar committees. The first was the Star Chamber court set up by an Act in 1487 to deal with overmighty subjects, though in practice it met rarely and withered away. This court was intended to hear complaints of maintenance, riot and abuses of privilege.

■ **Key term**

Royal servant: any person who served the King in the governance of the country – nobles, churchmen, gentry and lawyers.

■ **Cross-reference**

To review the details of Henry's policies towards the nobles, see page 76.

Later conciliar committees proved to be more durable. The most well known was Counsel Learned in the Law set up in 1495 to look after the King's interests as feudal landlord of England, so acquiring both the functions of a court and a debt-collecting agency. Under the leadership of Sir Reginald Bray, the Counsel Learned soon extended its role becoming increasingly unpopular with the wealthy landowning classes, especially over the supervision of bonds and recognisances. Following Bray's death in 1503, the Counsel Learned was taken over by Richard Empson and Edmund Dudley. It ceased to exist in 1509.

Key profiles

Richard Empson

Richard Empson was also a lawyer with a legal practice in Northamptonshire. He gained experience of royal service under Edward IV whom he served as Attorney-General for the duchy of Lancaster. He also gave public service as JP and MP, acting as Speaker of the Commons in the 1491 parliament. He rose to political prominence in the Counsel Learned in the Law.

Edmund Dudley

Edmund Dudley was a lawyer who made a name for himself as the main legal adviser to the corporation of London 1496–1502. He attended every parliament of the reign and rose to be speaker in the 1504 parliament. He was also a leading member of the Counsel Learned.

Cross-reference

Sir Reginald Bray is also mentioned earlier in this chapter, on page 73.

For the Yorkshire rebellion of 1489, refer to page 53.

Other counsels dealt with the outlying regions. After Northumberland's murder in 1489 during the Yorkshire rebellion, Henry set up a Counsel to rule the North nominally under Prince Arthur but in practice run by the Earl of Surrey. Similarly, a counsel in Wales and the marches was set up under Prince Arthur, then the Bishop of Lincoln after Arthur's death in 1502.

Parliament

The national assembly (parliament), both the Lords and the Commons, was called primarily by the King to do his business: to legislate and grant tax. It was not yet a permanent institution but was called as and when the King needed it; however, this does not mean it was unimportant or irrelevant.

Henry called seven parliaments. The first five were in the first decade of the reign and only one in the second half of the reign – this reflects Henry's growing security on the throne but does not mean that he devalued parliament. He legislated through parliament to strengthen royal authority over the nobles and the economy, and to ensure his law was applied across the realm. In this, he used parliament to emphasise that all power was derived from the crown, and that there was only one ruler in England.

Justices of the Peace (JPs)

Henry increased the status and workload of JPs in local government so curbing the power of the sheriffs. Every one of his seven parliaments passed laws relevant to the work of JPs. These amateur, unpaid justices were crown-appointed, crown-controlled

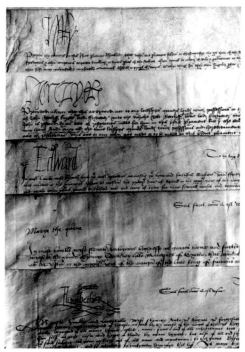

Fig. 3 *Tudor monarchs made effective use of the established institutions of government in England, including parliament. This photograph illustrates signatures on Acts of parliament*

Table 2 *Dates and main purpose of each of Henry VII's parliaments*

Date	Purpose
1485–6	To confirm kingship, pass Acts of Attainder, and vote revenues
1487	To deal with lawlessness and financial matters after the Battle of Stoke
1489–90	To fund the royal army for the expedition against France
1491–2	To fund the expedition against France
1495	To manage the threat from Perkin Warbeck
1497	To fund the possible war against Scotland
1504	To raise two feudal levies for Princess Margaret's marriage and Prince Arthur's posthumous knighthood

and crown-rewarded administrators of a great body of legislation. They mainly operated four times a year in the Quarter Sessions, a combination of law court and administrative meetings held in each county town, but also in less formal meetings and courts known as Petty Sessions.

Henry relied on his JPs to perform numerous duties ranging from serious disorder such as riots, unlawful assemblies, illegal retaining and extortion to less-threatening issues of poaching, gambling and unlawful games, and coinage; therefore he remained anxious about how efficiently they actually carried out their duties. If he became dissatisfied with a JP's performance, he could leave his name off the Commission of the Peace for the next year; meanwhile an act in 1489 set out procedures for making complaints against JPs, and in 1506 he issued a manual for JPs. All this suggests that Henry VII had the same difficulties as previous monarchs in enforcing his laws across his realm.

He increased the numbers but kept the same social mix of magnates, churchmen, lawyers and gentry among JPs.

The administration of justice

Henry VII has an excellent reputation as a justiciar. Historians have commented that he respected judicial independence because he retained the judges he had inherited from Richard III and only replaced them on their retirement or death. Most importantly in many historians' judgement, Henry appointed Sir William Huse as Chief Justice of the King's Bench in September 1485. Huse had the same role from 1481 so had served both Edward IV and Richard III. In 1486, the King consulted Huse about the legality of Humphrey Stafford's claim that he had been forced from sanctuary so could not face trial for high treason after the failed Lovell rebellion. Huse responded that he could not give the King advice on this matter before it came to court – a rebuff the King reluctantly accepted.

On the other hand, some historians have criticised Henry VII for having corrupted the administration of justice to secure his monarchy; however, this seems misplaced. He initiated a considerable amount of legislation to improve the effectiveness of common law, for instance

■ Key chronology

Some acts passed by parliament

1495 De Facto Act: anyone giving the King loyal service can not be attainted for treason.

1495 Parliament extends the role of JPs enabling them to decide on all offences except murder.

1497 Parliament prevents the Merchant Adventurers (page 94), setting an extortionate membership fee, which was intended to restrict new entrants into the cloth trade.

1497 Acts are passed to standardise and promote trade by setting up a new coinage and introducing standard weights and measures.

1489 Act to limit rural depopulation.

■ Cross-reference

The new coinage is referred to on pages 92–93.

Fig. 4 *Henry VII was interested in economic development and encouraged commerce. In this picture weights and measures are being tested to safeguard commercial integrity. You can see measures that were not up to standard being burned at the bottom right. There were severe penalties for using sub-standard weights, lengths and volumes*

Fig. 5 *The career of Giles Daubeney*

Revision exercise

Construct a fortune graph of Giles Daubeney's career from 1483 to 1508.

■ **Key terms**

Chancery: the court of the Lord Chancellor. It made decisions in the interests of equity or fair play that were not covered by the other courts.

Roman: the Pope was based in Rome, Italy. He claimed to be the successor to the apostle St Peter who was buried in Rome.

Catholic: means 'universal'. Christians believed there could only be one Christian Church. The Roman Catholic Church was the only established Christian Church in western Europe at this time.

Diocese: England and Wales were divided into 21 administrative areas, each called a diocese but also known as sees or bishoprics.

Livings: Bishops were able to earn a substantial income from the land and other sources of revenue that went with a bishopric.

Convocation: official assembly of senior clergy that usually coincided with the calling of parliament.

passing a series of acts to strengthen the law against perjury and riotous assembly, while a statute in 1496 allowed poor men to sue *in forma pauperis* which meant that they were not required to pay. It is important not to overstate the impact of these improvements, however, because common law still provided little protection in many cases, leading to a rapid increase in the numbers of cases being brought before the **Chancery** or the Counsel.

■ A closer look

Interlocking central and local government – the career of Giles Daubeney (1451–1508)

Giles Daubeney was a late medieval royal servant over the years 1483 to 1508. His career illustrates the importance of the King's relationship with his leading gentry in both central and local government, and the varied responsibilities they held.

The Daubeney family was a long-established English gentry family whose ancestors had accompanied Duke William from Normandy in 1066. The title 'Baron Daubeney' was also long established, but had fallen into disuse. Giles was born in the family heartland of South Ingleby in Devonshire in 1451. He rose to political prominence as a loyal servant of Edward IV, and fled into exile after the Buckingham rebellion in autumn 1483, after which he was attainted, but returned to fight for Henry Tudor at Bosworth, and prospered further under the new King, Henry VII.

Giles Daubeney was buried in Westminster Abbey in 1508.

Management of the Church

Henry VII was a devout **Roman Catholic** who recognised the Pope as spiritual leader of the Christian Church. The potential tension between such secular and spiritual leaders as monarchs and religious figureheads had resulted in great arguments, even bloodshed, between previous kings and popes. By the late 15th century, however, a *modus vivendi* had been established. The King ran the Church in England and the Church was loyal to the King, upholding the rule of law and confirming the sanctity of royal office through the coronation service.

Church appointments

Henry VII was able to use the Church to reinforce his royal power after 1485. He kept a tight control over church appointments, selecting loyal, well-educated churchmen to important state and episcopal posts. The Church also strengthened royal control across the realm through its administrative structure in which archbishops and bishops were responsible for running the churches in their **diocese**.

Henry followed a similar policy towards bishops who had supported Richard III to the policy he pursued towards any noblemen who had been loyal to the previous monarch. He allowed them to prove their allegiance to the Tudor dynasty and then entrusted them with significant responsibilities. Thomas Langton had been promoted by Richard III to the bishopric of St David's in 1483, then to that of Salisbury in 1485. After Bosworth, he was temporarily deprived of his **livings** and excluded from both parliament and **Convocation**; however, by 1493, he had been appointed Bishop of Winchester.

Key profiles

Leading churchmen

John Morton was Lord Chancellor as well as Archbishop of Canterbury before his death in 1500.

William Warham was Archbishop of Canterbury after Morton's death.

Richard Fox held various bishoprics including Exeter, Bath and Wells, Durham and Winchester. He had been trained as a lawyer, and served Henry VII as secretary and diplomat.

Relations with the papacy

There was no dispute between Henry VII and any of the three popes with whom he had to deal. Henry was glad to receive papal support and the popes needed English support to resist French and Spanish aggression in Italy. After Bosworth, Henry declared his obedience to Pope Innocent VIII who, in return, provided dispensation for the King to marry Elizabeth of York, and declared their children legitimate. The Pope did not object in 1486 over the judicial decision made during Stafford's trial that the right of sanctuary could not be pleaded in cases of treason. Henry reciprocated by contributing £4,000 in 1501 towards Pope Alexander VI's crusading levy.

A closer look

The pre-Reformation Church

It seems extraordinary that there was so little friction between Henry VII and the popes appointed during his reign given the turmoil in church-state relations under Henry VIII. Although there was no open conflict, changes that foreshadowed the Reformation were taking place, and a number of leading reformists were already in influential posts by 1509.

There were **heretics** in England during the reign of Henry VII. About 73 heretics were put on trial and, while most recanted their heresy, three were burned alive. These heretics were members of a small, underground illegal sect called the Lollards who believed that the Bible, as the direct Word of God, should be made accessible to laymen by translation into English. Furthermore, the Lollards denounced papal authority, preferring the King to be head of the Church, and rejected the Catholic doctrine of **transubstantiation**.

Lollards had very little support and little hope of undermining the power of the Roman Catholic Church in England. There were other critics of the Church, known as **anticlericals**, who did not wish to undermine the Church however but to reform it from within.

During the reign of Henry VII there were important changes in the intellectual life of the country. These reflected the European Renaissance, which widened interest in learning and discovery, inspired growth in education and spread **humanist** ideas. In England these changes had been enhanced by technological advances, such as William Caxton's printing press from 1476, and this continued after the establishment of the first proper paper mill in 1496.

Fig. 6 *This pre-Reformation panel painting shows the Last Judgement in which Christ, in his majesty, oversees the weighing of souls who are afterwards led away either to heaven (north) or hell (south)*

Cross-reference

To review the Battle of Bosworth, see page 34.

The trial of Stafford is discussed on page 46.

Henry VII's relations with the papacy are discussed on this page and with the Church in general on page 80.

Key terms

Heretics: people who challenged the ideas or doctrine of the Roman Catholic Church. Refusing to support Roman Catholic doctrine was known as heresy.

Transubstantiation: the Roman Catholic doctrine that believes that during Mass the bread actually changes its form into Christ's flesh, and the wine into his blood.

Anticlericals: people who were aware of the 'proven abuses', as they termed the customs of which they were critical, in the Roman Catholic Church. They were critical of the personnel, lifestyle and teaching of the Church.

Humanists: wanted to improve the quality of teaching and learning in the Church.

Humanists aimed to reform the teaching of the Church by ending the Church's monopoly of schools and the curriculum. They wanted students to examine literature, philosophy, the arts and science, as well as Church-based theology and religion. One leading humanist was William Grocyn who had studied in Italy and returned in 1500 to lecture at Oxford University on the ideas of Aristotle and Plato. John Colet was another significant influence on emerging humanist ideas. These ideas were important because they paved the way for the invitation to Erasmus to come and work in England between 1509 and 1514. Erasmus added strength to the existing movement to reform Church teaching.

Key profile

Erasmus (c.1469–1536)

Erasmus was the greatest scholar of early 16th century Europe. He travelled extensively meeting humanist intellectuals in the university cities of northern Europe including Cambridge and Oxford. He was a leading Renaissance writer who anticipated Europe would enjoy a golden age of Christian unity and peace after essential church reform. He wanted to improve the Roman Catholic Church but not destroy it for he regarded heresy as a threat to the Church. He influenced events in England through his personal friendship with leading churchmen and courtiers including John Colet, Thomas Wolsey and Thomas More, and Henry VIII's tutor, John Skelton.

A closer look

Humanism

Humanism was a distinctive culture of the social, political and intellectual elites in Renaissance Europe. It emerged in 14th century Italy and spread gradually to many states, including England, releasing a wave of intellectual and creative energy. The environment of the wealthy Italian cities fostered this energy. Humanists considered wealth to be a mark of distinction provided it was spent wisely. The Italian cities were frequently rocked by intense factional struggles, however humanists wrote that peace and greatness, in humanist language 'virtue', could be achieved.

Humanist ideas stressed the power and potential of humankind. Artists celebrated human achievement and explored ways to paint using three-dimensions to give their pictures greater expression and movement. Humanist scholars believed that human behaviour and knowledge could be enhanced through the power of education. They wrote on logic, rhetoric and the importance of grammar.

Humanists were also concerned about the condition of the Roman Catholic Church. These Christian humanists did not question Catholic principles, but did criticise some practices within the Church, in particular the quality of some Catholic priests, the ostentatious wealth of the Catholic Church, and the perceived reliance on Catholic ritual in the services rather than prayer and worship. They feared that some souls were led from God by these abuses. They believed that the Church should promote prayer and knowledge of the faith to enable humans to dedicate their lives to God.

Humanism was a very varied, and often contradictory, culture. Thomas Wolsey displayed many humanist traits yet opposed the vernacular Bible desired by other humanists, because he associated it with German heresy.

John Colet (1467–1519)

John Colet was educated at Oxford University. In 1493, he toured Europe, travelling through France and Italy so acquiring his love of learning and meeting leading scholars, including Erasmus. He returned to Oxford where he lectured on the New Testament, which he translated into English for his students. He rejected the Roman Catholic theory that the scriptures were 'mystical'; instead, he made his plain and easy to understand. In 1504, he became Dean of St Paul's Cathedral. On his father's death, he inherited a great fortune, which he spent on the school he founded, St Paul's School. Greek was considered an important subject in the school, so Colet wrote the first Greek grammar book to be printed in England.

Colet did not aspire to a formal break with the Roman Church but then neither did most of the Reformers. Colet was a keen reformer. His most significant contribution to the Reformation was his bold reading of the New Testament in Greek and translating it into English for his students, which was strictly forbidden by the Church. Later, he read the scriptures in English for the public at St Paul's Cathedral in London. Within six months there were 20,000 people packed in the church and at least as many outside trying to get in! Fortunately for Colet, he was a powerful man with friends in high places, so he amazingly managed to avoid punishment for this blatant violation of the church's 'Latin-only' policy.

3   *Adapted from English Bible History* (www.greatsite.com)

A closer look

Thomas More

Thomas More was an English lawyer, scholar, writer, MP and Lord Chancellor, who was executed for refusing to recognise the break from Rome in the 1530s. He was multi-talented, hence his epithet 'the man for all seasons'.

Born in 1478 in London, the son of a prominent judge, More was educated at St Anthony's School, London, and served as a page in the household of Archbishop Morton. He went on to Oxford University where he studied under the humanist intellectuals Thomas Linacre and William Grocyn.

More's early career was in the law. Like many London lawyers, he entered parliament in 1504 and gained experience of public service. He also served as one of two under-sherrifs in London, a position of considerable responsibility, where he earned a reputation for honesty. At this time he also developed a career as a writer writing *History of King Richard III* and *Utopia*, the name he gave to an imaginary society living on an island off the coast of the New World. This ideal society, where women priests, divorce and euthanasia

Fig. 7 *This portrait of the statesman and scholar Thomas More is by Hans Holbein. More appears serious and pensive as is appropriate for a lawyer-statesman who had to resolve great questions of law and statecraft*

were permitted, was written as a critique of his own society. The utopians were eventually converted to Christianity having been convinced by the trust and virtue of the 'one true faith'.

The major change in More's career came in 1516 when he moved into the King's government. By 1517, he was a counsellor and 'King's servant', and a year later was appointed to the Privy Counsel. His political importance continued to grow. In 1520, he accompanied the King to the Field of the Cloth of Gold and, in 1521, he was knighted for his assistance to the king in writing *In Assertio Septem Sacramentorum*. His appointment in 1523 as Speaker of the House of Commons was followed, in 1529, by his elevation to Lord Chancellor after Wolsey's fall from that post.

After 1529, More found himself in a terrible dilemma. He was devoted to the King and recognised the opinions of theologians at Oxford and Cambridge universities that the marriage between Henry and Catherine of Aragon had not been lawful. He, however, opposed the royal supremacy, the denial of the Pope's authority, as heresy. This principled opposition to the royal supremacy led to his martyrdom.

Learning outcomes

In this section, you have studied in detail the challenges Henry VII faced in securing his dynasty, and the decisions he made in both his domestic and foreign policies.

You have examined the threats from surviving Yorkists, imposters and internal rebellions, explored the vital relationship between the King and his nobility and upper gentry, and gained an understanding of the different roles and functions of central and local governement institution. You have analysed the importance of Henry VII's relations with foreign princes, including his need for international recognition. Finally, you have examined the nature of the pre-Reformation Church.

Examination-style questions

(a) Explain why Henry VII passed Acts of Attainder. *(12 marks)*

The answer to this question needs to demonstrate good understanding of any Act of Attainder. It was passed through parliament to punish a nobleman for treason. It is good practice to know at least one good example of such an act, e.g. the act passed against Thomas Howard after the Battle of Bosworth.

You need to investigate the different reasons. The King either passed Acts of Attainder through parliament to punish traitors or as a deterrent to other noblemen. Ideally, you will prioritise one reason and explain exactly why you think that was the most important reason.

(b) How successful was Henry VII in limiting the power of the nobility? *(24 marks)*

7 Financial management, the domestic economy and overseas trade

In this chapter you will learn about:

- why solvency was so important to Henry VII

- how the King obtained revenue and managed his finances

- the economic development of England, especially the expansion of the cloth trade and the start of overseas exploration.

The king wished to keep all Englishmen obedient through fear. He considered that whenever they gave him offence they were driven by their great wealth. Whenever any of his subjects, who were men of substance, were found guilty, of whatever fault, he fined them harshly. Such a penalty deprived of their fortunes, not only the men themselves, but also their descendants. In this way the population was less able to undertake any upheaval and, at the same time, all offences were discouraged.

1   *Polydore Vergil Anglica historia (written c.1513)*

Sir John Fortescue, a Lancastrian chancellor and author, wrote a book on *The Governance of England*, in which he warned of the dangers of poverty for a king. Henry had inherited a bankrupt throne yet had to pay for the **ordinary expenses** of government. This was very difficult in the early years: the royal finances were unable to fund the **extraordinary expenses** of the King's coronation and marriage, his royal progress, or to defeat Lovell in 1486, and in 1487 he did not have sufficient money to pay for the feast of St George at Windsor.

Financial management and the wealth of the crown

Fig. 1 *This woodcut shows coiners at work in the interior of a mint. They are stamping out and weighing the coins to make sure they have the correct amount of metal*

Key term

Solvent: the monarch needed to balance his books by making sure he covered his expenses with his income. In doing so, he remained solvent.

Sound financial management underpinned Henry's government. He needed steady and secure income for two key purposes:

1 To fund the ordinary and extraordinary expenses of government.
2 To continue his centralisation of power and discipline of the realm.

He inherited a bankrupt throne but bequeathed a **solvent** treasury, which is clear evidence of competent financial management. Some historians have criticised Henry VII for being a greedy monarch. Bacon commented on his love of money, and other contemporaries complained that his actions were sometimes unjust.

More recent historians, such as John Guy, have revised this interpretation. They recognise that Henry made the most of his various sources of revenue, which is scarcely surprising since he had spent much of his youth as a penniless exile, and that there was great continuity between his financial management and that of Edward IV. These historians also comment that his methods of financial management became increasingly rigorous as the reign developed, even to the point of unjust extortion through the Counsel Learned in the Law in the later years of the reign.

Ian Dawson explores the contradictory interpretations about Henry VII's financial management in Source 2.

Fear was the motive behind Henry's avarice. In 1496 a Florentine merchant wrote 'the king is rather feared than loved and this is due to his avarice'. The king's 'infinite' and 'immense' treasure was frequently noted by Milanese writers and was linked to his security as in 1497 'this kingdom is perfectly stable, by reason first of the king's wisdom, whereof everyone stand in awe, and secondly, on account of the king's wealth'. These sources show us an anxious but resolute and wise king whose prudence was turned to avarice by the everlasting threats to his crown and his dynasty.

However, consistent though this picture is, the same sources reveal other sides to Henry. In 1497 the Milanese ambassador described how he met the king 'fifty miles from London, where his Majesty is accustomed to spend the summer hunting'. Henry 'was adorned with a most rich collar, full of great pearls and many other jewels, in four rows, and in his bonnet he had a pear-shaped pearl, which seemed to me like something most rich'.

A very different source is the King's Privy Purse expenses, miscellaneous items paid for at Henry's personal request. In January 1494, for example, four actors of Essex received £1 in reward, as did the players of Wimborne Minster. Next day the King paid £2 to morris dancers while before the end of the month he had lost £2 at cards and laid out nearly £2 for clothing for Dick the fool, a jester. By far the largest sums were spent on jewellery and gold and silver plate, all used to maintain the majesty of the king's appearance.

2 ——————————————— *Ian Dawson, 'Henry VII: Out of the Shadows', September 1995*

Solvency was important but less important than the development of administrative techniques that increased the power of the crown and, therefore, reduced the possibility of large-scale rebellion. As in other areas of government, Henry appointed zealous agents, usually with legal training, to ensure revenue was collected. These agents benefited from Henry's patronage gaining increased status and personal wealth. The King carefully supervised their work, sometimes directly and at other times through royal spies or informants.

One such agent was Sir Edward Belknap who was appointed Surveyor of the King's **Prerogative**. He and his assistants worked on a commission basis to exact fines. They collected £7,000 in seven months and became hated as ruthless extortioners.

Exchequer and Chamber

Initially, Henry relied on the Exchequer to organise his finances. The Exchequer was a system that ran royal finances by employing its own officials; therefore, in effect, Henry sub-contracted financial management to the Exchequer. The Exchequer kept accurate accounts; however, it was historically considered to be slow and less efficient.

The previous Yorkist kings had relied on a different financial system to manage their finances. It was known as the Chamber system because financial management was part of the royal household and under the direct supervision of the King. It had, however, collapsed with the Yorkist dynasty and Henry lacked the financial experience to be able to reconstruct it immediately. He was by nature cautious and was not prepared to risk losing his throne by being bankrupt.

Gradually, he returned to the Chamber system. From 1493, the Exchequer lost its role in accounting for revenue from the crown lands. Instead, the land revenue receivers accounted to a counsel committee sitting in Chamber to be known as the Court of the General Surveyors. Everyone working in the Court of the General Surveyors took a bond to guarantee their work for the King. Therefore, their careful supervision and thorough investigation increased the revenue from crown lands.

Table 1 *Income from crown lands*

King	Year	Financial system	Annual income
Richard III	1484	Chamber	£25,000
Henry VII	1486	Exchequer	£11,700
Henry VII	1508	Chamber	£42,000

Henry's closest and most trusted servants were given important treasury roles from the start of the reign, but particularly after he began to transform his royal household into the royal treasury. The most important role, Treasurer of the Chamber, was filled by two men Sir Thomas Lovell (1485–92) and Sir John Heron (1492–1509). Under these two men the Chamber became the King's major financial office, where a wide range of financial documents were scrutinised and stored including lists of debts owed, recognisances, payments for land sales, wardships and collections of fines. The cash and jewels collected by the Chamber were stored in the King's Jewel House, which became in effect the King's private bank.

Key term

Prerogative: the powers that enabled the King to govern the realm effectively. Some of these powers were derived from the King's role as feudal overlord of the kingdom. These powers included the rights to raise money from various feudal levies. The Surveyor of the King's Prerogative was the man responsible for managing this income.

Cross-reference

Recognisances are explained on page 73.

Ordinary revenue

The King was expected to 'live off his own'. This meant he had to pay for the day-to-day expenses of government from his regular income. Henry went to great efforts to appoint administrators who would ensure these sources of ordinary revenue were efficiently managed.

Table 2 *Ordinary revenue*

	Explanation	Outcome
Customs duties *These were granted by parliament for life*	Henry took care to increase this source of income by cracking down on corrupt officials, and by twice updating the Book of Rates of Customs Duties.	Historians estimate customs duties rose from £33,000 to £40,000pa. This growth was, however, primarily due to the recovery in trade after the late medieval depression.
Crown lands *These were the King's most important source of revenue*	Henry VII had more crown land then previous monarchs. Some lands were confiscated under the Acts of Attainder; others were reclaimed after the Acts of Resumption.	Sir Reginald Bray developed techniques for estate management. The King's annual income from his royal estates rose: 1486: £12,000 1508: £42,000 Land revenue was inflated after 1503 partly because Henry VII did not have to grant lands to his Queen or son.
Feudal dues *These were derived from the King's historical role as the landowner who granted lands to his tenants-in-chief*	A tenant-in-chief had to pay **relief** to inherit lands on the death of his father. If the tenant-in-chief died without an heir, the land reverted (or escheated) to the crown. This had to be paid for in **escheats.** If the heir was a minor, the King had right to all income from the land as **wardship.** When the heir came of age he had to pay **livery** to the King before he recovered the lands. If there was an heiress, the king had a right to agree to her marriage as **marriage dues.** All tenants-in-chief were obliged to pay an **aid** to the King on the knighting of his eldest son and marriage of his eldest daughter.	Although feudalism was obsolete for military purposes, Henry was most zealous in this aspect of financial management. He set up the office of the Surveyor of the King's Prerogative under Sir Edward Belknap. Sir John Hussey was appointed Master of the King's Wards. The Counsel Learned in the Law also made great efforts to chase these profitable dues. The King's annual income from wardship rose: 1487: under £350 1507: £6,000 In 1502 Robert Willoughby de Broke paid £400 for livery of his lands.
Profits of justice *These came from the enforcement of law and order*	All court actions started with the issuing of royal writs and letters which had to be paid for in fees. Any fines imposed by the King's courts had to be paid directly to the crown.	The sums varied and many were not recorded in accounts so historians cannot estimate the income from these profits. They were, however, unlikely to have been a significant part of ordinary royal revenue.

Extraordinary revenue

The King was entitled to raise money from additional sources as one-off payments when he faced an emergency or an extraordinary – unforeseeable – expense of government. He was similarly determined to ensure these revenues were collected in full and efficiently.

■ Cross-reference

To recap on the Counsel Learned in the Law, look back to page 78.

Table 3 *Extraordinary revenue*

	Explanation	Outcome
Parliamentary subsidies	Parliament contributed to the King's revenue by granting him a directly assessed subsidy – a 15th was the rate of tax on the moveable goods of laymen, and a 10th was the rate of tax on the income of the clergy.	Each subsidy yielded a total of approximately £29,000. It seems that Henry VII achieved efficient tax collection.
Loans *These could be raised speedily*	Voluntary loans could be raised from richer subjects, e.g. merchants, the city of London.	In 1485, Henry VII raised over £10,000 in loans. He repaid these loans. Over the reign, Henry raised some £203,000 in loans.
Benevolences	These were loans that were forced with the threat of sanction, and were not repaid. These obligatory loans could not be seized, but had to be handed over.	In 1491, the King raised £48,000 to fund the invasion of France.
Bonds and recognisances *These were raised for political and financial purposes*	A bond was a lump sum of money payable only if a condition was not observed. A recognisance was formal acknowledgement of a debt.	Payments were enforced by the Counsel Learned in the Law.
Feudal obligations	All tenants-in-chief were obliged to pay an **aid** to the King on the knighting of his eldest son and marriage of his eldest daughter.	£30,000 was collected on the posthumous knighting of Prince Arthur.
Clerical taxes	Convocation (the Church assembly) matched each parliamentary subsidy. Another source of income from the church was vacant bishoprics. When a bishop died, the King might not appoint a successor, and so keep the revenue.	Each clerical grant raised approximately £9,000. Later in the reign, several bishops died enabling Henry to raise over £6,000pa from vacant bishoprics.
The French pension *This was a one-off payment*	In 1475, Edward IV had agreed an annual pension from France in the Treaty of Picquigny.	In the Treaty of Etaples of 1491 Charles VIII of France agreed to repay arrears in the French pension amounting to a total of £159,000 over several years.

■ Activity

Revision exercise

Historians have tended neatly to break Henry's income down into ordinary and extraordinary revenue but this is not a separation that Henry himself would have recognised. It is based on the 15th century chancellor and constitutionalist, Sir John Fortescue, who identified two separate expenses: ordinary and extraordinary.

Henry's income was much more complex because the various incomes were derived from his various roles:

■ as King

■ as landowner

■ as feudal overlord.

Draw a spider diagram in which you re-allocate the various sources of royal income to these three roles. You will find that there is considerable overlap between the roles and incomes.

Main developments in the domestic economy

The domestic economy at the end of the 15th century

England was an agricultural country with the vast majority of the population involved in some form of farming. It is important to understand that there were many farming regions and practices; that some regions maintained a medieval open field system, some open fields were being enclosed, and other regions never had open fields. In some areas, notably Norfolk and the south and east Midlands, enclosure was a problem long before 1485. Enclosure meant hedging and cultivating waste ground, consolidating agricultural strips and dividing common pasture, and, above all, ending common rights to a piece of land by taking it under single ownership.

Industry was dominated by the wool and cloth 'industry'. Manufacturing techniques were backward. The threads of the raw wool were carded (untangled) by hand, spun into thread on a spinning wheel, and the thread was woven on a handloom. Such 'industry' took place in individual farmworkers' homes, although some processes such as fulling, where the wool was cleaned, and dyeing were completed outside. Other industries included mining tin, lead and coal; metal working; leatherwork; shipbuilding; and paper making.

Fig. 2 *An early 15th century image of the important cloth industry. Women are shown carrying out the separate production stages from washing and carding the wool, to spinning the yarn, and finally weaving the cloth at the loom*

England was a trading nation, but the profits of trade were not, yet, a major source of income for the crown. Imports included wine and wood from France, wrought iron from Spain, and cod from Scandanavia. The nature of imports indicates that the wealthy enjoyed a luxurious lifestyle – sweet wine, raisins, dyes and glass. The most important exports were wool and cloth, but other exports included barley and malt.

Between 90 and 95% of trade was internal trade. The road network was extensive, though the amounts carried by cart or packhorse were small, and the routes were, at times, impassable. Where possible, traders used rivers and the coast. The amount of coastal trade was massive with, among many commodities, bulk carriage of coal from Newcastle, tin from Cornwall, and grain.

London was the largest city. Norwich, Bristol, Newcastle and Coventry numbered about 10,000, and there were hundreds of small market towns. These urban areas were centres for a wide variety of crafts and trades. The guardians of these crafts industries were the urban guilds. The guilds controlled entry to the craft, kept watch over quality and production levels, enforced apprenticeship regulations, and set wages and prices.

Economic developments

Although Henry VII had no economic policy as modern leaders would understand the phrase, he was interested in economic matters, as he was interested in any issue that affected his personal wealth or the condition of the people. The King's interest in economic matters was not comprehensive but directed at particular areas of the economy such as, in particular, those of coinage and trade. During the reign, parliament passed 50 statutes concerned with economic matters; however, most of those statutes were driven by interest groups, such as the merchants of the city of London, rather than the King's government. There was relatively little crown-directed economic growth or change over the reign of Henry VII.

Fig. 3 *This is an early 16th century woodcut that shows the importance of sheep tending in England. The shepherds are shown with their flocks and dogs, as well as their crooks for handling the sheep. They clearly passed the time with music as the figure on the left is holding bagpipes and there are pipes on the ground*

Agriculture

The most important sector of the national economy was agriculture. 90% of the population were **peasants** who lived off the land, usually struggling for survival. This is sometimes called **subsistence agriculture**; however, that is not accurate because the English economy was more developed by the late 15th century. All peasants had to pay rents, tithes and taxes; and many supplemented their income with **cottage industry**.

The most important influence on economic activity in the realm was the harvest. It determined whether there would be abundant food or widespread starvation and disease. It seems 1485 was a really good harvest but the other harvests in 1486–9 were only average. The 1490s were a golden decade with 5 out of the 10 harvests proving plentiful, and only one being deficient. Four bad years followed from 1500 to 1503, but from 1504 to 1509 the harvests were average to good. These fluctuations in the harvest were reflected in the fluctuations in the prices for basic foodstuffs, and so had direct impact on the size of the population and the condition of the people.

There was already one significant change taking place in the pattern of farming in England – the decline of the traditional open-field system with its attendant strips, 3-course rotation and common land. The growing profitability of wool encouraged enterprising landowners to **enclose** land and to **engross** farms. Both processes made farming less labour intensive and, therefore, caused rural depopulation, especially in the rich arable farmlands of the Midlands. Henry VII passed legislation in 1488 and 1489 to prevent the depopulation but the acts were never enforced.

Wool was important because it was used to clothe everybody. English wool, partly processed into broadcloth, was the main ingredient of the Flemish cloth industry based in Antwerp that clothed people in Germany and eastern Europe. The great increase in foreign demand for this broadcloth raised the prices of English wool, and made it worth converting land from arable to pastoral, hence enclosing fields and engrossing farms.

Industry

There was limited industrial advance during Henry VII's reign. The most important industries continued to be those most directly associated with the wool and cloth trade, centred in Yorkshire, East Anglia and the West Country. The industry remained cottage-based, but the emergence of the Merchant Clothiers, or cloth merchants, who collected the wool, thread, and/or cloth, then collected it for export, marked the beginnings of a more capitalist organisation of the trade, which took some control away from the individual producers. The 'putting out' system grew in the second half of the 15th century. Capitalist production proved more flexible and could be more easily adapted to consumer demand. Distributors might, for example, insist on some variation to a product in order to meet market demand and increase sales. Such practices helped increase exports so that, for example, the export of cloth by the Hansa merchants increased five-fold between the beginning and the end of the 15th century.

Other industries took place across the kingdom and recent historical research suggests that reliance on customs records has led historians to underestimate the scale of industrial development beyond the wool and cloth industries. However, most were small scale and, principally, in the form of handicrafts. Usually all the stages of the manufacturing

Key terms

Peasants: small-scale farmers who had the right to farm land.

Subsistence agriculture: where the farmers grew enough food to support their families without any surplus.

Cottage industry: small-scale manufacturing that took place in people's homes, sometimes on simple machinery, e.g. spinning wool into yarn on a spinning wheel, or weaving yarn into cloth on a hand loom.

Enclosure: rearranging open fields into fields separated from each other by fences or hedges.

Engrossing: amalgamating small farms into one larger farming unit by a single owner.

Fig. 4 *A charcoal smelting furnace in the 15th century. This furnace is heated by charcoal but soon it would be replaced by coal that is cheaper and more plentiful. The Weald was the main iron-producing region in Britain at the end of the 15th century*

■ Cross-reference

Sir Giles Daubeney is profiled in more detail on page 80.

process were undertaken by the single skilled craftsman in each town. There was little heavy industry and what there was was located out of town where water and raw materials were readily available. The coal industry exported little of its production for most was consumed domestically or used in iron smelting or lime burning. By 1508–09, 20% of the value in export trade from Newcastle was in coal. In 1486, a water-powered pump was bought to pump water out of the coal mine near Finchale in County Durham. Iron making was undertaken sporadically; sometimes using charcoal, an alternative smelting fuel to coal, in the Forest of Dean and the Weald of Kent and Sussex. Another important industry was the building industry for, although any surviving records are very incomplete, there is evidence of significant building projects in the manor houses built by gentry families. Metal working was established across the country, particularly in the Midlands where labourers in Coventry made nails, and Sheffield already had a cutlery industry.

There is limited evidence of the King having a role in the development of the industrial sector of the economy. In 1496, the crown sponsored the building of a blast furnace at Newbridge in the Kentish Weald, as part of an iron smelting works to make armaments for the Scottish war; and in 1509 cast-iron guns were successfully made in England for the first time.

Changes to the coinage

It is very difficult to find evidence that Henry VII took any initiative in the wider economy; but it seems that he was interested in reforming the coinage for both economic and political reasons.

There had been little development in the English coinage since the reign of Edward III but Henry VII introduced new denominations in gold and silver and new designs. His interest was apparent from the start of the reign. In November 1485, he granted the titles master of Monies and keeper of Exchange in the Tower to his trusted friend Sir Giles Daubeney. These titles were held under indentures that set out the value and weight of these new coins in great detail.

Henry VII also introduced a shilling piece which was the first coin ever to have a true portrait of the King. He was depicted wearing the closed crown (a symbol of imperial power) in a conspicuous and deliberate copy of Maximilian's coin cast in 1487 for his son Philip.

■ The expansion of overseas trade

England was a trading nation, but trade was not the primary source of crown income. This is clear from the fact that revenues from trade provided £40,000pa in 1509 – only a fraction of royal revenue. At the heart of the King's decision making concerning trade was a balance

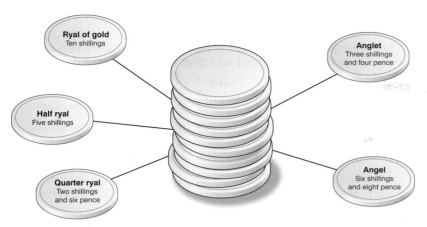

Fig. 5 *Henry VII's new coins, 1485*

Ryal of gold
Ten shillings

Half ryal
Five shillings

Quarter ryal
Two shillings
and six pence

Anglet
Three shillings
and four pence

Angel
Six shillings
and eight pence

between exploiting commercial interests to serve his dynastic needs, and the monarch's genuine desire to encourage growth in shipping, exports and maritime exploration.

Trade with Burgundy

Foreign relations were inextricably linked to trade. England's primary trading relationship was with Burgundy because England's main export was wool and woollen cloth, and the main European cloth trading centre was Antwerp. Henry realised the need for good trading relations with Burgundy but he faced an implacable political enemy in Margaret, Duchess of Burgundy. He was always prepared to jeopardise his trading relationship with Burgundy to put political pressure on the rulers of Burgundy. As a result, trade with Burgundy proved inconsistent.

In 1493, Henry placed a ban on all English trade with Burgundy after Maximilian backed Perkin Warbeck. This was a drastic embargo that proved to be economically damaging but was deemed to be politically necessary.

In 1496, Henry signed the *Intercursus Magnus* (Great Settlement) with Philip after Burgundy withdrew support for Warbeck. This trade treaty gave English merchants the right to trade freely throughout Burgundy, except in Flanders.

In 1506, Henry signed the *Intercursus Malus* (Evil Settlement) as part of the Treaty of Windsor. This trade treaty gave English merchants such privileges in Burgundy that the Burgundians never implemented it.

Trade with France

There was similar inconsistency in England's trading relations with France, for both countries used trade as a bargaining chip in diplomatic relations.

- In 1487, France imposed restrictions on trade after Henry backed Breton independence against French ambitions.
- In 1492, both countries agreed to reduce restrictions on trade as part of the Treaty of Etaples.
- In 1495, France ended all restrictions on English trade to secure English neutrality in the Italian Wars.

Exploring the detail
Population

The population of England continued the long-term trend of slow and steady growth up to 1509, although the pace of increase would pick up in the reign of Henry VIII.

London was the only city of significant size in England with a population of about 60,000 by 1509. Harvest fluctuations and growth in the population did result in price inflation, an economic problem that would become more serious as the 16th century unfolded. It is clear from these statistics that by 1522 England had embarked on the Tudor population explosion so that the population would reach 5.2 million by 1640.

1430	c.2.1 million
1522	c.2.3 million
1545	c.2.7 million

Cross-reference

To recap on England's relations with Burgundy and France, including the significance of Perkin Warbeck, look back to pages 54 and 65.

Fig. 6 *An English merchant counting his money. Merchants could make personal fortunes. They often invested their money in property. There are still Tudor merchants' houses in many towns across the country*

The cloth trade

The wool and cloth trade was most important, accounting for 90% of all exports. The trade was changing long before Henry VII's reign from the export of raw wool to the export of broadcloth. This development continued under Henry VII with the continued ascendancy of the **Merchant Adventurers**, and the continued decline of the **Merchants of the Staple**.

Henry used the Merchant Adventurers as a means to limit the trading rights enjoyed by foreign traders in England, particularly to undermine the privileged **Hanseatic League**, also known as the Hansa.

In 1487, Henry banned the export of unfinished cloth by any foreign merchants and, in 1489, he ended the Hansa's privilege that they controlled the export of bullion from England. He modified this policy however when he needed the Hansa's support to secure his kingship because he could not afford to offend such a powerful interest as the Hansa. Finally, in 1504, Henry restored all the Hansa's privileges; at this point he was trying to gain custody of the Earl of Suffolk, a Yorkist fugitive in Germany.

Shipping

Henry showed similar inconsistency in his decisions over the state of the shipping industry. He did little for the English navy, leaving it in a weaker state than the Yorkist kings – Edward IV had 16 ships, Richard maintained an effective and vigilant naval force, but Tudor let it decline. Henry began his reign with seven ships in 1485 but allowed the number to fall to five by 1488, where it remained throughout the reign. It can be argued, however, that since Henry's defensive foreign policy ensured England was never at risk, the weakened navy was not a serious issue.

Conversely, Henry passed Navigation Acts in 1485 and 1489. These specified that English ships and crew had to be used in certain trades, to encourage English shipping and shipbuilding and to end dependency on foreign ships; although their scope was narrow, being principally concerned with the Gascon wine trade. The acts had limited success; in 1509 half of trade was still carried out in foreign ships. Henry did try to encourage improved ship maintenance by paying for the construction at Portsmouth of the first dry dock.

These developments in the shipping industry were important as English seamen were seeking to explore new lands.

A closer look

Exploration

Portugal and Spain had taken an early lead in the Age of Reconnaissance, the search for new lands, wealth and goods, after their royal families increasingly acted as patrons of voyages of discovery. In 1504, five Portuguese ships entered Falmouth harbour carrying 380 tonnes of spices and pepper because the Portuguese had cornered 75% of Europe's spice market. Henry did not initiate any overseas discovery but realised the economic possibilities and acted as patron for trans-Atlantic voyages that would mark the start of English participation in overseas discovery.

This was not a new idea. From 1480, Bristol merchants had certainly been undertaking voyages of discovery westwards, though historians have little information about these early explorations. It is possible that these merchants were looking for new fishing grounds having

Fig. 7 *This mid-19th century picture shows an interpretation of John and Sebastian Cabot's discovery of North America*

been forced from Icelandic waters by the growing power of the Hanseatic League. They had discovered new fishing grounds in the seas around Newfoundland, now known as the Grand Banks, and they may possibly have reached Newfoundland itself – although they were actually searching for the mythical 'Isle of Brasil'.

Henry VII visited Bristol in 1486 and 1496, so would have learned of these voyages. He was therefore receptive when John Cabot, from Genoa, asked him to sponsor his voyage of discovery to the wealthy parts of Asia by sailing westwards. Henry judiciously backed Cabot and his three sons provided their voyage did not antagonise either Spain or Portugal. He specified in the letters patent that any lands Cabot discovered were to be occupied in the King's name.

One small ship, the *Matthew*, set out with 18 men on the first expedition in May 1497. It made landfall on the American continent in June, though historians debate the exact location. Cabot returned to the King and was rewarded with an annual pension.

The King was even more enthusiastic about the second expedition in 1498 when six ships were sent out, one fully equipped by the King himself. John Cabot never returned and there is no record of the fate of the other ships or men.

Overseas exploration developed further under Henry VII for he issued subsequent letters patent to other men in 1501 and 1502. A company called Adventurers to the New Found lands was in existence by 1506; however, by this time it was clear that the New Found lands were not Asia.

One of John Cabot's sons, Sebastian, won Henry VII's patronage when he set out again in 1508 to search for the north-west passage to Asia. He may have found the Hudson Strait and possibly Hudson Bay, but when he returned he found that Henry VII was dead and the new King far less sympathetic to such enterprises. It was not until the second half of the 16th century that an English voyage of discovery again became an attractive prospect for venture capital.

A closer look

Historiographical debate: Chrimes v. Carpenter

Historians reconstruct the past to explain and to make judgements. They draw upon documentary evidence found in archives in order to substantiate these judgements. Where historians choose to research has an immense bearing on the information they find, and therefore the history they write.

In 1972, Professor Chrimes wrote the definitive account of the reign of Henry VII. Chrimes had been a civil servant in the Second World War and so chose to research in the archives of public administration. Chrimes interpreted Henry VII as a conventional late medieval ruler who distrusted administrative innovation, but was strong and achieved stability. Above all, Henry was his own man, for he determined the governance and financial management of the realm. Throughout, Chrimes presented the King as the leader of a powerful top-down state that ran sound finances and, through wise legislation and increasing reliance on the middle class, put the nobles in order. Chrimes did concede that Henry extended his royal rights against the leading nobles by exploiting his hold over them as feudal lord.

A later analysis of the reign by Christine Carpenter in 1997 was less positive. An academic historian, her real interest is in the history of families in Warwickshire and how they reflect national trends. She built on recent local studies of individual noble families that show a crisis in government revealed especially by the fall of Sir William Stanley. These political crises suggest that the state was less secure because government had alienated its natural allies, the nobility. She interpreted Henry VII as a leader who did not understand how to rule alongside, rather than over, the nobility, but sought to control them with excessive severity and, in doing so, he actually undermined, destabilised and weakened monarchy in England.

Learning outcomes

In this section you have studied the financial management of the country, and gained an understanding of the main economic trends of the period. You have explored in detail the importance of financial solvency to Henry VII, and how he exploited his ordinary and extraordinary sources of revenue, sometimes even going beyond the bounds of ethical conduct. You have examined developments in the English economy, especially the impact of enclosure, and gained understanding that there were few significant economic advances, even in the wool and cloth trade.

 Examination-style questions

(a) In what ways did Henry VII increase his income from crown lands? *(12 marks)*

(b) How important were Henry's financial policies in strengthening solvency in England over the years 1485 to 1509? *(24 marks)*

In answering this question you need to be well informed about Henry VII's financial solvency. This means that you need to be able to explain what 'solvency' was and why it was so important to Henry VII. Always bear in mind the fact that Richard III had been unable to finance a fleet in 1485 to prevent Tudor from crossing the Channel. You will need to base your answer on the understanding that Henry VII's constant concern was his desire for dynastic security.

The best answers will analyse the nature of dynastic security in late 15th and early 16th century England. You will explore the inter-relationship between financial management and other areas of royal policy such as the King's relations with foreign powers and the domestic nobility. One fruitful line of enquiry might be an examination of the negative impact of some of his financial policies on his dynastic security.

The answer should reach a well-supported judgement about the importance of the various factors.

In this chapter you will learn about:

- the problems Henry VIII faced when he inherited the throne of England in 1509

- the reasons for the rise of Thomas Wolsey.

Key chronology

Princes Arthur and Henry

18 January 1486	Henry VII marries Elizabeth of York.
19 September 1486	Birth of Prince Arthur at Winchester.
28 June 1491	Prince Henry is born at Greenwich, London.
14 November 1501	Prince Arthur marries Catherine of Aragon.
2 April 1502	Prince Arthur dies at Ludlow Castle and Prince Henry becomes heir to the throne of England.
21 April 1509	Henry VII dies.
11 June 1509	Henry VIII marries Catherine of Aragon.
22 June 1509	Coronation of King Henry VIII and Queen Catherine.

Fig. 1 *This is an anonymous portrait of Henry VIII from about 1520. He clearly enjoyed fine clothes and the trappings of royal power, and at this stage of his life remained in good physical condition*

This portrait of Henry VIII presents a very strong image of the King. The jewels and fine clothes all show a king who is confident, secure and powerful. Early Renaissance portraits like this were usually head and shoulders studies with the hands sometimes resting on a shelf and sometimes with the fingers entwined. There are very few portraits of Henry VIII before 1525.

The King is the most handsome potentate I ever set eyes on, above the usual height, with an extremely fine calf to his leg, his complexion very fair and bright, with auburn hair combed straight and short, in the French fashion, and a round face so very beautiful that it would become a pretty woman, his throat being rather long and thick… He speaks French, English, and Latin, and a little Italian; plays well on the lute and harpischord, sings from a book at sight, draws the bow with greater strength than any man in England and jousts marvellously.

1 *From Ian Dawson,*
***The Tudor Century**, 1993*

■ **Exploring the detail**

The Renaissance and the ideal prince

The Renaissance was a time of great optimism and confidence. Scholars rediscovered classical studies and subsequently explored mathematical, scientific, theological, historical, cultural and philosophical thinking. This 'new learning', or Renaissance thinking, spread across Europe through humanist education.

A Renaissance prince was identifiable as being learned, courteous, poetic and well dressed. He could run, jump, swim, fight and ride perfectly. He should be supremely eloquent, able to persuade other princes, nobles and ambassadors. The ideal prince was embodied in a book by Bernard Castiglione *The Book of the Courtier*, based on his own experiences in the court of Urbino where the Duke of Urbino assembled a court of noblemen and intellectuals in his magnificent palace.

His physical appearance certainly impressed foreign visitors. Pasqualagio, a Venetian ambassador, wrote in 1515:

■ Government and authority

The new King: the personality of Henry VIII

Henry VIII came to the throne of England a young, ambitious Renaissance prince of 17 years old. He looked impressively regal being six foot and two inches (188 cm) tall, fair haired, and athletically built. He knew how to dress to impress so wore rich and fashionable clothes. He had been the heir to the throne since his brother's death in 1502, yet surprisingly his father had not fully prepared him for kingship. Firstly, Henry VIII had had no practical experience in governance, for his father had not sent him to Ludlow Castle to learn the arts of government, as was usual for a Prince of Wales, after his eldest son's premature death at Ludlow. Secondly, Henry VII had made no provision for his son's marriage despite the importance Henry Tudor attached to the continuation of his dynasty.

Henry VII died, it is alleged, overworked, worn out by the cares of state, and prematurely aged after several years of declining health. The effigy on his tomb, however, has a slight indent above his left eyebrow – an indication that he may have died of a stroke. J. J. Scarisbrick captures the energy of the new reign after Henry's marriage and coronation in *Henry VIII* (Source 2).

The Court settled into an almost unbroken round of festivities – revels and disguisings, maying, pageants, tilts and jousts, interspersed with long days in the saddle or following the hawks and long nights banqueting, dancing and making music. Now, in January 1510, Henry burst into the queen's bedchamber at Westminster one morning with ten fellows dressed as Robin Hood's men for dancing and pastimes with the abashed ladies; now, on the following Shrove Tuesday, he disappeared in the midst of a banquet in honour of foreign ambassadors given in the parliament chamber and returned with the Earl of Essex dressed in Turkish fashion, laden with gold decoration and with two scimitars hanging from his waist. Six others were dressed as Prussians, the torch bearers as Moors.

The royal regime was astounding. In the course of a progress in 1511 Henry exercised himself in shooting, singing, dancing, wrestling, casting of the bar, playing at the recorders, flute and virginals, and in setting of songs, making of ballads and did set two Godly masses, every one of them of five parts, which were sung sometimes in his chapel. The rest of the time might also have been spent playing cards, tennis and dice.

He was a prodigy, a sun king. He lived in, and crowned, a world of lavish allegory, mythology and romance. Court pageants portrayed the roses and pomegranates of England and Spain. Above all this was a world of chivalry – of Fame, Renown, Hardiness, of Sir Gallant and *Coeur Loyal*.

2 *J. J. Scarisbrick, **Henry VIII**, 1981*

A closer look

Henry VIII – a Renaissance prince

Henry was born at Greenwich in June 1491 and brought up in a close family unit in the royal nursery at Eltham Palace, surrounded by siblings and cousins. This nursery was closely supervised by his mother, Elizabeth of York, who saw it as an opportunity to reconcile the next generation of Yorkists and Lancastrians. The young prince developed into a confident and self-assured young man in contrast to his elder brother Arthur who was being prepared for his role as king away at Ludlow Castle in the Welsh Marches.

Education was the hallmark of a Renaissance prince so the poet John Skelton was engaged to act as the prince's tutor. Henry was clearly a very able child who soon mastered Latin and French, and developed a working knowledge of Spanish and Italian. He read widely, acquiring great knowledge of classical writers such as Homer, Ovid, Virgil and Cicero and becoming well versed in history having studied Caesar, Livy and Tacitus. His formal education also included mathematics, astronomy and theology.

There is evidence that the education soon paid dividends. At the age of eight, Prince Henry received Thomas More and Erasmus at Eltham Palace. Erasmus later wrote that the young prince already had regal presence commenting specifically on his grace and poise. Such was the influence and reputation of the young prince that, even such a dignitary as Thomas More, prepared for the reception by writing a Latin text in honour of Prince Henry. Erasmus, however, was embarrassed to have arrived empty handed and within three days had completed an ode entitled 'A Description of Britain, Henry VII and the King's Children'.

Fig. 2 *Henry VIII enjoyed princely pursuits such as taking part in tournaments. He spent much of his youth in tiltyards where he learned to joust magnificently. This is an early 16th century Flemish image of a tournament*

Henry, in true Renaissance tradition, was also encouraged to become a skilled sportsman and musician, and to take an interest in the arts. He loved the tiltyard and the hunt, as well as training in physical combat. He played several musical instruments, composed music, and learned to dance. He was heavily influenced by the popular literature of the day – the courtly romances at the Court of King Arthur. As a new king, he aspired to be the perfect knight – chivalric, honourable, just and glorious in war.

Cross-reference

Thomas More and Erasmus are covered on pages 82 and 83.

The new reign: personal monarchy in action

The new reign was marked by the introduction of three changes:

1 The removal of Empson and Dudley and the abolition of the Counsel Learned in the Law.
2 The marriage to Catherine of Aragon.
3 The declaration of war against France.

■ Cross-reference

Richard Empson and Edmund Dudley and The Counsel Learned in the Law under Henry VII are described on page 78.

The removal of Empson and Dudley and the abolition of the Counsel Learned in the Law

Henry VII was perceived to have tyrannised members of the gentry and nobility and to have imposed extortionate financial penalties such as bonds and recognisances through the Counsel Learned in the Law headed by Richard Empson and Edmund Dudley. Henry VIII rejected such punitive actions as unjust. The two enforcers, Empson and Dudley, were arrested and imprisoned in the Tower of London. Tension between the King and his political nation was further defused during the first parliament with the abolition of the Counsel Learned in the Law. The King also set up Commissions of Oyer and Terminer across the country to hear grievances against the late King's agents. These commissions uncovered only petty complaints and little evidence of any sustained oppression; nevertheless Empson and Dudley were executed to satisfy public demand for revenge and the King's need for a fresh start.

■ Key chronology

The Spanish marriage

1509

22 April Henry VII dies.

27 April Henry VIII announces his intention of marrying Catherine of Aragon.

11 June Henry VIII marries Catherine in the Franciscan church at Greenwich.

23 June Coronation of Henry VIII and Queen Catherine in Westminster Abbey.

Fig. 3 *Catherine of Aragon was highly educated, intelligent and virtuous*

The marriage to Catherine of Aragon

Henry VII had insisted that Catherine of Aragon should stay in England after Prince Arthur's death in 1502 for several reasons. The King needed to retain the Anglo-Spanish connection even though relations between himself and Ferdinand had deteriorated. As part of the marriage alliance, Catherine had brought a dowry that Henry refused to repay. Henry VII wanted to keep open an option that Catherine might now marry Prince Henry, an arrangement made possible after the Pope issued a decree or 'bull' in 1504 giving papal dispensation, although he also negotiated for his surviving son to make other marriages.

Catherine was not simply a passive victim. She was ambitious and determined to fulfil her destiny by becoming queen of England; so much so that after 1506 she was the official Spanish ambassador at court working for her father to improve Anglo-Spanish relations, and therefore her own chance of marriage to Prince Henry. Henry VIII, however, believed his father's conduct towards his daughter-in-law had been neglectful and dishonourable.

The declaration of war against France

Henry wanted to go to war as a warrior king to become an imperial king. His young courtiers or 'minions', such as Lord Henry Stafford, Thomas and William Parr, Thomas Boleyn, William Compton and Nicholas Carew, were similarly bored by the period of protracted peace and wanted

■ Cross-reference

Henry VIII's war against France is discussed in more detail on page 116.

the chance for adventure, glory and profit. It took time to reverse his father's pacifist policy and remove his father's pacifist advisors, before he could assemble a pro-war Counsel and prepare for war against France.

Activity

Thinking point

How far did the following three new policies set Henry VIII apart from his father, Henry VII?

1. The decision to marry Catherine of Aragon.

2. The imprisonment and execution of Empson and Dudley.

3. The war against France.

The Counsel

Henry VIII inherited his father's established Counsel.

- William Warham, Archbishop of Canterbury and Lord Chancellor.
- Richard Fox, Lord Privy Seal.
- John de Vere, Earl of Oxford.
- Thomas Howard, Earl of Surrey and Lord Treasurer.

Key profile

Richard Fox

Richard Fox was a bishop and lawyer who had served Edward IV, joined the Tudor court in exile, served Henry VII and continued to serve Henry VIII. He was Keeper of the Privy Seal from 1487 to 1516, often acted as Counsellor, and was frequently sent to represent the King as ambassador. Fox recognised Wolsey's administrative skills and acted as his patron bringing him in to Counsel during 1510.

Fig. 4 *William Warham. A long lasting Archbishop of Canterbury who held the Primacy from 1503 to 1532*

Henry VIII came to the throne with an established Counsel, unlike his father who had spent the weeks after Bosworth assembling his Counsel. The Counsel had served the old King who was, by nature, cautious and inclined to work hard. Henry VIII, however, was a young man who desired glory and adventure. Relations between the new King and his Counsel were bound to be strained. In the early months of his reign, Archbishop Warham and Richard Fox advised the King to avoid conflict with France, advice that fell on deaf ears.

Relations between the King and his Counsel were made more complex by the political influence of Henry VIII's grandmother, Lady Margaret Beaufort, who directed the new King's affairs at the start of the reign, although her influence was short since she died soon after her son. She had taken a personal dislike to Thomas Wolsey, a man who would play a key role in developing the pro-war policy after 1512. Henry VIII was looking for an outlet from the affairs of state, so he was impressed by Wolsey's enormous capacity for hard work and unparalled organisational skills.

The tensions between the counsellors and divisions over policy within the Counsel soon became public knowledge, and opened up factional in-fighting. The main line of division was between those counsellors who opposed war against France and those who backed the war, known respectively as the anti-war and pro-war factions.

Cross-reference

Lady Margaret Beaufort and her role in affairs are outlined on page 44.

The Counsel and institutions of government such as parliament continued to provide the King's formal machinery of advice and consultation under Henry VIII, however policies and decisions were increasingly determined at court and, in particular, in the household department – the Privy Chamber.

The court and the Privy Chamber

Fig. 5 *Henry VIII surrounded by his court. The courtiers provided entertainment, spectacle and advice for the King and, in return, tried to influence the King and benefit from his patronage*

The court remained the source of patronage and political influence where personal and family fortunes were made and broken. There were two politically important sections to the King's court: the Chamber; and the Privy Chamber. The latter was established by Henry VII in the 1490s to provide a place for his personal servants. Under Henry VII the Privy Chamber was small and modestly staffed. At its head was the Groom of the Stool who assisted the King when he sat on the close-stool, otherwise known as the toilet. The men of the Privy Chamber kept Henry VII washed and dressed, fed and watered leaving him free to work and rule as he wished.

The growing importance of the Privy Chamber

The Privy Chamber served a different function under Henry VIII, although the change was not apparent until 1518. The King relied on a new group of much younger favourites, the 'minions' (a word derived from the French word 'mignons' meaning 'darlings'). He also admired and emulated the structure of the French court where the monarch's favourites were identified by the title 'Gentlemen'. When Henry chose to formally recognise his minions as 'Gentlemen of the Privy Chamber' he transformed the Privy Chamber into a small but prestigious part of the royal household.

From this time, the Gentlemen of the Privy Chamber were increasingly careerist politicians who expected money and titles for their services to the King. Gradually it took over management of the King's affairs from the Chamber. Under Henry VII the Treasurer of the Chamber had managed the King's finances while the Groom only had a small account for Privy Chamber expenses that he actually drew from the Chamber itself. By 1529, the royal finances had been split into two between the still larger Chamber and the Privy Purse, at this time supervised by

■ Cross-reference

To recap on the Chamber, see page 87.

Further aspects of Henry VIII's government and his domestic policies are discussed on page 109.

Henry Norris, one of the Gentlemen of the Privy Chamber. The Privy Purse was no longer funded by money drawn from the Chamber but had its own royal treasury known as the Privy Coffers.

Similarly, the Privy Chamber gained access to the royal signature, known as the sign manual. This was a very important state role because the sign manual was the equivalent to the great seal that authorised any state paper. Henry VII was an orderly and disciplined king who signed documents; however, Henry VIII notoriously hated paperwork and would delay signing. The Gentlemen of the Privy Chamber were most favourably placed to sense when he was in the best mood to sign papers.

David Starkey, 'Court and Government' explains how the Privy Chamber functioned (Source 3).

> Quite soon we see State Papers accumulating in the hands of the Sir William Compton, the Groom of the Stool, or Henry Norris who submitted them for signature at a propitious moment after supper or during mass. These were papers prepared by Wolsey's own secretariat. But the Privy Chamber also took a less passive role. There survives a 12-page letter book for the latter part of 1517. Its contents are very mixed. Some letters are on state business, like the workings of the enclosure commission, but most deal with the personal interests of Henry's intimate attendants.
>
> Four of the letters deal with the suit of William Coffin of the Privy Chamber to marry the wealthy widow, Mrs Vernon of Haddon Hall, Derbyshire. Opposing Coffin was Wolsey himself, who wanted the widow for one of his own servants. But Coffin backed to the hilt by Nicholas Carew, the most dominant member of the Privy Chamber, was able to procure the king's own signature, and so inflicted public defeat on the minister, 'whereat', as Compton smugly reported, 'my lord cardinal is not content with all'. So the Privy Chamber's access to the sign manual was a valuable weapon in the armoury that turned the newly appointed Gentlemen into some of Wolsey's most feared rivals.

3   *David Starkey, 'Court and Government' in John Guy (ed.),*
__The Tudor Monarchy__, 1997

The rise of Thomas Wolsey to 1515

Thomas Wolsey was an academic and churchman who rose through the ranks of noble and royal service to achieve the position of royal chaplain. This post gave him access to the King and court; however, his political position was far from central or secure in 1509. He had attended Henry VII's funeral but was not invited to Henry VIII's coronation, probably due to Margaret Beaufort's influence. After her death he secured several court positions including royal almoner and registrar of the Order of the Garter but his real breakthrough came in June 1510 when he was appointed to the Counsel. He had been recommended for this appointment by his current patron Richard Fox, who recognised the younger churchman's abilities and potential to serve the crown. At this stage his role, as a low-ranking counsellor, was to keep anti-war Fox informed about the actions of the pro-war faction.

By 1512, it was clear that Henry was serious about his plans for war and that Surrey's pro-war faction in Counsel had won the argument. Wolsey was ambitious for further advancement that could only be secured if he served the King; the King wanted war and glory, therefore Wolsey must deliver the victory. He switched allegiance to support the war where his

Fig. 6 *Thomas Wolsey. A man from relatively humble origins who loved display and wealth, and grew to live in royal splendour. In 1515, he was appointed both Cardinal by the Pope and Lord Chancellor by the King*

Key chronology

Key chronology

The early years of Thomas Wolsey

1472/3 Thomas Wolsey is born in Suffolk, the son of an Ipswich butcher. His family is clearly wealthy as Wolsey is well educated.

1487/8 He graduates from Magdalen College, Oxford with a BA (Bachelor of Arts) aged 15 years of age, then he pursues an academic career, adding further academic honours such as an MA (Master of Arts).

1497–1500 He is appointed fellow and bursar of the college.

1498 He is ordained as a priest.

1500 He is forced to resign for overspending on the building works to complete the college tower.

Activity

Thinking point

Why did Wolsey rise to political prominence so rapidly?

administrative skills were required to manage the organisation of the vast military and naval supplies needed to fight against France.

A closer look

Thomas Wolsey before 1509

Thomas Wolsey left his early academic career at Oxford somewhat under a cloud, and pursued a new career in the Roman Catholic Church. He made full use of his network of personal contacts for his patron was the Marquis of Dorset, whose three sons he had tutored at Magdalen College school. It was vital for a young man from a relatively humble family to have a patron if he was to make his way up the social and political ladder, and Wolsey was fortunate in his patrons.

Dorset helped Wolsey embark on a career as chaplain in various influential households, until he was appointed chaplain to Sir Richard Nanfan, deputy of Calais. In Calais, he became increasingly involved in official matters and political life where his undoubted skills impressed Nanfan who recommended Wolsey to Henry VII. As one of Henry VII's chaplains, Wolsey had access to the court where he observed court politics, he extended his network of contacts, especially when he was sent to embassies in Scotland and Flanders, and he prospered with lucrative rewards such as the deaneries of Lincoln and Hereford.

Wolsey's personal skills

- Intelligence: brilliant mind.
- Eloquence: the power to persuade was a key skill in 16th century politicians.
- Immense capacity for hard work.
- Administrative and organisational talents.
- Ambitious.
- Ability to network.

Wolsey rose very rapidly to political dominance and was soon well rewarded, accumulating great rewards for his advice and efficiency. Each appointment brought him additional influence and wealth in both church and secular affairs.

Table 1 *Wolsey's personal power base: his religious and secular roles*

	Church affairs	Secular affairs
1513	Dean of York Bishop of Tournai	
1514	Bishop of Lincoln Archbishop of York (now a peer of the realm)	
1515	Cardinal (now a prince of the Church entitled to wear scarlet robes)	Lord Chancellor *Warham resigned the post and retired to Canterbury*
1516		Lord Privy Seal *Fox resigned and retired to Winchester*

Wolsey was able to consolidate his hold on power because his patrons now stood out of his way when both Warham and Fox retired to their church appointments. Other influential men, who might have blocked his path, stood aside.

- Charles Brandon, the Duke of Suffolk had long been a favourite of Henry VIII's. Suffolk might have retained great political influence and opposed Wolsey's emergence as chief minister. Wolsey, however, managed to win Suffolk's political gratitude and loyalty. In January 1515, Henry VIII sent Suffolk to accompany his sister, Mary Tudor, back from the French court after the death of her husband, King Louis XII of France. Mary and Suffolk were secretly married on the return journey provoking great anger from the King. Wolsey offered to mediate with Henry to prevent the pair being expelled from court.

- Thomas Howard, Earl of Surrey, was now restored to the Dukedom of Norfolk, but failed to resist Wolsey's inexorable rise to dominance.

- Edward Stafford, the Duke of Buckingham, was a serious opponent. He despised Wolsey, and was inclined to despise the King for trusting Wolsey. Buckingham was a powerful enemy for he had great estates, fortified castles, armouries and many servants, above all he had a claim to the throne through Thomas of Woodstock, fifth son of Edward III. In 1521, Wolsey persuaded the King that Buckingham was guilty of treason and the Duke was executed.

By 1515, Wolsey had consolidated his position as the King's 'chief minister'. This title was not an official post but reflected his dominance over Church and state, and the fact that he had sidelined his political rivals. He would hold on to his unquestioned political power until 1525.

John Guy analyses the struggle between Wolsey and Buckingham in Cardinal Wolsey (Source 4).

Cross-reference
More information on Richard Fox can be found on pages 40, 81, 101 and 118.

Cross-reference
More information on the marriage of Mary Tudor and Louis XII of France is to be found on page 120.

Fig. 7 *Henry VIII talking with Wolsey. The King was actively interested in foreign policy but content to leave the domestic economy and affairs to his chief minister*

Edward Stafford, 3rd Duke of Buckingham, was among those nobles who found it difficult to adapt themselves to their Tudor roles as courtiers and servants of the Crown. He was among those who felt a contradiction between his ducal standing and a royal policy calculated to ensure the subordination of the nobility. In short, Buckingham stood for chivalry and noble privileges. He regarded Wolsey as an upstart.

They had clashed in various ways. As Lord Chancellor Wolsey insisted that law enforcement in his courts of Chancery and Star Chamber should be governed by the golden rule of equity 'Do as you would be done by!' – Christ himself had commanded in the sermon on the mount. This amounted to a frontal assault upon the mafia-type methods associated with 'bastard feudalism'. He prosecuted Sir William Bulmer for illegal retaining. Wolsey's attack on Sir William Bulmer was, indirectly, an attack on Buckingham whose livery Bulmer had worn.

Thereafter Buckingham was heard grumbling about the king's counsellors. And when he allegedly threatened that he would kill Henry VIII as his father had been willing to kill Richard III, Henry and Wolsey struck. It culminated in Buckingham's trial and execution.

4

*John Guy, **Cardinal Wolsey**, Headstart History Papers, date unknown*

Wolsey as patron of the arts and learning

Erasmus recognised Wolsey as a great patron of arts and learning. Wolsey founded lectureships in Oxford in theology, civil law, medicine, philosophy, mathematics, and Greek and rhetoric. He also found the funds to establish Cardinal's College, Oxford to house 500 students each year, although this college was refounded on a smaller scale after 1529 by Henry VIII as King's College, then later renamed Christ Church College. He saw the need for a feeder school to Oxford University so set up Ipswich School, which was later dismantled.

Wolsey had an insatiable desire to accrue and flaunt personal wealth. His building projects at York Place, The More and above all at Hampton Court were architectural triumphs. The buildings housed his art collections, libraries and all manner of Renaissance refinements and achievements.

■ A closer look

Hampton Court

In 1515, Wolsey celebrated his investiture as cardinal in a spectacular ceremony in Westminster Abbey that, for pomp, matched any king's coronation; and he soon began to equal the King in palace building. He secured the lease on a manor on the River Thames at Hampton, some 15 miles west of London. The site had the advantage of being upriver and, therefore, the water was cleaner.

Wolsey demolished the existing building, which had once belonged to Giles Daubeney, and replaced it with a grand red-brick house decorated with turret and tall chimneys and surrounded by elaborate formal gardens and a moat. The architectural design of two courtyards was historic as it mirrored colleges in Oxford, but was also modern as the palace had the most advanced sewers. No expense was spared, for the new palace boasted **mullioned glass windows**, and was ornately decorated with a splendid clock tower and **medallions** of Roman emperors. These medallions were carved for Wolsey by the Florentine sculptor di Maiano in the style of those commissioned for the Cardinal of Amboise in his palace at Rouen. Wolsey clearly intended his palace to be a Renaissance cardinal's residence.

Wolsey's palace was said to have 1,000 rooms. The first courtyard, the Base Court, contained accommodation for his household with 45 additional guest rooms. He kept 280 beds, each with silk hangings, ready for visitors. The inner courtyard, the Clock Court, included the great hall, banqueting chamber, gallery and chapel. The public rooms and private apartments were adorned richly. Some had splendidly-carved wood panels, while others were decorated with friezes and paintings. Wolsey impressed his visitors with his collection of priceless tapestries and 60 carpets.

Hampton Court Palace became the physical manifestation of Wolsey's wealth and political influence. Contemporaries were aware of this, and some became very jealous. In c.1523, John Skelton wrote verses to attack Wolsey for being ambitious and greedy (Source 5).

■ Key terms

Mullioned glass windows: a vertical bar separated each compartment of a window.

Medallions: a panel, usually round or oval, containing a sculpture.

Why come ye not to court?
To which court
To the King's Court
Or to Hampton Court?
The King's Court
Should have the excellence,
But Hampton Court
Hath the pre-eminence

5

John Skelton

It was said that Wolsey ordered Skelton's arrest but the poet avoided him by fleeing into sanctuary.

Fig. 8 *The palace at Hampton Court was built for Wolsey in the style of a Renaissance cardinal's palace*

The relationship between king and minister: master or servant?

The nature of the relationship between Henry VIII and his chief minister in the years 1515 to 1529 is fundamental to an analysis of Tudor political history. The topic has been debated intensively by generations of historians.

▪ **Traditional interpretation**: A. F. Pollard claimed that Wolsey achieved a 'prime ministerial' dominance over policy making for 14 years, a view also held by G. R. Elton who wrote that Wolsey tried to rule as king when he was not king. He had enormous power through his religious authority as Archbishop of Rome and Cardinal Legate, and through his lay position as Lord Chancellor. Furthermore, he manipulated his influence over the King to exclude any rivals at court. He assumed great personal power, determined English foreign policy, and dominated the Court of Star Chamber.

▪ **Revisionist interpretation**: Wolsey is seen by other historians as a man who followed instructions. He had to follow policies that reflected the King's will, greed and desire for conflict. Wolsey desired peace but was forced to declare war intermittently to satify the King. S. J. Gunn argued that Wolsey was determined to enforce the King's laws, and faced opposition from contemporaries who failed to realise that he served the royal will. Eric Ives noted that Wolsey never owned the policy, for it was always the King's policy.

■ **Resolving the conflicting interpretations**: Henry was a young man in the years that Wolsey held political power. John Guy stressed his view that the King regarded the older man not as a servant but as a friend, even a junior partner. He trusted Wolsey to calculate the policy options and rank them for his royal consideration, to edit his correspondence, and control the information flowing from central to local government.

Conclusion

The personality of Henry VIII was central to the governance of the country. Two personal characteristics of the new King were that he was very willing to listen to the Counsel of his favoured ministers or personal friends – the notable example being Sir Thomas Wolsey – and he was ready to entrust his chief minister with the routine administration of diverse state affairs. Wolsey, his chief minister from 1515, enjoyed immense political power though it was counter-balanced both by the growing political influence of the young Gentlemen in the Privy Chamber and by established government structures such as the Counsel, the law courts and parliament. The chief minister and Gentlemen were essentially courtiers, who surrounded the King alongside many other powerful families and aspirant interests, and who competed for the royal patronage by serving the King.

The weakness in Wolsey's authority, that became apparent after 1525, was that the King did not know of, or approve, everything that the minister did. By 1525, Wolsey was struggling to manage the King's foreign relations and financial solvency, then policies started to go wrong. At this point, the King was not obliged to stand by his minister.

Summary questions

1 How far was Wolsey's rise to power due to his own personal qualities?

2 Why has Wolsey's career given rise to such different interpretations?

9 Henry VIII in England and Europe

In this chapter you will learn about:

- the internal government of England during the first two decades of Henry VIII's reign

- how Henry VIII experienced very different foreign relations from his father.

The first twenty years of Henry VIII's reign, were years of domestic peace and tranquillity. His reign promised a steady development of government, under a respected and able king who was the undoubted master of the country. Henry was prepared for kingship and was accustomed to the deference due to a royal prince since he had been heir to the throne since the age of ten. When he became king, aged seventeen years, Henry appeared to be totally self-confident, to be a carefree and trusting man; in contrast to his father who had been prudent and cautious.

Henry's court experienced one of those occasional periods of classical ease. With no urgent domestic problems, with an inheritance which, if less munificent than is sometimes thought, was, thanks to his father, at least free from debt, Henry could afford the luxury of concentrating on the princely pastimes of diplomacy and war.

1

*Adapted from C. S. L. Davies, **Peace, Print and Protestantism**, 1995*

Activity

Challenge your thinking

1. How much of Source 1 is opinion and how much is fact?

2. Using the material in Chapters 8 and 9 and the heading 'Personal strengths and weaknesses', write a short character profile of Henry VIII in 1509. Then write another profile for 1529. Compare Henry VIII to his father, Henry VII, whose personality was analysed at the start of Chapter 6 on page 71.

Domestic policies

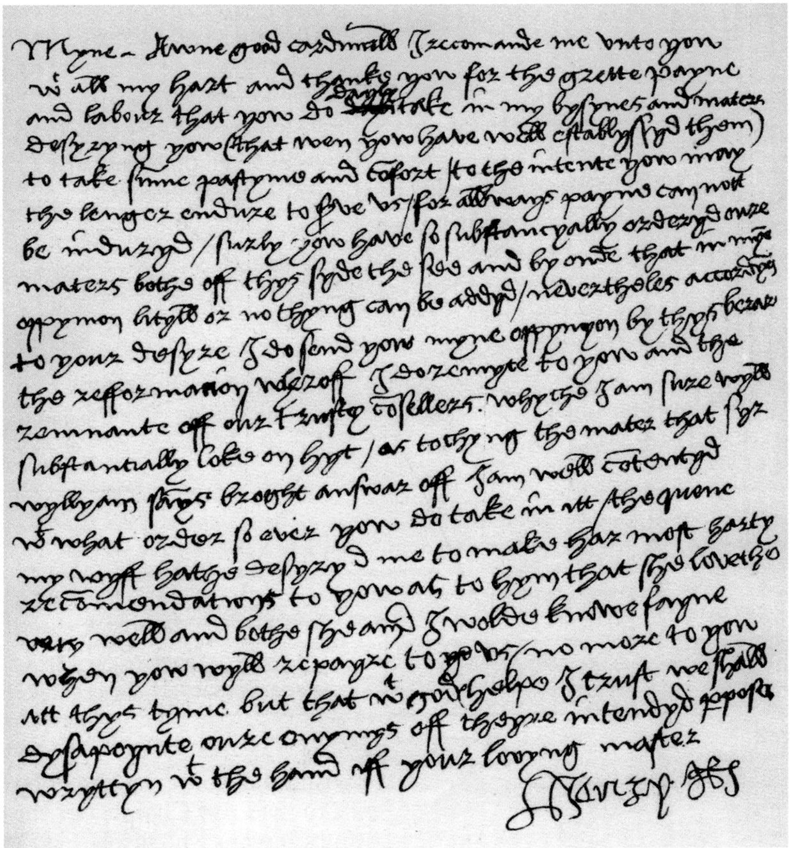

Fig. 1 *In this letter, Henry VIII thanked Wolsey for the trouble he had taken with domestic and foreign affairs, and urged him to take some 'pastime and comfort'. The letter concludes with a friendly greeting from the Queen. It is good evidence that the two men enjoyed a close relationship, sometimes referred to as a partnership*

Cross-reference

For information on policies concerning the Church, see page 132.

Key term

Treasurer of the Chamber: when Henry VII became King he appointed Lord Dynham to be Treasurer of the Exchequer. Thomas Lovell was appointed to be a senior member of the royal household. As Henry VII moved financial management from Exchequer to Chamber, he reappointed and renamed the post. Thomas Lovell became the first Treasurer of the Chamber but in 1492 was succeeded by Sir John Heron.

In the Tudor period, the aims of domestic policy were rarely spelled out clearly. It was accepted that a monarch was expected to keep law and order; to administer the country efficiently; and to raise taxes when necessary. All Tudor monarchs feared internal rebellion, since they had no standing army or police to re-establish royal authority, so any serious failure of domestic policy that caused rebellion would bring criticism.

Administrative efficiency

There was no major reform of government administration under Wolsey who, acting as Henry VIII's 'business manager', preferred to keep and further develop the administration established by Henry VII. Henry VIII kept most of his father's experienced officials to ensure continuity in government. Sir John Heron had been appointed **Treasurer of the Chamber** by Henry VII and kept that post until 1524.

In 1526, the King demanded reform of the royal household after he concluded that he had been denied access to sufficient counsellors through Wolsey's executive control over appointments to the Counsel. Wolsey, with characteristic political skill, turned this challenge to his own political advantage in the Eltham Ordinances for the Regulation of the Court. The Eltham Ordinances effectively boosted his control over both the Counsel and the Privy Chamber, but did not improve administrative efficiency.

Local government and Justices of the Peace

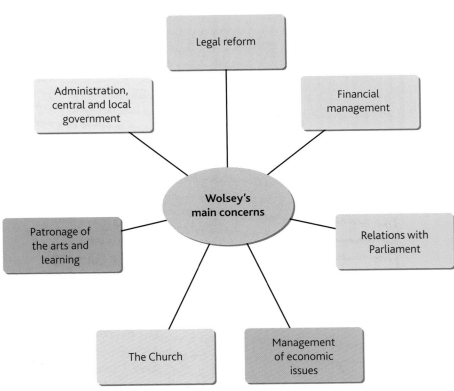

Fig. 2

Although national politics were decided at court and Counsel, relationships between the court and the country were key to national political stability. Central government needed the support of local magistrates especially the Justices of the Peace (JPs).

Henry and Wolsey continued Henry VII's policy of building links between the country and the court. Many local magnates and JPs were invited to attend court and participate in a ceremony of personally swearing allegiance to the King who sat under a gold canopy in Chamber. The name of each man was recorded in a special book as a 'King's servant', some of whom were given unsalaried positions at court and some were given nothing. The 'carrot' for those who received a position at court was the hope of further patronage. Some JPs did indeed rise to the Privy Chamber or the Counsel. The 'stick', however, for any King's servant who disobeyed the rules, as Sir William Bulmer found out when he wore the livery of the Duke of Buckingham in the King's presence, was that he could be hauled into the Court of Star Chamber.

Royal authority also passed from court to the country. Wolsey's household was a noted training place for local government. He named his dependants and placed them as commissioners to assess and collect subsidy, or on county benches to dispense the King's law. An example is Ralph Pexsall who served Wolsey as clerk of the Crown in Chancery until 1522, then was appointed to local government in Surrey, Berkshire and Devon.

Wolsey used his powers in the Star Chamber to reduce alleged corruption and maladministration in the counties. One example of his work is the case of Sir Robert Sheffield. Sheffield was a former member of the King's Counsel, Speaker of the House of Commons and JP in Lincolnshire and Nottinghamshire. He was brought before the Court of Star Chamber accused of aiding and abetting homicide in his counties and was sent to the Tower, where he died.

The courts of law also served a positive function in ensuring administrative efficiency. Wolsey insisted that as many JPs as possible should attend Star Chamber to be 'sworn in' and then to hear a homily on the duties of JP and the links between central and local government. He knew the crown needed active JPs to implement its policies.

Legal reforms

As Lord Chancellor, Wolsey was well placed to reform the many abuses of the legal system. He was intellectually interested in the whole process of law making, despite his lack of legal training. Each day, he presided in the Court of Chancery, clearly enjoying the majesty of a judge, although his effect was minimal judging by the amount of work handled by that court. Chancery continued to function as it had under John Morton and William Warham.

Wolsey had greater impact on the work of the Court of Star Chamber. Noblemen, because of their influence, were frequently able to avoid justice. In 1516, he put forward his principles that any crime should be punished, regardless of rank, and that justice should be cheap and impartial. He planned to use the Court of Star Chamber to achieve these principles, and correspondingly the caseload rose from 12 cases pa to 120 pa. Wolsey openly asked for complaints to be brought to the court promising that social status would be no barrier to justice or protection against prosecution. He investigated all manner of complaints ranging from criminal offences to abuses of power, many of which were committed by senior members of the Counsel.

Wolsey's legal reforms are not beyond criticism. Sometimes his judicial investigations smacked of personal vendetta. When Wolsey prosecuted Henry Standish, Bishop of St Asaph for **praemunire** in the Star Chamber he appeared to be getting revenge for a previous legal argument, won by the bishop, after which Wolsey publicly had to submit on his knees to Henry VIII.

Another serious criticism of the reforms is that Wolsey did not appear to plan ahead for the increased workload. He was unable to hear all the suits in Star Chamber and the hastily-established overflow tribunals also became log-jammed. By 1529, the Court of Star Chamber had almost collapsed under the workload so many of the suits had to be remitted to local commissioners or even abandoned.

Financial management

Tax reform

Wolsey's most significant and lasting achievements were in tax reform. The old system of **fifteenths and tenths** was inefficient as it raised insufficient income.

Wolsey aimed to replace these taxes with a directly-assessed subsidy. He was assisted by John Hales, a judge in the Court of Exchequer

Exploring the detail

The Eltham Ordinances, 1526

Wolsey reduced the size of the Privy Chamber from 12 to six gentlemen. He took advantage of this to remove his chief opponents – William Compton was removed and replaced as Groom of the Stool by the politically-neutral Henry Norris.

Wolsey arranged for Counsel Attendant on the King to be made up of 20 counsellors. In practice, Wolsey used his political influence to ensure the nominated 20 counsellors were often absent on the King's business, leaving only a sparsely attended Counsel that he could manipulate.

Cross-reference

To review central and local government under Henry VII, including the Court of the Star Chamber, see pages 73–74.

Cross-reference

The Court of Chancery is also mentioned on page 80.

Key terms

Praemunire: a law that made any acknowledgement of papal power illegal in England.

Fifteenths and tenths: parliament granted a directly-assessed subsidy – a 15th was the rate of tax on the moveable goods of laymen, and a 10th was the rate of tax on the income of the clergy.

from 1522, who drafted the legislation required for assessment and collection. Together, Wolsey and Hales moved towards a system whereby taxpayers were assessed individually under oath by local officials who were to be supervised by centrally-appointed commissioners. When parliament granted a subsidy, every adult (except married women) had to be assessed, but only those adults whose incomes exceeded a prescribed limit had to pay tax. The limit varied from subsidy to subsidy.

The reform of the tax system caused problems because many of the propertied classes, those hit hardest by the new assessments, not surprisingly resented the new subsidy assessments. In 1523, parliament voted subsidy at 4 shillings in the £ on goods and land, but eventually less than half the anticipated £800,000 was raised. Even worse, the subsidy was collected in instalments rather than as the lump sum intended. There was growing resistance when the second instalment of the subsidy was due in February 1525.

The Amicable Grant, 1525

In 1525, Wolsey had to raise money to pay for the war against France but, being already at loggerheads with parliament, he did not want to risk calling a new parliament to raise the subsidy. Besides, the 1523 subsidy was still being collected. Instead, Wolsey instructed his commissioners to raise a non-parliamentary tax which he called the 'Amicable Grant' to appeal to patriotic sentiments. Tax payers, however, did not receive the demand amicably but rebelled at the imposition of a forced loan. Wolsey backtracked and simply requested a benevolence, a 'voluntary' contribution from selected tax payers to the crown.

By this time the damage was done. Discontent grew, resulting in opposition across the English counties that ranged from refusal to pay to full-scale revolt. The most serious resistance was at Lavenham in Suffolk where 10,000 men took part in a very serious uprising which threatened to spread to the nearby counties of Essex and Cambridgeshire. The revolt was suppressed for the King by the Dukes of Norfolk and Suffolk.

The King had caused the discontent by planning an expensive war but Wolsey was left to take the blame for the crown's disastrous financial management. He had to publicly pardon the Lavenham rebels and even pay the leading rebels' prison expenses! No further taxation was attempted after this.

It is important to keep this revolt in context. The resistance to the Amicable Grant was the most serious breakdown in law and order in England whilst Wolsey was the King's chief minister. For most of the time the country was at peace, and some families prospered as is evident through the contemporary investment in houses and homes. William Moreton was a member of the Cheshire gentry who rebuilt the east wing of his family home, added a chapel, and the remarkable five-sided bay windows. George Cavendish also commented on this period of stability when he wrote 'I never saw this realm in better order, quietness, and obedience than it was in the time of his authority and rule; nor justice better administered with indifference [impartiality]'.

Relations with parliament

Wolsey did not prove adept in managing parliament and called only two parliaments – in 1515 and 1523.

The 1515 parliament was dominated by worries over Church affairs in the aftermath of the Hunne case. The wrangling was so intense that Wolsey dismissed parliament even before it voted on his taxation.

■ **Cross-reference**

For the war against France, see page 119.

Wolsey's relationships with parliament in 1525 is covered on page 110.

Fig. 3 *The construction of Little Moreton hall began around 1450. It is sometimes called a 'Magpie house' because of the black and white, asymetrical half-timbering*

The 1523 parliament was overshadowed by the need to raise funds to fight the war in France. As chief minister, Wolsey chose to go to parliament to persuade, or bully, the House of Commons into voting the subsidy. The Speaker, Thomas More, reminded the Lord Chancellor that he had no constitutional right to enter the Commons.

Relationships between Wolsey and parliament were so bitter that Wolsey avoided calling a meeting. In 1525, he chose, instead, to raise additional revenue by the ill-fated Amicable Grant.

Economic issues

Enclosure

Tudor England suffered from serious economic problems that caused social tensions. There was poverty, with food shortages, high prices, unemployment, crime and depopulation. The principal cause of these social ills was the increase in population from its late medieval low point. Renaissance humanist thinkers, such as Thomas Wolsey and Thomas More, believed that one task of government was to find remedies to these economic and social problems; however, they did not understand the population increase, and instead blamed the problems on the enclosure of fields.

The enclosure of open fields and common lands was, therefore, perceived to be evil by the humanists, and was expressed in the phrase 'sheep ate up men'. The humanists based their theories on the ideas of classical authors such as Plato, Cicero and Aristotle. The classical authors judged that immoral and irresponsible landowners were driven by personal greed,

Cross-reference

The Hunne case is discussed on page 131.

The Amicable Grant is detailed on page 112.

Cross-reference

To recap on the beliefs of the humanists, see page 82.

To refresh your knowledge of economic issues, including enclosure, under Henry VII, see pages 90–91.

rather than public good, when they chose to convert land from arable to pastoral by trampling on the rights of the community to common land.

Government had already passed legislation to restrict enclosure in the year 1489, then between 1514 and 1515. In 1517, Wolsey launched a national enquiry into how effective the previous legislation had been, which uncovered evidence against 264 landlords and corporations, such as some Oxford colleges. Although some cases proved time consuming, most were speedily resolved with clear verdicts being brought against the enclosers. Afterwards, some 74 landowners entered into recognisances to rebuild demolished farmhouses or to restore lands to arable. These statistics can be interpreted as evidence that Wolsey was earnest in his determination to reverse some of the enclosures.

He was, however, less passionate in his policy against enclosure in 1523 when he agreed to suspend his enclosure policy, unpopular with landowning MPs and members of the Lords, in order to secure their support for the parliamentary subsidy to fight the war against France. At the same time, he also granted an amnesty for landowners who had enclosed land. Such a deal, however, raises suspicions that he campaigned against enclosure only to weaken his wealthy opponents who were profiting from enclosure, rather than out of any humanist principle. It is certainly true that his attempts to deal with the problem of enclosure made him few friends among the nobility or propertied classes.

Profiteering

Wolsey stated a desire to resolve other social evils besides enclosure. In particular, he wished to protect ordinary people from extortionate overcharging for basic foodstuffs. He dealt with food racketeers from the Court of Star Chamber. In 1518, he fixed poultry prices in London and investigated the scarcity of other meats including beef, mutton and veal, although there were no long-term improvements in the prices and availability of meat for the capital. Such interventions angered London butchers and provincial cattle farmers.

He issued proclamations against grain dealers who profiteered in grain. In practice, however, he did little to enforce the measures. In 1520 six grain speculators were brought before him but he referred the cases back to their local justices, claiming he was too busy to deal with the problem.

 Activity

Challenge your thinking

What were Wolsey's aims in domestic policy and how successful was he?

Wolsey's aims in the management of domestic policy might be identified as below. For each aim, consider where he had success and where he failed to achieve his aims.

Wolsey's aim	Evidence of success	Evidence of failure
To serve the King		
To discredit opponents		
To apply humanist ideals		
To raise standards		
To fund the King's policies		
Any other aim		

Activity

Thinking point

Which policies created the most opposition?

Wolsey's domestic policies certainly created enemies. Identify policies that can be described as 'enlightened' and those that were mismanaged. Then identify Wolsey's resulting political enemies.

Opposition caused by Wolsey's constructive enlightened policies		Opposition caused by Wolsey's mismanagement of his policies	
Opposition	Policy	Opposition	Policy

■ Foreign policies

Henry VIII's foreign relations were conducted under the same constraints as his father's. European power politics had been dominated since 1494 by the Italian Wars. The King of France persistently tried, and failed, to win control over Naples, Sicily and Milan. The warfare in southern Europe meant that English foreign policy in northern Europe was little more than a sideshow in European terms, however much it meant to Henry VIII personally. All he could do to claim his title 'King of France' was invade France from the north, usually in alliance with the Duke of Burgundy, to put pressure on the French government in Paris.

Another constraint, which Henry VII also recognised, was the need to constantly readjust English foreign relations to changes in European politics. The defining point in foreign relations came in 1519, when Charles Hapsburg was elected as Holy Roman Emperor combining that role with his existing powers as King of Spain and Duke of Burgundy. His victory in the imperial election over Francis I meant there were two immensely powerful, rival dynastic powers in Europe – the Hapsburg and Valois families; consequently, conflict between Hapsburg and Valois was imminent. Henry and Wolsey now, in theory, had a choice of one of two allies, although English economic interests were much more closely tied to the Hapsburgs because the English cloth trade depended on the markets of the duchy of Burgundy.

Henry VII had conducted foreign policy essentially in a defensive manner, making a virtue of non-commitment. Henry VIII was unable to continue this policy

Activity

Revision exercise

Look back to Chapter 5, page 60, to read about Henry VII's foreign relations. Use this information as a basis to outline the situation in Europe in 1509 regarding: the aims of foreign relations; England's allies and enemies; the major issues in European affairs.

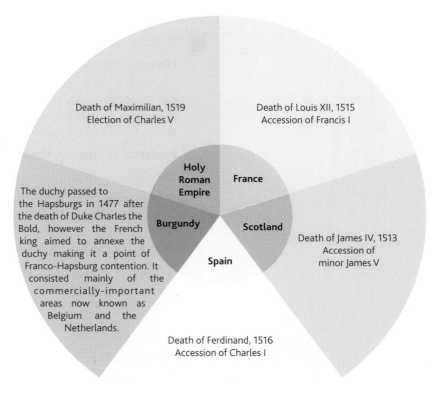

Fig. 4 *The main players in English foreign relations, 1509–29*

(a)

Annual ordinary income of the three monarchs

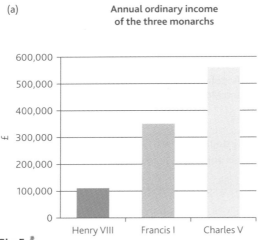

(b)

Size of the population

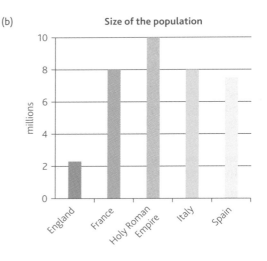

Fig.5

Cross-reference

The ideal of a Renaissance prince, and Henry VIII's upbringing in light of this, are described on page 99

for two important reasons. His own nature was war-like, and, as a Renaissance prince, he desired adventure, victory and glory. Europe was dominated by the enmity between the two dynastic rivals, Francis I and Charles V, who set the tone and context for relations between princes in Europe.

A final restriction was that foreign policy always had an impact on domestic issues. Henry VIII wanted to build a reputation as a warrior king but there was little support in England for war because of the consequent high tax demands and disruption to trade and the domestic economy.

A closer look

Historiographical debate

The traditional view of Henry's (or Wolsey's) foreign policy, expresssed by historians writing before the 1960s, was that it was unrealistic, costly, failed to achieve significant territorial gains and was conducted for the benefit of his unreliable allies rather than English interests.

Evidence to support the traditional interpretation

The claim to the title 'King of France':

■ Henry's primary aim was to recover the title to the kingdom of France and so rebuild an English empire on the continent; however, Wolsey did not secure this title.

War against France 1512–14:

■ English troops were sent to Bayonne to assist Ferdinand recapture Navarre rather than to secure realistic English interests.

■ English troops took Therouanne and Tournai, both were soft targets. These 'victories' assisted Maximilian more than Henry VIII.

War against France 1523–5:

■ Charles V dissuaded Henry from his plan to capture Boulogne, which would have been realistic and useful, and encouraged him to campaign against Paris.

- Henry came within reach of Paris but was let down by the absence of the promised imperial reinforcements.
- Charles V refused to honour his treaty obligation that he would marry Mary Tudor.

Costs:

- Henry spent about £1,400,000 fighting wars between 1512 and 1525.

A more modern interpretation, developed by Peter Gwyn, is that Wolsey did consistently pursue English interests, sometimes through war, but also through diplomacy, and secured some significant achievements. He understood the need for flexibility in foreign relations and juggled the conflicting interests of the rulers of France and the Holy Roman Emperor. Even historians who are sympathetic to Wolsey are not wholly positive about foreign relations, and they do recognise the failures in the period from 1526 to 1529.

Evidence to support the modern interpretation

The claim to the title 'King of France':

- The importance of this claim was not in actually achieving it but to use the claim as a lever to force concessions out of the French.

The diplomatic value of Therouanne and Tournai:

- These towns were useful also as negotiating tools to use in diplomatic bargaining.

Diplomatic achievements:

- The Peace of London 1518 was Wolsey's most significant achievement in foreign relations as, while it proved prestigious, it avoided the danger of diplomatic isolation after Francis I marked his victory over the Swiss at the Battle of Marignano by signing treaties with several European powers.
- At the Field of the Cloth of Gold 1520, Wolsey appeared to be reconciled to France. He intended to put pressure on Charles V to give him good terms in an alliance. This shows Wolsey had a flexible approach to foreign relations.
- At the secret Treaty of Bruges 1521, Wolsey secured a realistic alliance with Charles V.

> **Activity**
>
> ### Challenge your thinking
>
> 'England's dealings with her neighbours during the years 1513 to 1529 were muddled, costly and shameful.'
>
> 'Henry and Wolsey were successful. After 1513, Henry was internationally regarded as a figure of splendid chivalric kingship, a reputation enhanced by the Field of the Cloth of Gold.'
>
> Which of these statements is the more accurate assessment of foreign relations in the years 1513 to 1529?

> **Activity**
>
> ### Revision exercise
>
> As you read through the rest of this chapter, identify the main events in foreign relations for each country. Use the table below to help you.
>
> | France | Burgundy | Holy Roman Empire | Spain | The Papacy | Scotland |
> |--------|----------|-------------------|-------|------------|----------|
> | | | | | | |

Fig. 6 *Europe in 1487*

Relations with France to 1521

Relations with France were fraught from the start of the reign because the new King dreamed of war against France to reclaim the ancient right of English kings to the throne of France. One interest group on the Counsel advised Henry VIII to avoid such a costly overseas commitment, however another faction counselled war against France. The anti-war faction held the early advantage. Archbishop Warham and Richard Fox advised the King to:

- secure a peace treaty with France in March 1510
- discuss the possibilities of war with Counsel in 1511, then dismiss the proposal as expensive and dangerous.

From 1511, however, the anti-war faction lost ground to the ascendant pro-war faction led by the Earl of Surrey. There are several reasons for this change in political fortunes.

1 By 1511, Surrey had won the argument in favour of war against France in Counsel.
2 Catherine of Aragon encouraged her new husband, Henry VIII, to declare war against France. She knew such action would reinforce her father's position as he annexed the kingdom of Navarre from France.
3 One of the key anti-war factions, Lady Margaret Beaufort, died a few months after her son. This proved useful to both the King and Thomas Wolsey.

Cross-reference

To recap on Henry VIII's Counsel and the immediate issues facing them, see pages 101–102.

Information on the European situation during the reign of Henry VII, including Navarre and the League of Cambrai, can be found on page 59.

Fig. 7 *A painting that records a series of events at the magnificent Field of the Cloth of Gold. Henry VIII arrived in the lower-left section, met and embraced the King of France in the upper-central section, and watched the tournament in the tiltyard in the upper-right section*

4   The international situation changed. The League of Cambrai formed in 1508 by the Pope to attack Venice had been too successful. The French, in particular, had considerable success in northern Italy, and the Pope now saw the French as a threat. He resumed his previous policy of playing off France and Spain against each other by forming the Holy League in 1511. The Holy League was a papal, Spanish and Venetian alliance against France, which England joined in November 1511.

Henry was drawn in 1511 into the anti-French Holy League with the Pope, Venetians, Swiss and Ferdinand of Spain. The Holy League was diplomatic preparation for his first war against France. By 1513, he also had an alliance with the emperor Maximilian. The war eventually provided Henry with several desired victories in northern France but proved to be a short-lived success. In 1514, Henry was deserted by both his allies, Ferdinand and Maximilian, so had to make terms with France.

The war against France

By February 1512, Henry was in a position to move towards a declaration of war against France by restating the ancient claim of the King of England to the kingdom of France. He called his second parliament to approve a subsidy for the war. The war had two distinct phases, beginning badly but then becoming much more successful after the project was re-engineered by the rising star of Henry VIII's government, Thomas Wolsey.

Phase 1: to April 1513

Henry was guided by his father-in-law Ferdinand of Spain under whose guidance he sent an expedition, led by the Marquis of Dorset, to help the Spanish. The English army landed near Bayonne in south-west France but proved ill-disciplined and achieved little more than to distract the French while Ferdinand achieved his objective of taking Navarre. Meanwhile, Henry's fleet was defeated off Brest. During this naval engagement Admiral Edward Howard, one of Henry's close friends, was killed.

Phase 2: to August 1514

Wolsey prepared and equipped a new army of 30,000 men to be led by the King himself when it set out from Dover bound for Calais. This time the army was allied to the Holy Roman Emperor, Maximilian, so advanced towards Flanders as agreed capturing the French fortress of Therouanne which was a threat to Maximilian's territories in the Netherlands. A French cavalry force, sent to relieve the fortress, was easily defeated by the superior numbers of English soldiers in a skirmish later glamourised with the title 'The Battle of the Spurs'. Soon afterwards the English laid quick and successful siege to the French city of Tournai. These various achievements gave the King the military glory he craved enabling him to return home in triumph.

The war in France continued after the King's departure but proved costly, so pressure for peace grew, especially after Ferdinand, then Maximilian, settled their differences with the King of France. Henry was greatly pleased with his military glory.

Anglo-French relations after 1514

Anglo-French relations remained tense for several reasons. The accession of Francis I in 1515 brought another 'young gun' to European politics who Henry VIII considered a rival. The Pope immediately feared further French aggression in Italy and appealed to his ally, Henry VIII, for support. Francis stirred unrest in Scotland against the English regent, Queen Margaret, who was Henry's sister.

Francis soon confirmed his status as a dynastic power in Europe. By September 1515, he had won a sweeping victory over the reputedly invincible Swiss at the Battle of Marignano in 1515, forced a treaty on the Pope, taken control of Milan and forced Queen Margaret to flee from Scotland. Wolsey searched desperately for allies against this expansion of French power, but failed. At this time, the European powers were engaged in extensive treaty making: Francis gained substantial land when he signed the Treaty of Noyon with Ferdinand's successor, Charles I; and Maximilian made peace with Francis I. England was isolated and diplomatically insignificant.

Wolsey seized the moment. Continuing Anglo-French tension became the spring-board for his greatest diplomatic triumph in the Treaty of London 1518, also known as the Treaty of Universal Peace. The treaty was made possible by Pope Leo X who called for peace between the warring states of Europe and international cooperation in a crusade against the Moslems who had been attacking Italy. Wolsey jumped on the papal bandwagon and suggested the core of European peace should be an Anglo-French peace treaty, but it should be strengthened by a non-aggression pact signed by the other nations who would collectively guarantee future peace. In securing this treaty, Wolsey demonstrated astute diplomatic judgement that brought glory on the King and built his own international reputation as peacemaker of Europe.

The consequent improvement in Anglo-French relations was evident at the Field of the Cloth of Gold in 1520, named after Henry VIII's magnificent marquee made of cloth of gold. There was jousting, wrestling, music and ostentatious wealth at this magnificent meeting between Henry VIII and Francis I, although nothing of diplomatic value was achieved.

Alison Weir vividly describes the events at the summit meeting between Henry VIII and Francis I in Henry VIII (Source 2).

The summit meeting later came to be known as the Field of the Cloth of Gold, in commemoration of the lavish display made there; some even called it the eighth wonder of the world. It cost Henry an estimated total of £15,000, while it took the French ten years to pay for their share of it.

Everyone was ordered to attend 'in their best manner, apparelled according to their estate and degrees'. The courtiers on both sides had nearly ruined themselves buying rich materials and accoutrements. King Henry was his usual peacock self, and would appear each day in a series of increasingly spectacular costumes; for months the king had been importing great quantities of rich fabrics, including 1,050 yards of velvet.

On 7 June, the Feast of Corpus Christi, as the cannons boomed simultaneously from Guisnes and Ardres, the two kings, accompanied by a host of courtiers, rode from their respective headquarters to meet each other. Henry VIII wore a cloth of gold and silver, heavily bejewelled, with a feathered black bonnet and his Garter collar; he rode a bay horse hung with gold bells that jangled as it moved, and he was attended by the Yeomen of the Guard. Francis I, in cloth of gold and silver encrusted with gems, and sporting white boots and a black cap, was flanked by his Swiss Guards. At the perimeter of the Val d'Or, the kings paused, then, to the sound of trumpets, they galloped alone towards each other, doffed their bonnets, and embraced whilst still on horseback.

There followed two weeks of courtesies, feasting, jousting, dancing and midsummer games, in which the two courts vied for supremacy.

2
*Alison Weir, **Henry VIII**, 2002*

Relations with the Holy Roman Empire to 1521

Henry had built an alliance with Maximilian in 1513 and co-operated with the emperor during the first war against France. Anglo-Imperial relations remained on a steady footing and Maximilian was one of the signatories of the Treaty of London; however, Maximilian's death three months later undermined the principles of peace. The growth of the English cloth trade to Flanders confirmed the benefits of sustained Anglo-Imperial co-operation.

The election of Charles V to the title Holy Roman Emperor in 1519 created an empire powerful enough to challenge the might of France. Wolsey had to work hard to preserve good relations with Charles V, meeting him twice in 1520, although Wolsey refused the emperor's invitation to join a war against France. Wolsey, at this stage, again demonstrated his flexible and deft handling of foreign relations.

He needed every ounce of skill to serve the King. Henry was enthusiastic about the Hapsburg alliance, which he planned to seal with marriage between Princess Mary and Charles V. Wolsey, however, desired peace. Over the period to 1521, England gradually moved into an alliance with the emperor and towards a declaration of war against France.

English response to the Hapsburg-Valois wars

Outbreak of war, April 1521

Francis I declared war on Charles V in April 1521 by invading Luxembourg. In August 1521, a conference was called at Calais, attended by representatives from France and the Empire, to find a way to avoid further conflict. Wolsey was chosen, as international peacemaker, to

Fig. 8 *Charles V was a monarch who ruled large areas of Europe from western Europe, to Italy and the Mediterranean, and who oversaw some of the explorations of the New World*

Cross-reference

Information on the cloth trade is to be found on page 90.

negotiate a peace deal; though both sides were, in reality, playing for time. He, therefore, could no longer win international plaudits as a peacebroker. Besides, he knew that Henry was looking to join the conflict, so the time had come for England to ally – either to Hapsburg or to Valois.

Double-dealing was typical of foreign relations during this very complex period of diplomacy. While the Calais conference was underway, Wolsey travelled to meet Charles V at Bruges where they secretly agreed to declare war on France if Francis refused to make peace. This treaty would be kept secret until Francis had paid the next instalment of the French pension, after which Charles agreed to compensate England for pension payments lost during the war. At this time, Charles also confirmed his intention to marry Princess Mary, Henry VIII's daughter by Catherine of Aragon, who was now five years old.

In 1522, England declared war on France. English troops were sent to Picardy where it soon became apparent that Charles V was much more committed to the fighting in northern Italy, especially after he successfully recovered Milan, than to the fighting in northern France. English fortunes improved in 1523 when the Duke of Bourbon, a powerful French nobleman, raised his army against Francis. Plans were swiftly drawn up for a three-pronged attack on Paris by the Dukes of Suffolk and Bourbon, and imperial forces from the Netherlands. Only Suffolk came close to Paris but was abandoned by his allies so had to return to England in disarray. Henry lost interest in the war and Wolsey returned to his natural habitat – the negotiating table.

Between the autumn of 1523 and early 1525, Wolsey made no positive contribution to the Hapsburg-Valois wars. He resisted Charles V's requests to send another English army to northern France while he opened secret negotiations with the French, although these achieved little. Charles V knew, through his agents, that his ally was likely to desert him.

The diplomatic revolution: English response to the wars, 1525–9

In the years to 1525, Wolsey had pursued the traditional line in English foreign relations, which was, essentially, pro-Imperial and anti-French. From 1525, however, the alliance with Charles V did not serve English interests for several reasons and Wolsey looked to build an alliance with France. This was a risky policy reversal because many Englishmen, particularly the conservative faction at court, opposed this new direction in foreign relations and it threatened diplomatic isolation if Francis and Charles settled their enmity at England's expense. By August 1525, Wolsey had opened negotiations for peace with the French, and the subsequent talks soon led to the Treaty of the More.

The creation of the anti-Hapsburg League of Cognac in 1526 confirmed the shift in diplomatic policy. The League included France and the Italian states (Venice, the papacy, Florence and the Duke of Milan). England gave financial assistance.

The diplomatic revolution was more marked in 1527 after the Sack of Rome, when the Pope effectively became the emperor's prisoner. Wolsey realised that he had even less chance of securing Henry VIII's marriage annulment so became more committed to the anti-Hapsburg position. Firstly, he signed the Treaty of Westminster, which declared perpetual peace between England and France, even with plans for the recently widowed Francis to marry Princess Mary. Later, in the same year, Wolsey travelled to Amiens to sign the Treaty of Amiens, an Anglo-French agreement to attack Charles V.

Exploring the detail

Reasons why the Hapsburg alliance failed to serve English interests from 1525

- Charles V opposed the annulment of the marriage between Catherine of Aragon and Henry VIII. This opposition became even more significant after the sack of Rome in 1527.
- Francis I had been heavily defeated by the imperial army at the Battle of Pavia, 1525. Charles was the dominant dynastic power in Europe so no longer needed his alliance with the English.
- Charles rejected Henry's proposal for an Anglo-French attack on France to capitalise on Pavia.
- Charles cancelled his proposed marriage to Princess Mary, agreed at Bruges in 1521.

Activity

Thinking point

Here are three reasons why Charles V did not wish Henry VIII to annul his marriage to Catherine of Aragon. Using the table below, consider the pros and cons of each reason. Then conclude which reason you think was the most important.

Reason	Evidence to support the reason	Evidence to counter the reason
To protect family honour		
To weaken the Tudor dynasty		
To prevent Henry VIII from making another marriage		

Exploring the detail

The Sack of Rome, 1527

In 1527, starving, mutinous soldiers in the army of the Holy Roman Emperor Charles V, commanded by the Duke of Bourbon, moved south and sacked Rome. They indulged in an orgy of looting and destruction that shocked the rest of Europe. Charles did not order the sacking, as he was in Spain at the time, but he benefited from it. The Pope was taken prisoner and therefore completely subdued. Charles V could order the Pope to refuse Herny VIII's request for annulment.

In January 1528, England declared war on Charles V. Wolsey imposed a trade embargo on the English cloth trade with Burgundy, as Henry VII had done, planning to put pressure on Charles to negotiate. In retaliation, Charles V ordered English merchants to be held hostage. The trade embargo led to widespread unemployment in England and coincided with a very poor harvest, economic conditions that culminated in trouble across the south west, south east and East Anglia by March 1528. Wolsey had no choice but to lift the embargo and face another humiliating climbdown.

The so-called 'Ladies' Peace' of 1529, also known as the Treaty of Cambrai, was negotiated by Margaret of Austria and Louise of Savoy to settle the conflict between France, the Empire and the Pope. The Treaty excluded English interests leaving England diplomatically isolated, and therefore unable to influence negotiations between Charles and Francis. This Treaty confirmed Charles' victory over Henry VIII.

It is important to remember that this diplomatic revolution was pushed through by the King. Wolsey preferred to be flexible; to keep his options open and to negotiate with both Francis and Charles. After 1525, however, he lost this flexibility because the King insisted on a rigid policy: oppose Charles V.

Fig. 9 *The illuminated title page for the Treaty of Peace signed between Henry VII and Francis I of France at Amiens*

Relations with the papacy

Henry VIII had good relations with the papacy until their disagreement over the annulment of the King's marriage to Catherine of Aragon.

Some historians, notably Alan Pollard writing in 1929, argued that Wolsey, as cardinal and papal legate, actually conducted foreign relations in the interests of the Pope. Pollard also argued that Wolsey was ambitious and aspired to become Pope himself. In 1527, when the Pope was effectively held prisoner by Charles V, Wolsey did put himself forward as a temporary pope, though this proposal soon lost any favour.

Cross-reference

The annulment of the marriage of Henry VIII and Catherine of Aragon is covered on page 132.

Henry VII's embargo on the cloth trade with Burgundy is discussed on page 93.

Key chronology

Relations between England and the papacy

1511 Holy League: England and the papacy sign the anti-French alliance.

1518 Pope Leo's call for 'Universal Peace' is reflected in the Treaty of London.

1519 Martin Luther publishes his criticisms of the Roman Catholic Church, and the papacy in particular.

1521 Henry publishes his fierce defence of the Pope and the Church In *Assertio Septem Sacramentorum.*

1526 League of Cognac: both England and the papacy sign this anti-Hapsburg alliance.

After

1527 The Pope is a prisoner of Charles V and, therefore, not free to make independent policy decisions so the King's 'Great Matter' becomes a contentious issue.

1529 League of Cambrai: the Pope signs the settlement that leaves England isolated.

Cross-reference

More information on Wolsey and his aims and objectives is to be found on page 103.

Later historians, inlcuding David Potter, have revised this view after examining Wolsey's immense efforts to secure the marriage annulment despite prolonged papal opposition, and have concluded that Wolsey really did put the King's interests before those of the papacy. They also comment that England was a small country with only medium-sized power, and the priority was to survive as European alliance shifted during the unpredictable Hapsburg-Valois wars.

Key profile

Pope Clement VII

Pope Clement VII was a member of the powerful Medici family from Florence. He had a high reputation for his political skill and was an accomplished diplomat, personal attributes he would need during his papacy. He was elected Pope in 1523 at a time when war raged between France, England and the Holy Roman Empire. He chose to back the French in an attempt to free the papacy from domination by the Holy Roman Empire.

A closer look

Historiography and foreign relations

Traditional interpretation

Historians tried to 'pigeon hole' Wolsey's foreign policies by applying, or attempting to apply, a coherent policy or consistent motivations. A. F. Pollard analysed Wolsey's foreign policies and found an on-going concern for the papacy. Pollard explained this concern as part of Wolsey's insatiable desire for ecclesiastical promotion, claiming that he ultimately dreamed of being pope.

Professor Scarisbrick also found evidence of a coherent policy. He wrote that Wolsey wanted peace. This is a challenging case since Wolsey rose to power as a war-monger and England went to war three times in the period he served as chief minister. Scarisbrick argued that the King was so obsessed by honour, glory and war that he ignored the chief minister's counsel for peace.

Revisionist interpretation

Revisionist historians do not try to see a consistent policy but regard Wolsey as pragmatic and opportunist. He needed to provide the King with the honour and glory required by a Renaissance prince. Wolsey knew from the start that England's involvement in the Hapsburg-Valois wars would prove fruitless but warfare was fundamental to the cult of Henry VIII's personal monarchy.

Wolsey was creative and flexible in his thinking. He needed to win honour and glory but this could be done through peace as much as war. The Peace of London 1518 and the Field of the Cloth of Gold were both testimony to Wolsey's wheeling and dealing, and energy. S. Gunn makes the point that Wolsey could exploit any opportunity to make peace or war.

Relations with Scotland

Scotland remained a great threat to Henry VIII because of its traditional alliance with France, since the main thrust of Henry's foreign relations was anti-French. James IV was married to Henry's sister Margaret but this did not secure his loyalty to the English monarch. As an Anglophobe, James had a history of supporting anti-Tudor impostures so there was little surprise that he intervened in the Anglo-French war in 1512 when a Scottish army marched on England with the intention of diverting English troops from France. This intervention, however, proved disastrous when the Scottish army was routed and King James killed at the Battle of Flodden Field in 1513.

The new king of Scotland, James V, was only 17 months old. Queen Margaret initially became regent but she had little support among the leading Scottish nobles who were encouraged by Francis I to resist her. She handed the regency over to the Duke of Albany, who was the heir to the throne and a cousin to the young King.

Anglo-Scottish relations remained tense throughout the Francophile Albany's governorship. When Henry prepared for the second war against France in 1523, he tried to remove the threat of invasion from the north by offering the Scots a 16-year truce and marriage between James V and Princess Mary, on condition that Albany was removed. The Scots refused so Henry sent an English army to ravage the borders.

There was a marked improvement in Anglo-Scottish relations after Albany departed in 1524 and the French had been defeated at the Battle of Pavia in 1525. The subsequent diplomatic revolution meant there were friendly relations between England and France, and therefore with Scotland too. James V was now old enough to begin ruling as King, encouraged by the resurgent Anglophile party at the Scottish court.

Summary questions

1. Who were England's enemies and friends in Europe in the years 1509 to 1529?

2. In what ways did English foreign policy change over the years 1514 to 1517?

3. Why did English foreign policy appear so inconsistent in the years 1517 to 1525?

4. Why was Wolsey unsuccessful in foreign affairs in the years 1525 to 1529?

Activity

Revision exercise

Research the Battle of Flodden, one of the most significant battles in Anglo-Scottish history.

Exploring the detail

The Battle of Pavia, 1525

During the Italian Wars, Francis I was determined to reclaim Lombardy from the Duke of Milan. The French army crossed the Alps and pushed the Milanese army back to Pavia. The French encircled the city walls for several months engaging in skirmishes and artillery bombardments, before deciding to starve the defenders out. The Milanese were reinforced by troops from Spain and the Holy Roman Empire, who made a surprise attack, and inflicted disastrous defeat on the French army.

Activity

Revision exercise

Construct a fortune graph of foreign relations 1509 to 1529. Plot the fortunes of English foreign relations with each European power: France; the Holy Roman Empire; the papacy; and Scotland. (You may wish to review the guidance on the fortune graph for Henry VII's foreign relations on page 70.)

Wolsey and the Church

In this chapter you will learn about:

- why historians disagree about the state of the Church in England before the Reformation

- why it was so important for Henry VIII to secure his succession

- the impact of the arrival of Anne Boleyn at court

- why Wolsey fell from power.

Fig. 1 *Cardinal Wolsey riding in procession to Westminster Hall, preceded by his great crosses, one for being Archbishop the other for papal legate, and his cardinal hat*

Key term

Sacraments: the seven sacraments were seven important religious ceremonies that Catholics received during their lifetime – baptism, confirmation, marriage, Extreme Unction, the Eucharist (mass), penance, and Holy Orders.

Cross-reference

The ideal of a Renaissance prince is described on page 99.

To review the ideas of the humanists and the anticlerics, including the Lollards; to recap on the condition of the Church during the reign of Henry VII; and to re-read the detailed profiles on Thomas More and John Colet, look back to Chapter 6.

Further information on Richard Fox can be found on pages 40, 81, 101 and 118.

Thomas Wolsey is discussed throughout Chapters 7, 8 and 10.

The condition of the Church

Before the coming of the Reformation in England, the Roman Catholic Church, with its round of services and **sacraments**, was widely accepted as the spiritual basis of daily living. The overwhelming majority of ordinary people believed and worshipped – no doubt with occasional grumbles – but essentially without fundamental criticism of the Church. There were critics – but these were very much the minority and they came from the educated elite. Humanists wanted to see the Roman Catholic Church retained, but improved by the removal of abuses. Among the critics were a very few people who were converts to the new Protestant faith. They believed the Roman Catholic Church contained fundamental flaws. These Protestants who challenged the fundamental ideas and doctrines of the Roman Catholic Church were known as heretics.

Humanism and anticlericalism

In the early days of Henry VIII's reign, the humanists were optimistic that the 'proven abuses' in the Church would be addressed. In 1511, John Colet, Dean of St Paul's Cathedral, preached a sermon to the assembled clergy in Convocation in which he outlined the major problems and abuses in the Church. This sermon did not, however, mean the Church was about to be radically reformed. Colet was addressing senior churchmen who had not been appointed by the King for their spirituality but for their education and their administrative skills. It was, therefore, inevitable that senior clergy like Richard Fox and Thomas Wolsey were often absent from their sees on the King's business.

Sir Thomas More was also working to reform the Church. More's visionary book, written in 1516, entitled *Utopia* about an ideal fictional island, criticised contemporary society, especially the Roman Catholic Church. He wanted to cleanse the Church of all its abuses and make it into a more effective institution by returning to the true faith. There is little evidence, however, that More weakened the Catholic Church or opened it up to Protestant attack.

Proven abuses

The humanists and anticlericals drew attention to a range of 'abuses' that they perceived to be endemic in the Roman Cathlolic Church. These were criticisms of church practices rather than principles.

Table 1 *Abuses in the Church*

Abuse	Detail about the abuse	Comment on the abuse
Lower clergy lacked knowledge about the faith	Many parish priests had limited education and little knowledge of Latin.	In 1511–12, Archbishop Warham visited 260 parishes in Kent. He found only four ignorant priests.
Financial abuse	The main complaint was against tithes paid directly to the Church. The sale of **indulgences** to secure time off from **purgatory** was a significant abuse.	In 1517, the Pope ordered the sale of indulgences. This finally prompted Luther's 95 Theses.
Simony	It was an offence to buy or sell any Church office.	In an age of patronage, it is difficult to assess how common the practice was.
Nepotism	This was the practice of making church appointments to members of your own family.	Thomas Wolsey secured church posts for his son. This highlights another problem – churchmen did not keep their vow of celibacy!
Absenteeism	This was often linked to pluralism. Sometimes a king kept a post vacant so the revenue would pass to the crown.	Absenteeism did not mean Church life stagnated. Absent bishops appointed deputies to carry out their episcopal duties.
Pluralism	Many clergymen held more than one Church office at the same time. Thomas Wolsey was a notable pluralist.	John Fisher, Bishop of Rochester, was an example of a pious churchman who worked hard to eliminate pluralism from the middle church ranks of deans and archdeacons.
Church services relied on pomp and ceremony	The Church had become more superstitious.	Financial extortion associated with relics is a good example of this abuse.
Religious houses were rich institutions that failed to use their wealth to support education and charitable purposes	This was the part of the Church most open to criticism.	Some monasteries had a reputation for extravagant standards of living rather than the poverty, chastity and obedience expected of Benedictine monks.
Privileges of Church courts	The Church had its own law courts run under canon law.	The Hunne case is an excellent example of the abuse of Church courts and prisons.

Key terms

Indulgences: Roman Catholics believed that they could reduce the time they had to spend in purgatory if they purchased an indulgence, or several indulgences.

Purgatory: Roman Catholics believed that at the Day of Judgement souls were sent to one of three places. The wicked went to everlasting hell, the virtuous to heaven, but most souls were sent to be cleansed in purgatory. The time spent being purged could be reduced by financial support for the Church, e.g. if a man left money in his will for private masses to be said after his death.

Cross-reference

The Hunne case is outlined on page 131.

Fig. 2 *There was little support for Lutheran doctine in England before the Reformation. In this woodcut, Pope Leo is supervising the burning of Luther's books after the first Diet of Worms in 1521 to restrict the spread of Protestantism in Europe*

Protestantism

The most significant Protestant critic of the Church in England before 1529 was William Tyndale, another humanist and scholar. He was strongly influenced by Lutheran ideas after Martin Luther published the 95 Theses, an event that marked the start of the Reformation in Germany. Tyndale widely criticised the Church for the poor quality of the clergy, the sale of indulgences, the doctrine of purgatory and, most importantly, for the use of Latin rather than the vernacular in all Catholic services and publications.

Tyndale's impact on religious affairs in England before the Reformation was limited, however, because he lived overseas where he translated the Bible into English. He published it abroad, although many copies found their way into England despite the strict laws against heresy.

It is important not to overstate the degree of support for Tyndale in England. Not one member of the nobility became Lutheran but instead all noblemen remained loyal to the Catholic Church before 1529. Besides, many humanists rejected Tyndale, including More who wrote 'A Dialogue Concerning Heresies' in 1526 primarily as a condemnation of Tyndale.

■ Key profile

Martin Luther

Martin Luther was an Augustinian monk who began to question the Pope's authority over the Church. In 1517, the Pope tried to raise money by selling indulgences and Luther became an outspoken critic of the Papacy. In that year he published *Disputation against Scholastic Theology*, questioning the Catholic theology he had been trained in. Two years later he nailed his 95 Theses to the door of the university church at Wittenberg.

Luther believed that Christians could reach salvation other than through the Roman Catholic Church. He did not believe that any man could be saved through ceremonies, sacraments or indulgences, but that man would be forgiven by God through His Grace. God was all-powerful and would forgive men's sins provided they had faith.

■ A closer look

Key anticlerical figures

William Tyndale

Tyndale was educated at Oxford but forced to live on the continent because of his heresy. He translated the New Testament into English because he believed, like Luther, that it should be available in the vernacular. His New Testament was smuggled into England in 1526. He also wrote *Obedience of a Christian Man*, in which he argued the Pope had usurped the power of the King of England, and it was time for the King to reclaim his sovereignty. Anne Boleyn had a copy, and historians know that Henry read this, despite it being heretical, because it is annotated in his own handwriting.

Thomas Cranmer

Cranmer was a humanist-educated Cambridge scholar. He was chaplain to Anne Boleyn's father, Lord Rochford, and he became a great ally of the Boleyn family and a staunch supporter of Henry VIII through the break from Rome. Cranmer was a keen reformist who, in 1530, wrote *Collectanea Satis Copiosa*. This was a collection of precedents from the scriptures, the early Church and British history, drawn together as proof that Henry VIII was an imperial power not subject to any other earthly authority. The *Collectanea* was clearly directed against the Pope who, it claimed, had usurped the King's sovereignty; therefore it was built on Tyndale's *Obedience of a Christian Man*.

Cranmer later supported the publication of Tyndale's New Testament in England, and would himself write Prayer Books in English in 1549 and 1552. He was burned for his heresy in the reign of Mary Tudor.

Activity

Thinking point

'Superficial similarities conceal fundamental differences.' Examine the similarities and differences between humanist and Protestant critics of the Roman Catholic Church in England before the Reformation.

Continuing support for the Roman Catholic Church

There is considerable evidence that few questioned the **liturgy** or practices of the Roman Catholic Church. The Church had many loyal defenders during the years leading up to 1529 who followed the public lead given by their King. Henry VIII's response to Luther's 95 Theses was to write *Assertio Septem Sacramentorum* – a defence of the seven sacraments at the heart of the Catholic faith. The Pope demonstrated gratitude to the King for this open defence against the Lutheran challenge by awarding him the title *Fidei Defensor* (FD, literally 'Defender of the Faith').

Other literature provides plentiful evidence of Catholic support since printing presses in England produced more conservative publications than Protestant or anticlerical tracts. An example of these conservative publications is *The Pilgrimage of Perfection*, a popular Catholic handbook published by William Bond in 1526, followed the next year by *The Directory of Conscience*. Even more convincingly *The Primer*, a well-established medieval collection of Latin and English devotional works, sold 41 editions in the years from 1521 to 1530.

Further evidence that Catholicism was flourishing in the 1520s was the way in which ordinary citizens were leaving significant sums of money in their wills to various religious causes ranging from church building to private masses, and from religious houses to

Key term

Liturgy: the form of public worship of a specific religious group. It can be formal such as the elaborate ritual of Catholic mass. It can also refer to the standardised order of events during a religious service.

Fig. 3 *This is a procession of clergy and nobility riding through the streets of London to Parliament in 1512. The figures are wearing their ceremonial robes and are carrying symbols of their offices. Three figures are identified by name and by their coat of arms – the Archbishop of Canterbury, the Bishop of London and the Duke of Buckingham*

church ornaments. The new steeple of Louth church, in Lincolnshire, cost an immense £305 and took 15 years to complete.

According to the historian Christoper Haigh, on the whole, people in England seem to have accepted the condition of the Roman Catholic Church in England without question. Christopher Haigh's research into the evidence of bequests in wills suggests that most people were satisfied with the Church and trusted their parish priest. The Church was fixed in the heart of local communities providing protection against evil and the way to salvation, services from baptism to the Last Rites, and varied practical assistance including alms, hospitality, health care and education.

A closer look

The Church before the Reformation – historiographical debate

The state of the Church in England before the Reformation is a key debate amongst historians.

Geoffrey Elton studied Tudor state documents to find evidence that all was not well with the Church. Elton, a refugee from totalitarian Europe, harboured immense faith in British institutions of government so readily accepted state records as the basis of his judgements.

> The changes which came over the Church sprang from deep causes, from the condition of the Church and the anomaly of its privileged position within a growingly more centralised national state... Hostility to clergy and papacy drew support from various intellectual and religious movements – remnants of Lollardy, noticeable among the lower orders, humanist dissatisfaction with the existing condition of the Church, the beginnings of Lutheranism in the English universities – but it is more to the point that they came to involve the interests of the Crown.

1

*G. R. Elton, **The Tudor Constitution**, 1982*

Andrew Dickens researched into Lollardy and the spread of Protestantism in Yorkshire. He found evidence that ordinary people in England were taking on continental ideas about the Church and demanding change. Dickens wrote in the 1960s, a period dominated by active people power, hence his 'bottom-up' interpretation of the causes of the Reformation.

> Anticlericalism probably owed less to the actual faults of the clergy than to a gradual shift in the attitudes of lay society. Lay resentment against tithes and against the moral jurisdiction and the heavy probate fees of the church courts, the rise of lay education, the import of Bibles in English, the declining reputation of the Roman Curia, the survival of Lollardy and neo-Lollard anti-church opinion, the inveterate hostility of the common lawyers, the long-remembered scandal of Richard Hunne, the colourful but disastrous experiment with Thomas Wolsey; all these influences and many more had created a sharply critical atmosphere, particularly in London.

2

*A. G. Dickens, **The English Reformation**, 1999*

Christopher Haigh's research into wills left in Lancashire revealed widespread satisfaction with the Church and little evidence of a yearning for reform. He concluded that the Reformation was imposed 'top-down' on the realm by the King and his ministers.

The parish priest was, after all, the dispenser of saving sacraments, the pastor and reconciler, and one of the leaders of the village. The high level of recruitment to the clergy does not suggest that laymen were contemptuous of priesthood.

From the point of view of the parishes, the Reformation was an external, autonomous event, which they had in no sense chosen, caused or contributed towards. If we seek the origins of the Reformation, we shall find them not in any general 'anticlericalism' but in the aspirations of particular interest groups: the common lawyers who coveted ecclesiastical legislation and the Court politicians who aimed to make or salvage careers by taking advantage of the king's concern for the succession.

3   *Adapted from Christopher Haigh (ed.),* **The English Reformation Revisited***, 1987*

Key profile

Thomas Cromwell

Thomas Cromwell trained as a lawyer and entered parliament in 1523. He became the King's most important minister from 1532. He was a Protestant reformer who rose to political prominence through his good relationship with Anne Boleyn.

The extent of anticlerical feeling

It is difficult to assess accurately the levels of anticlerical feeling. One of the most celebrated anticlerical cases concerned Richard Hunne; indeed Thomas More discussed the case at length in his *Dialogue of Heresies*. The background to the case was one of the most contentious issues – Church demands for mortuary payments. Richard Hunne, a London merchant, refused to pay the mortuary fee after his infant son died in 1511. The grieving father responded with a series of law suits during which his house was searched and a large quantity of Lollard literature was found. Hunne was arrested as a suspected heretic by the Bishop of London. Hunne was found dead in his cell having probably been strangled. Popular opinion in London was outraged by this case; however, it does not prove that the country was ripe for religious reformation.

It is clear that support for anticlerical ideas was localised, tending to emerge in urban communities with higher numbers of educated people, often with access to new Protestant ideas from the European mainland. Merchants, lawyers, and chroniclers in London and the main ports, and intellectuals in the university cities of Oxford and Cambridge therefore determined the anticlerical hotspots. Typical anticlerical activists were found in a group of young men who met at the 'White Horse' tavern in Cambridge to discuss the state of the Church and the need for reform. Amongst those debating the best solutions were Robert Barnes, a scholar and prior who spoke publicly against arrogant priests, and Thomas Cranmer, later Archbishop of Canterbury.

Historians also examine a range of contemporary writing to gauge the level of anticlerical feeling. Geoffrey Chaucer wrote *The Canterbury Tales* in the 1380s and 1390s taking great pleasure in satirising the churchmen on the pilgrimage, including the pardoner and the summoner. Edward Hall, a Londoner who was educated at Cambridge University, before becoming a lawyer and MP wrote *Chronicles* recording the depth of anticlerical feeling in London. Simon Fish, a lawyer, wrote *A Supplication for the Beggars*, in which he begged the King to take action against the greedy churchmen. These written sources are useful but have to be considered as the works of literate activists rather than as evidence of widespread public opinion.

Wolsey and policy towards the Church

Many humanists were optimistic that Wolsey would introduce effective church reforms in the spirit of Erasmus. Wolsey certainly listened carefully and sympathetically to the case put by leading humanists such as John Colet and Thomas More. In 1519, Wolsey announced he would summon a legatine Counsel to overhaul the Church.

As **papal legate** from 1518, Wolsey had sweeping powers to reform both the regular and the secular clergy but he proved to be surprisingly ineffective. He had plans to reform the lifestyle of the **regular clergy** but took only limited action when he introduced new statutes for the Benedictine and Augustinian Orders; intervened in some monastic elections; and removed four inappropriate monastic heads. As far as the **secular clergy** were concerned he had a plan to set up 13 new English bishoprics, but this was incomplete.

Far from reforming the Church, Wolsey actually undermined it by paving the way for the general **dissolution of the monasteries** during the later 1530s. Between 1524 and 1529, he dissolved 30 religious houses and used the money to found and endow new colleges at Ipswich and Oxford.

The King's 'Great Matter' and the reasons for the fall of Wolsey

The question of annulment

Cross-reference

Humanists, including Thomas More, Erasmus and John Colet, and their ideas are discussed on pages 82–84.

Key terms

Papal legate: this prestigious appointment by the Pope meant that Wolsey was the most powerful churchman in England, he could claim precedence over the Archbishop of Canterbury.

Regular clergy: the monks and nuns who lived their lives according to regulations in religious houses.

Secular clergy: churchmen who served the everyday world as priests and bishops.

Dissolution of the monasteries: the name given to Thomas Cromwell's policy after 1536, during which he forced the closure of all religious houses. He seized their assets and sold their land to raise revenue for the King.

Fig. 4 *This painting by Marcus Stone (1840–1921) depicts the rivalry between Catherine of Aragon and Anne Boleyn. Catherine, standing in a doorway, watches the King and Anne flirt with a picture of the Queen behind them. Anne, an accomplished courtier, had been playing the lute for the King watched by a gathering of courtiers. Wolsey looks on, apparently helpless. The little dog is an ironic touch because it represents fidelity*

The first duty of royal marriage was to secure the succession. Catherine of Aragon had several miscarriages, gave birth to three infants who were still-born or died within a week of birth, and to two infants who died within weeks of birth. She and Henry had one surviving child, Princess Mary, born in 1516.

By 1527, Henry VIII had an acute succession problem and had decided he needed to annul his marriage to Catherine of Aragon. He had no prospect of a legimate son because Catherine was 42 years old and was unlikely to conceive another child. Henry had an illegitimate son, Henry, Duke of Richmond, by his mistress Bessie Blount; however, he needed a legitimate heir to secure the Tudor succession, for he feared political chaos would result from Princess Mary's succession. There was no precedent for a female ruler in England.

Other factors influenced his desire for an annulment. His marriage to Catherine of Aragon now had less political value than in 1509 because the Spanish-Imperial alliance had been replaced after 1525 with pro-French foreign relations. Wolsey drew up the League of Cognac 1526 as an anti-imperialist stance after the Emperor Charles V's sweeping victory over France at the Battle of Pavia.

In the meantime, Henry had become infatuated with Anne Boleyn who, coyly, refused to become his mistress. Anne had served Henry's younger sister Mary while Queen of France. After Mary returned to England, Anne remained at the French court in the service of the new Queen, where she became a highly-skilled courtier.

Key profile

Anne Boleyn

Anne was the second daughter of Sir Thomas Boleyn and Elizabeth Howard, daughter of the Duke of Norfolk. The Boleyn family made their way up at court where Sir Thomas had been an Esquire of the Body, a companion in arms, to Henry VII. He further developed his court career under Henry VIII when he was sent on a diplomatic assignment in 1512 to the Netherlands. Here the Archduchess agreed to take Anne as a *fille d'honneur*. Two years later Anne moved to the court of the King of France, to serve in the Queen's household. She was an accomplished courtier by her return to England.

Thomas Boleyn rose rapidly on the back of his daughter's success at court. He was granted the title Lord Rochford and in 1529, immediately after the fall of Wolsey, was created Earl of Wiltshire. Similarly, his son, George Boleyn, rose swiftly becoming a trusted member of the King's Privy Chamber.

The most famous portrait of Anne Boleyn confirms contemporary opinion that the Queen was not beautiful but was certainly attractive to men, in particular her eyes were dark and alluring. Her face was thin, she had high cheekbones, a small mouth and a pointed chin. Her daughter, Elizabeth, inherited these features. Anne was an accomplished and well-educated woman, with a lively interest in creative arts and theology. She sang and played the lute well, had mastered many complex dance steps, and wrote poetry.

Key chronology

Marriage of Henry VIII and Catherine of Aragon

11 June 1509 Henry VIII marries Catherine of Aragon.

By 1527 Henry VIII decides his marriage is not lawful.

1528–9 Cardinal Campeggio arrives to hear the case for annulment with Cardinal Wolsey in a legatine court.

1529 The Reformation parliament is called.

Cross-reference

The Spanish-Imperial alliance is covered on page 121.

Fig. 5 *This is the most famous portrait of Anne Boleyn and has become the definitive image of Anne with the famous 'B' pendant. It is not contemporary but is thought to be a copy of a lost original*

David Starkey analyses the early stages of the relationship between Henry VIII and Anne Boleyn (Source 4).

In France she learned her musical skills and her extraordinary gracefulness and poise in dancing. The French court, even more than its English counterpart, was a centre of literary and artistic patronage. Here she picked up the interests of a sparkling Renaissance court, and refined her own natural gifts of intellect.

Unmarried and distinctly eligible, Anne Boleyn was unleashed on the English court at the beginning of 1522. She was not a great beauty but extraordinarily attractive and stood out in any company. She was tall, and had a fine head of dark hair, but the reason for her attractiveness lay partly in her French-trained accomplishments, and partly in a kind of animal magnetism which was extremely hard to define, but which could perhaps be most simply described as sex appeal.

The game of courtly love so much favoured by the Tudors offered great scope to a young woman of wit. Queen Catherine had never really had an opportunity to play it for she had only ever known the English court as queen, however her ladies were expected to participate with enthusiasm. The court was always short of women and boredom was a constant enemy, so this relatively harmless pastime was very popular. Normally the exchange of compliments and tokens, the arch dialogue and clandestine assignations meant very little.

Some time during the winter of 1525–26 she began to play the game of courtly love with the king himself. Imperceptibly a conventional game of courtly love became a serious affair. By the summer of 1526 she knew that she had hooked a very dangerous fish.

 *David Loades, **Henry VIII and his Queens**, 1994*

Philippa Gregory's historical novel *The Other Boleyn Girl* described Anne's first significant appearance at court in 1522. The story is narrated by Anne's elder sister, Mary, who was also the King's mistress. This novel is a work of fiction based on historical research.

Cardinal Wolsey sent a message to the queen asking us to take part in a masque on Shrove Tuesday, which he was to stage in his house, York Place: a great masque, a fortress named Chateau Vert and five ladies to dance with five knights who would besiege the fort.

The arrival of the master of the revels to teach us our steps for the dance was the signal for a savage battle fought with smiles and the sweetest words as to who would play which role. In the end the queen intervened and gave us our parts. She gave me the role of Kindness, the king's sister Queen Mary got the plum part of Beauty, Jane Parker was Constancy. Anne herself was Perseverance.

We were to be attacked by Indian women – in reality the choristers of the royal chapel – before being rescued by the king and his chosen friends. We were warned that the king could be disguised and we should take great care not to penetrate the transparent ruse of a golden mask strapped on a golden head, taller than anyone else in the room.

It was a great romp in the end, much more of a play-fight than a dance. George flung rose petals at me and I drenched him with showers of rosewater. When we ladies came out from the castle and danced with the mystery knights it was the tallest knight who came to dance with me.

The musicians finished the dance and waited, poised for the king's orders. 'Unmask!' he said and tore his own mask off his face. I saw the king of England, then gave a wonderful little gasp. Anne, fast as a snake, unpinned my mask so that my golden hair tumbled down like a stream over the king's arm.

 5   *Philippa Gregory, **The Other Boleyn Girl**, 2002*

David Loades makes reference to the same event in his book *Henry VIII and his Queens* (Source 6).

Her first public appearance was in a pageant connected with a tournament held on Shrove Tuesday, the assault on the *Chateau Verte*, in which Anne appeared as the allegorical character Perseverance. Her sister, Mary, featured in the same pageant as Kindness, and the Duchess of Suffolk as Beauty.

6   *David Loades, **Henry VIII and his Queens**, 1994*

The case for the annulment

Henry was a loyal Catholic so he interpreted the absence of a male heir as God's intervention. He became convinced that by marrying Catherine he had broken the law of God from the Old Testament, and that Pope Julius II had been incorrect to give the 1509 dispensation that preceded the marriage. Henry, an accomplished Biblical scholar, found a passage in the Old Testament book of Leviticus that confirmed his judgement; then concluded that his marriage had never been lawful before God. This was the case for an annulment, rather than a divorce.

Leviticus 20:21: 'If a man marries his brother's wife, they will die childless. He has done a ritually unclean thing, and has disgraced his brother.'

Henry recruited Richard Wakefield, the reader in Hebrew at Oxford University, to give his opinion on the Biblical passage. Wakefield advised him that 'childless' in Leviticus meant 'male childless' in Hebrew texts.

The Bible was not straightforward however, as opponents of the annulment were swift to point out. Another section of text in the Bible contradicted Leviticus for verses in Deuteronomy specifically stated that a man had a duty to marry his dead brother's wife.

Deuteronomy 25:5: 'If two brothers live on the same property and one of them dies, leaving no son, then his widow is not to be married to someone outside the family; it is the duty of the dead man's brother to marry her.'

(Extracts quoted from *The Bible - Good News Bible*, the Bible Society, Collins/Fontana, 1976.)

The role of Cardinal Wolsey

Once Henry had decided to proceed with the annulment, known as the 'Great Matter', he presumed that swift success was guaranteed. He consulted his chief minister, then asked him to liaise with the Pope and secure the annulment.

It seemed very straightforward. Wolsey advised the King that all he needed was the Pope to declare the papal dispensation invalid, so ruling that Henry and Catherine had never been legally man and wife, and the supposed marriage would be annulled. This should not be difficult as there were many precedents for such an annulment and the Pope owed

 Activity

Talking point

Think about other historical novels, or poems, paintings or films. One obvious point is that each is a source for the period in which it was written or painted rather than the period it is purporting to represent; for instance, Shakespeare's history plays are good sources for contemporary Tudor attitudes towards politics and society, rather than historical sources about Richard III or Macbeth.

1 Does this mean that imaginative writing and painting has no value to a historian?

2 Are there any circumstances in which such works can add to historical understanding?

 Cross-reference

For the rise of Cardinal Wolsey, including his appointments as Archbishop, Cardinal and Papal Legate, see page 104.

Henry a favour for his intervention and defence against Luther in *Assertio Septem Sacramentorum*. Besides, Wolsey himself had good contacts in Rome being both Cardinal Archbishop and Papal Legate.

With hindsight, it is clear that this decision was a watershed in the reign of Henry VIII. The King directed the Great Matter, as he had not directed any previous policy, for he not only decided that he wanted annulment but he insisted on the nature of the arguments Wolsey would present to the Pope. The minister tried in vain to persuade the King to adopt a less technical and more diplomatic approach as foreign policy and domestic public opinion swung against annulment. He worked very hard to secure the annulment for two years knowing he had to keep the King's favour, trust and affection to retain his power.

Wolsey made the Great Matter public in May 1527 when he, as Papal Legate, summoned Henry to appear before a stage-managed legatine court to address issues concerning the salvation of the royal soul. The search for annulment was now firmly in the public domain.

Catherine's response

Catherine of Aragon was a devout Catholic, a dedicated wife, and a proud and politically astute queen who had been trained from childhood to fight to defend her own interests. She opposed the annulment from the start as it would mean her only daughter would be declared illegitimate and removed from succession, and that she would be presented as a royal mistress not wife. She stuck to her argument that her marriage with Arthur had never been consummated, and that she had been a virgin when she married Henry, so the Leviticus argument did not apply. She knew that she had the judicial right to oppose the annulment by appealing to the Pope in Rome. Her overt, sustained opposition was a key reason for Henry's failure to secure the annulment and for Wolsey's ultimate fall.

Catherine was popular in England and came to be seen as the victim of Henry's sexual lust for another woman by many at court and within the royal family. Her marriage to Henry had been happy and politically successful so Catherine came to believe that her husband's head was being filled with evil thoughts by his advisors, especially Wolsey. Many at court shared this judgement, being jealous of Wolsey and resentful of his influence over the King.

There were other reasons for the failure to secure an annulment from the Pope. Henry was undiplomatic in asking the current pope, Clement VII, to agree that a previous pope had acted illegally by issuing the 1509 dispensations. More importantly, the Pope was not free to make such a decision. The Holy Roman Emperor, Charles V, held the whiphand in 1527 after the sack of Rome by imperial forces. The Pope was effectively Charles' prisoner. Charles V was Catherine's nephew and may have wished to protect Hapsburg family pride from the stigma of divorce. He certainly preferred to keep his rival, Henry VIII, in an heirless marriage rather than to let him loose on the European marriage scene.

Wolsey realised that he needed to campaign hard for the marriage annulment but his diplomatic position was precarious. England had no established links among the cardinals and had no permanent presence in the Papal Curia. Instead, Wolsey relied on a succession of individual missions to Rome by William Knight, Stephen Gardiner and Edward Foxe but these men proved to be ineffective as they did not understand the finer intricacies of papal politics.

Cross-reference

The Sack of Rome is described on page 123.

Key profile

Stephen Gardiner

Stephen Gardiner, an expert in canon and civil law, rose to prominence in the service of Thomas Wolsey, who made him his secretary. He was sent to Rome on several occasions to try to negotiate the annulment, but without success, although he was rewarded with the post of King's secretary. He acquired several church posts including the archdeaconry of Taunton and Norfolk, before he was appointed Bishop of Winchester in 1531. Gardiner's career continued into the reign of Mary Tudor.

There was intense activity and fevered speculation throughout 1528 over the annulment. Wolsey's agents' journeys were long and dangerous, generating agonising delays, there were rumours that the Pope had died, and further rumours that draft papal annulments had been sealed, followed by accusations of forgery. Other events added to the King's frustration, especially the fierce outbreak of sweating sickness during the summer of 1528. As the epidemic spread, Wolsey ended the legal term prematurely, the King fled from the capital, and even Anne Boleyn herself fell ill.

The Pope temporarily escaped from the emperor's control so was able to appear willing to hear the case for annulment. He sent a second legate, Cardinal Campeggio, to England to try the case with Wolsey. Henry was encouraged by this appointment because Campeggio was the absentee Bishop of Salisbury so favoured by the King. He arrived in December 1528 after a painfully slow journey from Rome and it became clear that Campeggio, like the Pope, was playing for time. He tried a new approach by trying to persuade Catherine to enter a nunnery. This would have solved the problem as it would have ended her marriage to the King while safeguarding Princess Mary's legitimacy and claim to the throne of England. Catherine refused to contemplate such a resolution.

Key profile

Cardinal Campeggio

Cardinal Campeggio was sent to England in 1518 as part of Pope Leo X's peace mission that culminated in the celebrated Treaty of London. Henry VIII rewarded Campeggio with the bishopric of Salisbury. He became even more important at the Papal curia under Pope Clement VII but lost everything in the Sack of Rome in 1527. Nevertheless, he was named legate to hear the annulment case in London, but was unable to resolve the question and returned to Rome.

As events drew out Henry was increasingly anxious about his wife's stubborn refusal, becoming furiously impatient and more convinced of the justice of his case for annulment. He was entrenched in his view that his marriage was unnatural. At Bridewell Palace in London, the King made a speech to assembled notables to counter growing hostility as tempers flared in this bitter public scandal.

The legatine court presided over by Cardinals Wolsey and Campeggio finally opened at Blackfriars on 18 June 1528. On the first day, Catherine made an emotional public appeal to Henry confirming the validity of her marriage and her right to appeal to Rome, and then walked out. After that, her defence was conducted, in her absence, by Bishop John Fisher who was vocal in his defence of the marriage from the start.

J. J. Scarisbrick vividly casts light on the drama of the Blackfriars Court (Source 7).

The extraordinary legatine court charged with the task of passing sentence on Henry's marriage opened on 18 June at Blackfriars. Henry appeared by proxy, but, to the surprise of all, Catherine came in person, attended by four bishops, to protest loudly against the judges and announce her appeal to Rome. Three days later the court met again. Henry and Catherine were both there. First the judges announced they had overruled Catherine's protest; then Henry, seated beneath a canopy of cloth of gold, spoke to the court about his great scruple, his desire only for justice and deliverance from doubt. When he had finished, Catherine suddenly rose to her feet and, moving round the court-room, came to Henry to kneel before him and deliver a long plea to him not to cast her aside, not to dishonour her and her daughter. Only Rome, she said, could settle this matter and hence to Rome she appealed. Having said this, she withdrew. Three times the crier called her back, but she paid no heed. She would never return. The court would declare her contumacious [disobedient], but she no longer acknowledged its jurisdiction, and it was left to her Counsel, particularly Fisher, to conduct her defence henceforth.

Fisher fought like a lion. Two sessions later, on 28 June, he unleashed a thundering speech affirming the validity of the marriage and proclaiming his readiness to lay down his life, as John the Baptist, for the cause of matrimony. This speech drew a stinging reply, probably composed and delivered by Gardiner in the king's name, in which Fisher was accused of arrogance, temerity [excessive boldness], disloyalty and other shortcomings.

 7   *J. J. Scarisbrick, **Henry VIII**, 1981*

On 18 July, Pope Clement recalled the case to Rome.

As proceedings went against the King and his minister, so their foreign policy unravelled. On 5 August 1529 France made peace with the Holy Roman Emperor at Cambrai so ending any slight hope Wolsey nursed of being able to further influence the Pope.

 Activity

Thinking point

Examine the implications in August 1529 of the argument over annulment for each of the following:

	Implications of the argument over annulment by August 1529
Henry VIII	
Catherine of Aragon	
Thomas Wolsey	
The authority of the Pope in England	

The decline of Wolsey

By August 1529, Wolsey was a spent political force in England, and an easy target for his political opponents who aimed to prosper from Wolsey's fall. There was no doubt that Wolsey was in disgrace and that Anne Boleyn, Norfolk and the rest of their faction were determined to be rid of him for good.

Henry actually protected Wolsey from the wrath and vengeance of his enemies after the failure of the legatine court in July 1529 by not instantly dismissing him, but waiting until the start of the Michaelmas law term on 9 October 1529. On this day, Wolsey, as Lord Chancellor, was required to be present at the opening of the courts of Chancery and Star Chamber. The King had to act against his erstwhile close friend and removed him from power.

Wolsey was expelled from the law courts, dismissed from his position as Lord Chancellor, and prosecuted for praemunire. He surrendered himself and his possessions to the King. Henry allowed him to retire to his house at Esher and keep the title Archbishop of York, although he confiscated all Wolsey's wealth.

In April the following year, Wolsey retired to York, where he started to correspond with French and Imperial agents, trying to launch a political comeback. This correspondence was presented to the King as treason by Wolsey's political enemies.

Following his arrest in November 1530, Wolsey began a slow journey south. He died of dysentery at Leicester Abbey on 29 November.

A closer look

What happened next? Catherine of Aragon and Anne Boleyn after 1529

The stalemate over the annulment continued for four years after the fall of Wolsey. The King had called parliament in 1529 to solve the crisis but the deadlock persisted. There are different historical explanations for this inertia. Some historians present the King as indecisive, hampered by the lack of a determined and clear-thinking chief minister, enslaved by factional strife, and unable to find a solution to the problem until Thomas Cromwell emerged in 1532. Other historians interpret the period as years of preparation for the dramatic and revolutionary break from Rome. The King needed to develop the concept of sovereignty and to test the strength of clergymen's resistance.

Two vital events in 1532 led to the break from Rome. After Warham's death, Henry was able to appoint a new Archbishop of Canterbury; he chose Thomas Cranmer. Anne Boleyn finally agreed to become the King's mistress, and fell pregnant. Henry VIII had nine months to ensure that his child, assumed male, would be a legitimate heir. He had to move speedily to end his marriage to Catherine of Aragon and marry Anne Boleyn.

Henry VIII secured the annulment by declaring that he, the King, rather than the Pope, had supreme power over the Church in England. He declared his supremacy through Act of parliament. Archbishop Cranmer then declared that the King's marriage to Catherine had been null and void. The Great Matter was resolved.

Reasons for the fall of Wolsey

Wolsey's fall from political dominance was gradual and brought about by many, often interconnected, reasons.

Key chronology
The fall of Wolsey

9 October 1529 Wolsey is dismissed from his position as Lord Chancellor and prosecuted, but is allowed to retire and keep the title Archbishop of York.

April 1530 Wolsey retires to York, from where he begins a correspondence that is regarded as treasonable.

November 1530 Wolsey is arrested, and dies on the journey to London.

Fig. 6 *Mother Shipton prophesised the important events yet to come. Most famously she prophesised that Wolsey, although Archbishop of York, would not see York. It now appears that the prophecies were hoaxes written after the events for none were published before 1641*

Cross-reference

To revisit the question of whether Wolsey was the servant or master of Henry VIII, return to page 107.

Information on the Amicable Grant is provided on page 112.

Political enemies

The chief minister had retained his political power from 1515 to 1525 because he was able to outsmart his opponents and because he had a golden touch. He had, however, made significant numbers of enemies, often very powerful men, who were waiting to get revenge. Over the 10 years he had confronted noblemen, Londoners, taxpayers, churchmen as he enforced the King's law and increased the King's revenues. Contemporaries resented his lavish lifestyle and perceived him to be *alter rex* (literally, the 'other king', implying that Wolsey was the master, rather than the servant). Wolsey found after 1525 that he was also a relatively isolated figure lacking the protection of influential friends and family.

The failure of the Amicable Grant

Wolsey began to lose his influence after the debacle of the Amicable Grant. This allowed his political enemies, notably the Dukes of Norfolk and Suffolk, an opportunity to begin to undermine the minister's influence over the King. Wolsey held some of the blame as he had failed to raise sufficient revenue from the 1523 subsidy, so had to resort to a forced loan or benevolence in 1525 to fund the war against Charles V. This controversial benevolence had been agreed by Counsel, yet became Wolsey's sole responsibility when it failed disastrously with the revolt in East Anglia that was suppressed by the Duke of Norfolk. Through this, the duke gained credibility with the King, whilst Wolsey's fortunes declined. Henry himself afterwards claimed he had no knowledge of the benevolence. Wolsey had no choice but to accept responsibility and the attendant public humiliation.

Opposition to Wolsey's foreign policy

The majority of Henry's courtiers, especially the Dukes of Norfolk and Suffolk, were pro-imperial-Burgundian, so opposed Wolsey's foreign policy reversal after 1525 when he created a French alliance, known as the League of Cognac 1526, against the Holy Roman Emperor. England did not actually join the League but was on the fringes and offered financial assistance. Foreign relations proved key to Wolsey's fall. His departure for Amiens in 1527, to agree a new Anglo-French treaty intended to put pressure on Charles V, meant he was absent from court on unpopular business. Wolsey's position was further weakened when the French were again defeated by Charles V in Italy. As a result, the Pope made a treaty with Charles V in 1529, and the French followed his example, leaving England diplomatically isolated. The vultures gathered.

Increasing isolation from the King

The great weakness in Wolsey's position became apparent. He was often separated from the King at a time when access to the King was crucially important in building and retaining political power. Previously, when the King went on summer progress around the country, Wolsey had stayed at Hampton Court or Westminster, effectively to carry on the business of government for the King. During the legal terms, Wolsey had been based at the law courts in Westminster but had gone to the court at Greenwich on Sundays to dine with the King and usually attend a Counsel meeting. He had communicated with the King regularly by letter or messenger, and this had proved sufficient to protect his position until 1525.

The Dukes of Norfolk and Suffolk along with Anne Boleyn's father, Lord Rochford, were based at the court in Greenwich where, from 1525, they increasingly replaced Wolsey as the King's chief confidants, as was particularly noticeable when they gave him advice on foreign policy. Before Wolsey left for Amiens in 1527, the King was already consulting Norfolk and Rochford about Wolsey's letters, but during the minister's absence he began to consult them on policy without reference to Wolsey. By March 1529, the King was showing all his European correspondence to Norfolk, Suffolk and Rochford. Wolsey's political influence was clearly waning.

Wolsey recognised this weakness in his ministerial position and so introduced the Eltham Ordinances for the Regulation of the Court, which were designed to restrict other advisors' access to the King. The King had become aware that Wolsey's immense executive power had left him short of counsellors at court at a time when he wanted to take more personal charge over foreign and domestic policy. He demanded that Wolsey should appoint more counsellors. This threatened a further weakening of Wolsey's hold on power.

Cross-reference

Further information on the Eltham Ordinances can be found on page 111.

Instead, Wolsey executed a superb triumph of style over substance with the Eltham Ordinances. These ordinances appeared to give the King the counsellors he desired, while in practice they reinforced Wolsey's ministerial power for 18 months. He nominated a Counsel of 20 men to advise the King but acknowledged that many would be absent on their own and the King's business, so he made provision that it would be sufficient for just two counsellors to be on hand to advise the King and dispense justice. Clearly, Wolsey intended to be one of those two men. He also used the Eltham Ordinances as an opportunity to reduce the numbers of gentlemen of the Privy Chamber, the King's body guard with whom he chatted informally, and to ensure his placemen were securely represented within the Privy Chamber. He was still a supreme political operator.

Anne Boleyn

The rise of Anne Boleyn however was a factor beyond even Wolsey's control.

In conclusion, Thomas Wolsey was defeated by a lethal political mix – the King's infatuation; Anne's skills and intelligence; the Boleyns' political contacts; and adverse European power politics. The conservative faction joined forces with the Boleyns and the Aragonese in bringing down the Cardinal. Such an unlikely political alliance was not hard. Henry was angry at his chief minister's failure to secure the annulment. Wolsey had failed him so paid the price.

Political life after Wolsey

The nature of political life changed with Wolsey's fall from grace as the King no longer relied on his chief minister but on various counsellors from a range of competing factions.

Conservatives

One faction is known by historians as the conservatives for they rebutted religious reform. They were both hostile to Wolsey and opposed to his pro-French foreign policy. The most celebrated men in this faction were the Dukes of Norfolk and Suffolk.

Boleyn family

Another faction was centred on the Boleyn family, but here there is political complexity as the Boleyns were members of the Norfolk family. Lord Rochford, Anne's father, was closely associated with the Dukes of Norfolk and Suffolk but clearly had enormous family interest vested in his daughter's political ascendancy.

The Boleyn faction was not anti-Wolsey from the start but considered the chief minister their best hope of securing an annulment so that the King was free to marry Anne Boleyn. They were reformists prepared to consider a radical religious solution if necessary. This was a relatively weak faction backed by only a few members of the Privy Chamber, notably Thomas Wyatt, Sir Thomas Cheney and William Carey, but with the backing of two future powerful men – Thomas Cranmer and Thomas Cromwell. The extent of Anne's personal political involvement remains unclear before the summer of 1529.

Aragonese

The final faction was much more discrete being a group of counsellors centred on Wolsey's replacement as Lord Chancellor, Thomas More. It included conservatives who were loyal to Catherine of Aragon including Bishop Cuthbert Tunstall, John Fisher and William Warham. They are known by historians as the Aragonese.

In this highly-charged and confused political situation Henry called parliament. This proved to be the first step in his domestic resolution of the Great Matter. The so-called Reformation parliament that lasted from 1529 to 1536 was ultimately the legislative route to his marriage to Anne Boleyn.

Cross-reference

For more details on Thomas More, see page 83.

Learning outcomes

In this section you have studied the nature of government and authority under Henry VIII, and the foreign and domestic policies during the period that Thomas Wolsey was his chief minister, exploring the nature of the relationship between the King and Wolsey. You have analysed the state of the Church before the Reformation in England, and learnt about the reasons for the breakdown of the King's marriage to Catherine of Aragon by 1529. Finally, you have examined the reasons for Wolsey's fall from power in 1529.

 Examination-style questions

(a) Explain why Thomas Wolsey emerged as the King's chief minister by 1515. *(12 marks)*

(b) How important was the Anglo-French alliance from 1526 in explaining Wolsey's fall from political dominance by November 1529? *(24 marks)*

AQA
Examiner's tip

In this answer you are expected to show sound factual knowledge about the Anglo-French alliance that Wolsey built for the King after 1526. The League of Cognac 1526 and the treaty signed at Amiens in 1527 are central to any answer. It is important to place Anglo-French relations in the wider context of the Hapsburg-Valois wars and to explain that this alliance altered the English customary pro-Burgundian stance in foreign relations. It is essential that you explain how this undermined Wolsey's hold on power.

You will need to extend your answer to consider other explanations for Wolsey's fall from power. You need to structure the answer carefully to avoid a list of factors, instead you need to develop links between the reasons. The links may be through interrelated affairs, such as foreign policy difficulties opened Wolsey up to criticism from his rivals; prioritisation of the most important reason; or through analysis of causation, possibly short-term and long-term causes.

5 Conclusion

■ England in 1529

The monarchy in England in 1529 was much more powerful and stable than it had been in 1483. This is particularly apparent in the King's relationship with his great nobility, for each king was suspicious of any potential challenger and took action to contain any threat and preserve their dynasty. The monarchy was also stronger because the Renaissance kings were acutely conscious of their majesty, which explains why the royal court had become a centrepiece of royal authority. Finally, both Henry VII and Henry VIII were strong kings, albeit with very different skills and styles, and imposed their authority as personal monarchs.

The system of government had also undergone significant changes. One difference was the development of a group of non-clerical and non-noble professional administrators at both central and local government. The first two Tudor Kings and their ministers devised methods to improve the effectiveness of royal government, sometimes through new counsels or the increased use of the existing courts of law. The Privy Chamber, introduced in the 1490s, was evolving into an influential body.

On the other hand, there had been few changes in the governance of the realm. The King was still understood to have been appointed by God but was still expected to rule by taking Counsel. He could consult whomever he wished in formal assemblies or through informal contacts. Ambitious men and families jostled to give that Counsel and so benefit from the rich rewards of the King's patronage. Factional strife was, as ever, a feature of English political life.

By the 1520s, the population of the country was beginning to expand rapidly, putting growing pressure on prices and wages. The expansion of the wool and cloth trades drove a move towards pastoral farming often accompanied by enclosure of common land, which proved unpopular. Despite these economic difficulties, England enjoyed a period of relative domestic peace in the years leading up to 1529. New buildings across the realm, which exhibited good architecture, are evidence of this stability. London, already a very prosperous port, now emerged as the pre-eminent port in England.

Religious life, however, was undergoing major upheaval by 1529. Attempts had been made to reform the Roman Catholic Church before 1483, notably by the Lollards, but the Church faced far more serious challenges in 1529. Anticlerical and humanist ideas circulated in the ports and university towns. The Lutheran ideas, however, that had taken hold in the German states on the continent, were far more threatening to the Church. The emergence of the King's Great Matter, unresolved in 1529, would soon prove catastrophic for the power of the Roman Catholic Church in England.

In Europe, England remained a peripheral power overshadowed by the kingdom of France and the Holy Roman Empire, and not yet involved in overseas expansion or exploration. Indeed, the King of England had yet to fully establish royal authority over his realm. Wales was more closely linked to the English crown after leading Welsh families, such as the Tudors, entered the English aristocracy, although some areas still retained Welsh law. English rule in Ireland had not strengthened by 1529 as most native Irish remained free of English law and obeyed their local clan chieftains. Even the Anglo-Irish nobility, who had most to gain by allying with the English King, were always unpredictable agents of royal authority. Scotland also remained hostile to English kings despite royal Anglo-Scottish marriages and the existence of an Anglophile faction in the Scottish court.

By 1529, England had developed significantly from the country that faced two usurpations in 1483, emerging as a country where the King's law was, more or less, obeyed. This apparent stability would soon be rocked by a new crisis, the English Reformation.

Glossary

A

annulment: the end of a marriage (annulment suggests that the marriage did not properly take place, unlike divorce, which is the end of a legal marriage).

anticlericals: people who were aware of the 'proven abuses', as they termed the customs of which they were critical, in the Roman Catholic Church. They were critical of the personnel, lifestyle and teaching of the Church.

attainder: the loss of rights when a man was convicted by parliament of treason or any other serious crime. It applied to a man's heirs too and meant the loss of the family estate.

attainted: the Act of Attainder 'attainted' nobles who rebelled against a monarch. The attainted noble lost his title, lands and sometimes his head. His heirs were disinherited.

B

bastard line of descent: a claim to the throne through illegitimate ancestors.

bond: a bond was a lump sum of money. The person involved recognised himself as owing the lump sum stated, which was not payable if the condition (usually good behaviour) was observed. If the condition was not observed, the sum stated was paid.

C

Catholic: means 'universal'. Christians believed there could only be one Christian Church. The Roman Catholic Church was the only established Christian Church in western Europe at this time.

central government: decision-making bodies who ran the country including the court, Counsel and parliament.

chamberlain: also known as the Lord Chamberlain, he was an experienced nobleman and member of the Counsel, also a personal friend of the King. He had administrative and political functions for he often spoke for the monarch in Counsel or in parliament, and he was responsible for organising court ceremonies.

conciliar: in this period, kings started to create small counsels to deal with particular problems.

constableship: a post given by a king to a loyal servant who was trusted to supervise a castle.

convocation: official assembly of senior clergy that usually coincided with the calling of parliament.

cottage industry: small-scale manufacturing that took place in people's homes, sometimes on simple machinery, e.g. spinning wool into yarn on a spinning wheel, or weaving yarn into cloth on a hand loom.

Counsel: (also King's Counsel) a group of advisors chosen by the King. This was the central administrative and decision-making body. Different sized groups of the Counsel were known by different names: the Counsel; the King's Counsel; the Great Counsel; the Royal Counsel; or the Privy Counsel.

D

diocese: England and Wales were divided into 21 administrative areas, each called a diocese but also know as sees or bishoprics.

dissolution of the monasteries: the name given to Thomas Cromwell's policy after 1536, during which he forced the closure of all religious houses. He seized their assets and sold their land to raise revenue for the King.

E

embargo: a ban on the export of English wool or woollen cloth to any Burgundian port.

enclosure: rearranging open fields into fields separated from each other by fences or hedges.

engrossing: amalgamating small farms into one larger farming unit by a single owner.

exhume: to dig up a body after it has previously been buried.

extraordinary expenses: these were one-off expenses that the King had to meet, often to wage a war or suppress a rebellion, but also to fund major spectacles such as a coronation.

F

faction: an alliance of powerful courtiers who shared common interests.

feudal: a system introduced by the Normans after 1066. The King owned all the land and distributed it among loyal servants. They, in return, attended court and Counsel, provided armies, and ran administration at central and local government.

fifteenths and tenths: parliament granted a directly-assessed subsidy – a 15th was the rate of tax on the moveable goods of laymen, and a 10th was the rate of tax on the income of the clergy.

G

governance: the process of ruling, both formal and informal or, in this case, the ways that Henry ruled the country through his ministers, parliament, the nobles and the gentry.

government: is the mechanism of government, in other words the institutions that enabled the King to govern the realm.

H

heretics: people who challenged the ideas or doctrine of the Roman Catholic Church. Refusing to support Roman Catholic doctrine was known as heresy.

humanists: wanted to improve the quality of teaching and learning in the Church.

I

imposters: another term for the young men who pretended to be Yorkist princes. Their pretences are also termed impostures.

indulgences: Roman Catholics believed that they could reduce the time they had to spend in purgatory if they purchased an indulgence, or several indulgences.

Inns of Court: the buildings in London that belong to legal societies that have the right to admit people to practise at the English bar.

issued writs: parliament was not permanent. Issuing writs was the process by which a monarch summoned both the Commons and the Lords to attend parliament.

L

Legatine Counsel: a special ecclesiastical court in which the case is judged by the Pope's ambassador(s), his legate(s).

letters patent: Royal order granted under the Great Seal – in this case to confirm the grant of a title.

liturgy: the form of public worship of a specific religious group. It can be formal such as the elaborate ritual of Catholic mass. It can also refer to the standardised order of events during a religious service.

livings: Bishops were able to earn a substantial income from the land and other sources of revenue that went with a bishopric.

local government: administration, revenue collection and law enforcement carried out at county level by JPs and sheriffs, and in parishes by churchwardens, constables and overseers of the poor.

Lollards: followers of the docctrine of John Wycliffe. They had their own translation of the Bible and were highly critical of many aspects of the Roman Catholic Church.

Lord Chamberlain: the noble who ran the King's household at court. This man was usually one of the King's closest personal friends and advisers.

M

magnates: the most powerful noble families.

Marcher Lords: the magnate families who owned huge areas of land and possessed near-regal powers in the south and east of Wales.

medallions: a panel, usually round or oval, containing a sculpture.

Merchant Adventurers: exported finished cloth from London.

Merchants of the Staple: exported raw wool through Calais.

modus vivendi: an agreement between people who agree to differ.

mullioned glass windows: a vertical bar that separated each compartment of a window.

N

national interest: to meet the needs of the country.

O

ordinary expenses: a king was expected to 'live off his own'. This meant the day-to-day expenses were to be met from the king's regular revenues.

oyer and terminer: the two words are used to describe the work of a commission set up to 'hear' the evidence that a serious crime has been committed and to 'finish' by giving the verdict and carrying out justice.

P

papal legate: this prestigious appointment by the Pope meant that Wolsey was the most powerful churchman in England, he could claim precedence over the Archbishop of Canterbury.

patronage: the disposal of land, gifts and offices of state by the King or his leading ministers. This was essential to win and maintain the loyalty of the political nation.

peasants: small-scale farmers who had the right to farm land.

Peer of the Realm: one of a class of nobles who may sit in the House of Lords (Duke, Marquis, Earl, Viscount, Baron).

perjury: not telling the truth while under oath before a court.

political nation: those men who were actively involved, at central or local government level, in the administration of the country.

praemunire: a law that made any acknowledgement of papal power illegal in England.

prerogative: the powers that enabled the King to govern the realm effectively. Some of these powers were derived from the King's role as feudal overlord of the kingdom. These powers included the rights to raise money from various feudal levies. The Surveyor of the King's Prerogative was the man responsible for managing this income.

Prince of the Church: a cardinal in the Roman Catholic Church.

progress: (as in royal progress around the country) a king's journey around the country to meet his subjects.

prorogation: when the parliament was dissolved at the end of the session.

purgatory: Roman Catholics believed that at the Day of Judgement souls were sent to one of three places. The wicked went to everlasting hell, the virtuous to heaven, but most souls were sent to be cleansed in purgatory. The time spent being purged could be reduced by financial support for the Church, e.g. if a man left money in his will for private masses to be said after his death.

R

recognisance: when a person formally acknowledged a debt or obligation. The recognisance was often enforced by a bond.

regular clergy: the monks and nuns who lived their lives according to regulations in religious houses.

renaissance: a rebirth of interest in Europe in arts and sciences, often patronised by lavish royal and ducal courts.

retained men: men who voluntarily contracted and obliged themselves to provide a certain number of soldiers for their noblemen.

Roman: the Pope was based in Rome, Italy. He claimed to be the successor to the apostle St Peter who was buried in Rome.

royal household: personal advisers and companions to the King. These men travelled with the King wherever he went and also attended Court.

royal servant: any person who served the King in the governance of the country – nobles, churchmen, gentry and lawyers.

sacraments: the seven sacraments were seven important religious ceremonies that Catholics received during their lifetime – baptism, confirmation, marriage, Extreme Unification, the Eucharis (mass), penance, and Holy Orders.

sanctuary: a place of safety in a church. In this case, Queen Elizabeth took refuge in Westminster Abbey.

secular: concerned with the affairs of this world, rather than ecclesiastical or monastic matters.

secular clergy: churchmen who served the everyday world as priests and bishops.

solvency: having enough income to meet all expenses.

solvent: the monarch needed to balance his books by making sure he covered his expenses with his income. In doing so, he remained solvent.

statute: laws passed by an Act of parliament and recognised as the supreme form of law above precedent or royal proclamation.

stewardship: another reward for loyal service – to manage crown lands.

subsistence agriculture: where the farmers grew enough food to support their families without any surplus.

summary execution: put to death without a time-consuming trial. This was illegal – the right to trial, established long before 1483, is a core feature of the English system of justice.

The Hanseatic League: a powerful trading coalition of German cities.

The house of Lancaster: descendants of Edward III's third son, John of Gaunt, Duke of Lancaster.

The house of York: descendants of Edward III's second and fourth sons whose families intermarried.

The Pale: land around a town that was under English control.

Transubstantiation: the Roman Catholic doctrine that during Mass the bread actually changes its form into Christ's flesh, and the wine into his blood.

tunnage and poundage: the right to raise revenue from imports and exports for the whole reign.

usurpation: the seizure of the throne. In this case Richard, Duke of Gloucester, was to take the throne from the rightful King, Edward V.

V

vanguard: the forefront of the army.

Bibliography

Broad coverage

There are textbooks that cover sections of the course.

Ian Dawson, *The Tudor Century*, Nelson, 1993.

Another book with useful diagrams and varied sources.

Allan Keen, et al., *England 1485–1603*, Collins, 1999.

Contains four relevant chapters on Henry VII, the age of Wolsey, social and economic change and the beginnings of the Reformation.

Derrick Murphy, Allan Keen, Michael Tilbrook and Patrick Walsh-Atkins, *England 1485–1603*, Flagship History Collins, 1999.

A useful general textbook.

Andrew Pickering, *Lancastrians to Tudors*, Cambridge University Press, 2000.

Gives an overview of the years 1450–1509, along with useful background information on the Wars of the Roses.

Caroline Rogers, *Henry VII*, Hodder, 1991.

Contains a detailed study of the first Tudor monarch with useful historiographical explanations.

David Rogerson, Samantha Ellsmore and David Hudson, *The Early Tudors* (Schools History Project), Murray, 2001.

Has many thinking skills activities in the first chapter on Henry VII and the early part of the chapter on Henry VIII.

John Warren, *The Wars of the Roses and the Yorkist Kings*, Hodder, 1995.

Examines the civil wars.

Detailed coverage

Christine Carpenter, *The Wars of the Roses*, Cambridge University Press, 1997.

This is a very detailed analysis of the politics and constitution of England 1437–1509. It will challenge the most able students.

John Guy, *Tudor England*, Oxford University Press, 1988.

Provides a clear narrative account of English history from *c*.1460 to 1603.

John Lotherington, *The Tudor Years*, Hodder, 1994.

A wordy analysis of the Tudor monarchs. It is useful to stretch and challenge the most able students.

Biographies

There are many excellent biographies of the main personalities.

S. Chrimes, *Henry VII*, Yale University Press, 1999.

A reprint of the classic biography originally published in 1972.

Sean Cunningham, *Richard III, a royal enigma*, The National Archives, 2003.

A much shorter biography with beautiful colour illustrations.

John Guy, *Cardinal Wolsey*, Headstart History Papers, date unknown.

An ideal booklet for most AS students. It presents the historiographical debate in accessible text.

Michael Hicks, *Edward IV*, Arnold, 2004.

A book in the 'Reputations' series that will enhance students' understanding of historiography but is challenging.

Rosemary Horrox, *Richard III*, Cambridge University Press, 1989.

This study of service is a modern analysis of the King.

Paul Murray Kendall, *Richard III*, Cardinal, 1973.

Another detailed biography of this most-controversial monarch.

David Loades, *Henry VIII and his Queens*, Sutton Publishing, 1994.

Detailed and lively, AS students will enjoy the text.

Charles Ross, *Richard III*, Methuen, 1981.

Ross wrote the definitive biography of Edward IV, so this is his sequel.

J. J. Scarisbrick, *Henry VIII*, Methuen, 1981.

A readable biography, again a reprint of the 1968 classic.

Alison Weir, *Henry VIII*, Pimlico, 2002.

A detailed and readable analysis of the King and his court.

Rebellions

Michael Bennett, *Lambert Simnel and the Battle of Stoke*, Sutton Publishing, 1987.

Another detailed study, recommended for advanced students.

Anthony Fletcher, et al., *Tudor Rebellions*, Longman, 2004.

Contains some useful sections on the rebellions in Yorkshire 1489 and Cornwall 1497.

Louise Gill, *Richard III and Buckingham's Rebellion*, Sutton Publishing, 1999.

An advanced book for AS reading but is worth recommending to gifted students.

Michael Jones, *Bosworth*, Tempus, 2002.

A study of the battle from a psychological perspective.

The Church in England before the Reformation

A. G. Dickens, *The English Reformation*, Batsford, 1999.
A detailed study of the popular support for reform.

Christopher Haigh (ed.), *The English Reformation Revisited*, Cambridge University Press, 1987.
A collection of essays for the more advanced student.

Articles

Ian Arthurson, 'Perkin Warbeck', *History Review*, September 1996.

Ian Dawson, 'Henry VII: Out of the shadows', *History Review*, September 1995.

S. Gunn, 'Cardinal Wolsey in context', *History Review*, March 1991.

John Guy, 'Henry VIII and his ministers', *History Review*, December 1995.

Jez Ross, 'Henry VIII's Early Foreign Policy 1509–29', *History Review*, December 2001.

Retha Warnicke, 'Anne Boleyn, Queen of England', *History Review*, March 2002.

Websites

www.johnguy.co.uk
This is John Guy's website. It has detailed pages aimed at AS and A2, as well as undergraduate material and public lectures for extension reading.

www.richardiii.net
This is one of many sites that debate Richard III's reign.

www.tudorplace.com
This site has detailed genealogical and biographical material on the Tudor dynasty.

Places to visit

Bosworth: battlefield site
Hampton Court
Little Moreton Hall
The Tower of London

Acknowledgements

The author and publisher would like to thank the following for permission to reproduce material:

p38: Fig. 11 & 12, from Michael K. Jones, *Bosworth 1485: Psychology of a Battle*, The History Press, 2003 (p. 225, p.226), courtesy of Geoffrey Wheeler and Bill Featherstone

Source texts:

p15 Sean Cunningham, *Richard III, a royal enigma*, The National Archives, 2003; p16 Adapted from Charles Ross, *Edward IV*, Methuen, 1981; p22 Extract from Thomas More, *The History of England*, c.1513, quoted in J. R. Lander, *The Wars of the Roses*, Sutton Publishing, 1990; p23 Quoted in P. M. Kendall, *Richard III*, Cardinal, 1973; p31 William Shakespeare, *Richard III*, Act 1 Scene 2, Hamlyn, 1958; p32 Sean Cunningham, *Richard III, a royal enigma*, The National Archives, 2003; p32 Paul Murray Kendall, *Richard III*, Cardinal, 1973; p33 A. F. Pollard, *Richard III and the Princes*, Sutton Publishing, 1991; p38 Quoted from Arthur Marwick, *The Nature of History*, Macmillan, 1989; p40 Extract from the proclamation of Henry Tudor. Quoted in S. Chrimes, *Henry VII*, Yale University Press, 1999; p42 Act for the Confirmation of Henry VII (1485). From G. R. Elton, *The Tudor Constitution*, Cambridge University Press, 1982; p44 Quoted in Ralph Griffiths and Roger Thomas, *The Making of the Tudor Dynasty*, Sutton Publishing, 1985; p46 From Michael Bennett, *Lambert Simnel and the Battle of Stoke*, Sutton Publishing, 1987; p57 From D. O'Sullivan and R. Lockyer, *Tudor England*, Longman, 1993; p58 From D. O'Sullivan and R. Lockyer, *Tudor England*, Longman, 1993; p71 C. Davies, 'The Making of Henry VII', from D. Rogerson, S. Ellsmore and D. Hudson, *The Early Tudors* (Schools History Project), Murray, 2001; p73 M. Condon, in John Guy (ed.), *The Tudor Monarchy*, Hodder/Arnold, 1997; p83 Adapted from English Bible History (www.greatsite.com); p85 Polydore Vergil Anglica historia (written c.1513). Adapted from D. Rogerson, S. Ellsmore and D. Hudson, *The Early Tudors* (Schools History Project), 'Tudors', Murray, 2001; p86 Ian Dawson, 'Henry VII: Out of the Shadows', *History Review*, September 1995; p98 From Ian Dawson, *The Tudor Century*, Nelson, 1993; p98 J. J. Scarisbrick, *Henry VIII*, Methuen, 1981; p103 David Starkey, 'Court and Government' in John Guy (ed.), *The Tudor Monarchy*, Hodder/Arnold, 1997; p105 John Guy, *Cardinal Wolsey*, Headstart History Papers, date unknown; p107 John Skelton; p109 Adapted from C. S. L. Davies, *Peace, Print and Protestantism*, Fontana, 1995; p121 Alison Weir, *Henry VIII*, Pimlico, 2002; p130 G. R. Elton, *The Tudor Constitution*, Cambridge University Press, 1982; p130 A. G. Dickens, *The English Reformation*, Batsford, 1999; p131 Adapted from Christopher Haigh (ed.), *The English Reformation Revisited*, Cambridge University Press, 1987; p134 David Loades, *Henry VIII and his Queens*, Sutton Publishing, 1994; p134-5 Philippa Gregory, *The Other Boleyn Girl*, HarperCollins, 2002; p135 David Loades, *Henry VIII and his Queens*, Sutton Publishing, 1994; p138 J. J. Scarisbrick, *Henry VIII*, Methuen, 1981

Photographs courtesy of:

Ancient Art & Architecture 102; Ann Ronan Picture Library 3, 11 (top), 60, 93, 97, 103, 121; Edimedia Art Archive 15, 39 (right), 99; Getty Images iv, 58; Getty Images/Bridgeman Art Library 16; Getty Images/Mansell 44; Mary Evans Picture Library 30, 47, 55; National Archives of Scotland 69; Photo 12 32, 119; Topfoto 18, 23, 28, 36, 39 (left), 72, 90 (top), 92; Topfoto/British Library/HIP 49, 129; Topfoto/Corporation of London/HIP 4, 105, 126; Topfoto/Fotomas 26; Topfoto/Gardner 113; Topfoto/ HIP 17, 20, 101, 107, 109; Topfoto/HIP/EE Images 81; Topfoto/Public Records Office/HIP 123; Topfoto/ Woodmansterne 43, 78; World History Archive 10, 11 (bottom), 41, 52, 65, 67, 79, 83, 85, 90 (bottom), 94, 100, 128, 132, 133, 140; www.southlakes-uk.co.uk 51

Cover photograph: courtesy of Alamy/Tony Wright/earthscapes

For further information concerning any pictures appearing in this book. Please email samuel@uniquedimension.com

Photo research by Unique Dimension Limited

Special thanks to Topfoto, The Southlakes Organisation, Ann Asquith and Dora Swick

Index